Margaret Thatcher's Case against Democratic Socialism and Keynesian Economics

Margaret Thatcher's Case against Democratic Socialism and Keynesian Economics

Markets, Monetarism, and British Politics in the 1970s

Eric R. Crouse

LEXINGTON BOOKS
Lanham • Boulder • New York • London

Published by Lexington Books
An imprint of The Rowman & Littlefield Publishing Group, Inc.
4501 Forbes Boulevard, Suite 200, Lanham, Maryland 20706
www.rowman.com

6 Tinworth Street, London SE11 5AL, United Kingdom

British Library Cataloguing in Publication Information Available

Library of Congress Cataloging-in-Publication Data Available

ISBN 978-1-7936-5017-7 (cloth)
ISBN 978-1-7936-5018-4 (electronic)

In memory of Professor Derek Chisholm (1948–2019)

Contents

Introduction

Britain experienced two stunning developments in the 1970s. Postwar Keynesianism fell out of favor and, for the first time, British voters chose a female prime minister. From the day Margaret Thatcher entered Parliament, she was a partisan woman who fought Labour Party "socialism" with more commitment than almost all other Tories of her day. When she became leader of the Conservative Party in the 1970s, she was the first leader to oppose the consensus views of both the Labour Party and centrist Tories who, in varying degrees, accepted Keynesianism and state ownership of industry. She had great faith in a market economy of less government intervention. Thatcher's economic stand against key Tory members was often cautious, but she paved the way for a significant realignment of the Conservative Party. In an argument with Tory centrist James Prior, she declared: "Standing in the middle of the road is very dangerous, you get knocked down by the traffic from both sides."[1] Rather than a biography of Thatcher, this book is a history of her political rise within the context of the British economy and persisting Keynesian and socialist ideas. The focus is on conflicting economic views, both within Thatcher's party and the Labour Party, and how economic stagnation and inflation resulted in the transformation of British politics and a greater expression of free-market ideas.

I

For decades, Keynesianism ruled in academia, the Bank of England, and Whitehall.[2] John Maynard Keynes (1883–1946) was born in England to a distinguished family; his father was a Cambridge University professor and his mother had been mayor of Cambridge. He attended the best schools, and his university education was at Cambridge. He wrote several important books, including *The General Theory of Employment, Interest and Money* (1936). The book is an unfortunate example of contorted and obscure writing, and it is difficult to find anyone who has read it cover to cover. However, it gave birth to a new branch of economics called "macroeconomics" that focused on national economies. Critical of the "misleading and disastrous" consequences of laissez-faire theory, Keynes rejected both the thinking that full employment was the normal state of the economy and that high unemployment was a temporary circumstance that eventually corrected itself.[3] He entrusted experts to manage the economy, thus giving credibility to the idea that government action could smooth the unpleasant side of boom-bust business cycles. When private investment waned, it was crucial for the government to borrow money, increase spending, and later, as the economy improved, run a budget deficit to repay past loans.[4]

Consistent with Thatcher's rejection of excessive government action, she saw Keynesian deficit financing of public expenditure as problematic. For conservatives such as Thatcher, both Keynesianism and socialism had the serious flaw of promoting greater government management of the economy that did not allow the best allocation of scarce resources. High taxes, big government spending, and overregulation stifled wealth creation. How could the British people benefit from government waste and a stagnant economy? Thatcher apparently understood how best to undermine the Labour Party and Keynesian ideas. She effectively criticized Keynesian policies without using the word. In the Cold War years, the term socialism was a safer target. The "socialist" Labour Party that she took to task consisted of mostly those who embraced rigorous Keynesianism. The social democrats in the party far outnumbered the hardline socialists demanding comprehensive public ownership. When one considers pragmatism over idealism, the Labour Party's preference for Keynesianism over hardline socialist control is not surprising. Some believed Keynesianism could be quite radical. There is the argument that Keynes wanted to see Britain adopt, in his own words, "liberal socialism." In his revisionist work, economist James Crotty claims that genuine Keynesianism, as understood by Keynes himself, was more socialist than many recognized.[5] Perhaps Thatcher's broad usage of the term socialism to fight Labour's economic ideas was not too far off the mark.

Thatcher appreciated the ideas of Austrian economist F. A. Hayek (1899–1992), who was one of the few dissenters concerned that Keynesian economics and inflation eventually went hand in hand. When Hayek was a student at the University of Vienna after World War I, he witnessed how hyperinflation wrecked the German and Austrian economies. The University of Vienna barely functioned due to a shortage of coal, light, and food.[6] Hayek also saw an alarming problem with the central planning of socialist economics that threatened liberty, the issue he discussed in *The Road to Serfdom*. Two years before the publication of Hayek's book in 1944, the British Labour Party declared in the pamphlet *The Old World and the New Society* that a "planned society must replace the old competitive system."[7]

According to Hayek, central planners believed that modern capitalism, hampered by monopolistic tendencies and technological changes, did not allow true competition. Echoing the Marxist doctrine of the "concentration of industry," central planners saw government control of production as necessary to ensure the best economy.[8] But Hayek argued that central planning was a form of slavery because economic and social goals required authoritarian action. When speaking of freedom, socialists promised a new freedom, notably freedom from necessity. Ironically, if it took coercion to realize this freedom, so be it.[9] To no one's surprise, Labour Party politicians did not view *The Road to Serfdom* as a serious book.[10] In subsequent decades, the Labour Party consisted of a wide range of socialists who shared the idea that competition was an unsuitable method for realizing a just and productive economy. They believed that replacing "heartless" competition with planning was the proper thing to do. Thatcher disagreed and she used Hayek's writings for intellectual ballast. Although *The Road to Serfdom* offered no direct criticism of the Keynesianism that many Tories favored, the evidence suggests few Tory centrists read the book.

Hayek's writings were an important component of Thatcher's economic education, but the work of American economist Milton Friedman (1912–2006) did as much or more to shape her thinking. Friedman became the most influential free-market scholar in America. Both of his parents were Jewish immigrants from Europe. Having humble economic origins, Friedman was a mild-mannered intellectual who was friendly and respectful of opposing ideas. The label "heartless" capitalist, only concerned with defending the rich, did not fit him. His skill in presenting insightful economic analysis in layman's terms was obvious to the many readers who followed his *Newsweek* column begun in 1966. Friedman's monetary theory that focused on the role of money in causing both inflation and cyclical disturbances offered a serious critique of Keynesian thinking. The ideal system is when the "money supply increases at a steady or neutral rate (the monetarist rule)."[11]

More so than Hayek, Friedman demonstrated a keen interest in the British economy and sought to correct what he saw as misguided thinking about the cause of inflation: "In Britain, the explanation that everybody gives for inflation is that inflation is caused by trade unions, the greedy, grasping laborers who force up the wages that cause inflation." This was wrong. He presented data of recent British economic history showing the clear link between quantity of money and inflation. To make his point about trade unionism, Friedman noted the trend was almost identical in Japan where labor unions were relatively small and insignificant. While visiting Britain, he took the unusual position of partly defending trade unionism: "Labor unions do a great deal of harm in many ways, but one thing of which they're innocent is producing inflation."[12]

Although his work on money supply set him apart from most British economists, Friedman's criticism of government intervention in the economy received wider support. Keynesian economists and policymakers were vulnerable. They relied on the Phillips curve, named after the Australian economist A. W. Phillips who noted the long-term inverse relationship between unemployment and inflation: when one increased, the other decreased. For example, when the unemployment rate increased (more people out of work), there was less upward pressure on wages and prices, thus less inflation. When the unemployment rate fell, the tighter labor market resulted in an increase in wages and prices. Following the logic of the Phillips curve, the Keynesian strategy of fighting inflation was to have the government decrease the amount of money to cool the economy and balance inflation and unemployment to an acceptable level.[13] However, the Phillips curve had no answer to the problem of both inflation and unemployment rising at the same time. Thatcher found the work of Hayek and Friedman helpful, but in her speeches she saw no need to get into specifics of their theories. Thatcher the politician voiced her opposition to state intervention, either Keynesianism or socialism, in simple terms: it was socialistic and wrong for Britain.

II

After World War II the British economy was in a mess. Britain had large debts, low currency reserves, severe physical damage by aerial bombardment of major cities, and acute shortages of necessities. One of many examples of economic difficulty was housing. Enemy bombing destroyed almost 500,000 homes and temporarily disabled a far greater number.[14] On July 25, 1945, Prime Minister Winston Churchill was out. Voters chose the Labour Party to lead the nation. Years later, Thatcher viewed this shocking election as "the logical fulfilment of the collectivist spirit" that dominated wartime Britain.[15]

Led by Clement Atlee, the Labour Party favored planning, controls, and nationalization as the appropriate economic direction for the British people. The formation of the Central Economic Planning Staff was indicative of the government's greater role in addressing economic problems. However, there were obstacles to planning. In 1946, Edward Bridges, an important civil servant, wrote: "We are trying to work a planned economy without labour controls and in conditions of general inflationary pressure in which financial incentives alone cannot be strong enough to take their place." Many in the party viewed the nationalization of industries as a promising way to control and plan the economy. They looked to the economic benefits of large-scale enterprises run by "experts"; nationalized industries could achieve economies of scale beyond the hopes of "fragmented, private entities."[16] There was also a moral component. In 1949, Labour Cabinet minister Aneurin Bevan asked: "What is national planning but an insistence that human beings shall make ethical choices on a national scale?" Overall, the economic record of the Atlee government was weak; there were too many crises and shortages.[17] Economic growth in Britain was slower than in western European nations and Japan. Lacking innovation and entrepreneurship, the central planning of the Labour Party appeared less efficient than the market economies of competitors.

Thatcher's initial attempts to enter Parliament failed. In the 1950 general election, she wanted to see the defeat of the government's "socialism." She campaigned hard, but she fell far short against her Labour opponent.[18] Although defeated again in the 1951 election, Thatcher was happy to see the Conservative Party return to power. For the next thirteen years, the prime ministers were Churchill (1951–1955), Anthony Eden (1955–1957), Harold Macmillan (1957–1963), and Alex Douglas-Home (1963–1964). The Tories, most of them supportive of Keynesianism, accepted much of the welfare state ushered in by the Labour Party. Any dismantling of progressive platforms was modest at best. Soon to be prime minister, Eden did not hide the role the Tory Party played in advancing and accepting bigger government. He declared in 1955:

> We denounce the Labour Party's desire to use the social services, which we all helped to create, as an instrument for levelling down. We regard social security not as a substitute for family thrift, but as a necessary basis or supplement to it. We think of the national health service as a means, not of preventing anyone from paying anything for a service, but of ensuring that proper attention and treatment are denied to no one.[19]

Tories were comfortable with an accommodationist approach that they believed most voters welcomed. Government expenditure as a percentage of GDP was similar for the Labour government ending in 1951 and the Tory governments of the 1950s. In the second half of the decade, Britain experienced low productivity, a declining demand for exports, and increased competition from other nations. Rather than turning to the free market for answers, the Tories turned to more state planning. Created in 1961, the National Economic Development Council represented a Conservative statism that Tories believed was capable of managing the economy.[20] Finally elected to Parliament in 1959, Thatcher later wrote that Conservatism "lacked fire" and its questionable "management of the economy" was in part responsible for the worsening economic conditions of the 1960s.[21] Others pointed to the economic incompetence of Tory leadership.

Throughout the 1960s, economists noted the slow rate of growth of the British economy compared to other nations. As early as 1961, Oxford economist Thomas Balogh, who later became an economic advisor for the Labour Party, wrote: "Unless we can increase our rate of growth . . . we shall have to stifle something."[22] Led by Harold Wilson, the Labour Party took power in October 1964. In the following month, the new government faced a sterling crisis when the market lost confidence in the pound. To keep the pound at $2.78, the intervention of late November almost depleted the cash resources of the Bank of England.[23] Britain continued to experience weak productivity, anaemic investment in private enterprise, and rising export prices. There was another sterling crisis in 1966 and in the following year the Labour government devalued the sterling by 14 percent from $2.80 to $2.40. Other economic problems included an increasing number of days lost to labour strikes and inadequate investment in new technologies.[24] The economy in the 1960s was troubling, but the next decade was far worse. Britain in the 1970s experienced appalling economic conditions and both the Tory Party and the Labour Party struggled to find a solution to the economic woes. As Thatcher saw it, there was a need for significant change.

III

Scholarship on Thatcher is massive; no other British prime minister since Winston Churchill has received as much attention as this controversial woman. The publication of biographies and many other books on Thatcher as early as the 1970s is a testimony of her influence and importance in modern British history. Recent biographies by John Campbell, Robin Harris, Graham Goodlad, and Charles Moore cover much of her early life and political rise and her domestic and foreign policies. For good reasons, the bulk of the Thatcher literature is of her time as prime minister (1979–1991). Those who offer significant discussion of her economic policies focus mainly on the "Thatcherism" of the 1980s.[25]

This study focuses on the 1970s and seeks to better understand Thatcher's interaction with the troubled British economy and her opposition to socialist thinking. Reading economic history can be a daunting task complicated by economic jargon and ideology. Avoiding confusing economic language, this introductory study overs a concise analysis of Thatcher's criticism of Keynesian and socialist economics. There is no discussion of key domestic events such as Britain joining the Common Market, the devolution issue of Scotland and Wales, and the development of the North Sea oilfields. Considerable attention is on the divisions in each party and the key representatives of the various factions. Although political memoirs are typically self-serving and occasionally revisionist, they do capture the emotions of political battle and the reality of strange and shifting alliances. The autobiographical accounts of both Tory and Labour politicians reveal interesting confrontations within each political party. The Labour Party consisted of mostly democratic socialists, and the Tory Party saw centrists dominating key positions within the party. However, there were others keen to challenge status-quo thinking.

Thatcher's challenge of the postwar consensus of Labour and Tory leaders was both dramatic and subtle. The story of a shopkeeper's daughter upholding free-market capitalism against social democratic ideas defended by Labour politicians, often from privileged backgrounds, makes for captivating confrontations. But there are interesting twists to the story. Prime Minister James Callaghan (1976–1979) angered many in the labor movement with economic statements more in sync with free-market thinking, and Thatcher, stimulated by new economic thinking, nonetheless proceeded carefully so as not to antagonize Tory moderates distrustful of free-market ideas. In the end, the issue of inflation altered British economics and politics and Thatcher was there to take advantage of the moment and score a victory over "socialism."

NOTES

1. Jim Prior, *A Balance of Power* (London: Hamish Hamilton, 1986), 106.
2. William Keegan, *Mrs Thatcher's Economic Experiment* (London: Allen Lane, 1984), 45.
3. John Maynard Keynes, *The General Theory of Employment, Interest, and Money* (New York: Harcourt, 1963), 3.
4. Steven Pressman, *Fifty Major Economists*, Third Edition (London: Routledge, 2014), 145.
5. Crotty writes: "The consistency and clarity with which Keynes presented and defended his radical, pro-democratic socialist theory and policies in *The General Theory* once again raises a question I posed earlier. How is it possible that one of the most important and influential books in the history of economic thought, written by one of the most important and influential economists who ever lived, came to be so profoundly misunderstood by the economics profession?" See James Crotty, *Keynes Against Capitalism: His Economic Case for Liberal* Socialism (London: Routledge, 2019), 308–9.
6. Pressman, *Fifty Major Economists*, 165. Sylvia Nasar, *Grand Pursuit: The Story of Economic Genius* (New York: Simon & Schuster, 2011), 275.
7. Bruce Caldwell, ed., *The Collected Works of F.A. Hayek Volume II, The Road to Serfdom Text and Documents: The Definitive Edition* (Chicago: The University of Chicago Press, 2007), 12.
8. Caldwell, ed., *The Collected Works of F.A. Hayek Volume II,* 91.
9. Caldwell, ed., *The Collected Works of F.A. Hayek Volume II,* 67, 76–78, 83.
10. Caldwell, ed., *The Collected Works of F.A. Hayek Volume II,* 21.
11. Mark Skousen, *Vienna & Chicago: Friends or Foes? – A Tale of Two Schools of Free-Market Economics* (Washington, DC: Regnery Publishing, Inc., 2005), 7.

12. Milton Friedman, "Is Inflation a Curable Disease?" Pittsburgh: Pittsburgh National Bank, Alex C. Walker Educational and Charitable Foundation, and the University of Pittsburgh Graduate School of Business, 1974. Alex C. Walker Memorial Lecture, 5 December 1974, 3–4, 20, https://miltonfriedman.hoover.org/internal/media/dispatcher/271086/full.

13. Alan Greenspan, *The Age of Turbulence: Adventures in a New World* (New York: The Penguin Press, 2007), 60.

14. Peter M. Scott and James T. Walker, "'Stop-go' Policy and the Restriction of Postwar British House-building," *Economic History Review* 72, no. 2 (2019), 719.

15. Margaret Thatcher, *Margaret Thatcher: The Autobiography* (New York: HarperPerennial, 2010), 38.

16. J.D. Tomlinson, "The Iron Quadrilateral: Political Obstacles to Economic Reform under the Attlee Government," *Journal of British Studies* 34, no. 1 (1995), 96, 105.

17. Richard Toye, *The Labour Party and the Planned Economy, 1931-1951* (Woodbridge, Suffolk; Rochester, NY: Boydell & Brewer, 2003), 206, 208, 241.

18. Thatcher, *Margaret Thatcher*, 51–52.

19. Quoted in Robert M. Page, "The Conservative Party and the Welfare State since 1945," in *The Conservative Party and Social Policy*, ed. Hugh Bochel (Bristol, UK: Bristol University Press, 2011), 28.

20. Nick Ellison, "The Conservative Party and Public Expenditure," in *The Conservative Party and Social Policy*, ed. Hugh Bochel (Bristol, UK: Bristol University Press, 2011), 42, 46–47.

21. Thatcher, *Margaret Thatcher*, 76–77.

22. Glen O'Hara, "'This Is What Growth Does': British Views of the European Economies in the Prosperous 'Golden Age' of 1951-73," *Journal of Contemporary History* 44, no. 4 (2009), 697.

23. Michael J. Oliver, "The Two Sterling Crises of 1964: A Comment on Newton," *The Economic History Review* 65, no. 1 (2012), 319.

24. For a helpful discussion of some of the key literature, see Hugh Pemberton, "Relative Decline and British Economic Policy in the 1960s," *The Historical Journal* 47, no. 4 (2004), 989–1013.

25. John Campbell, *Margaret Thatcher: The Grocer's Daughter Volume One* (London: Jonathan Cape, 2000) and *Margaret Thatcher: The Iron Lady Volume Two* (London: Jonathan Cape, 2003); Robin Harris, *Not for Turning: The Life of Margaret Thatcher* (New York: St. Martin's Press, 2013); Graham Goodlad, *Thatcher* (London: Routledge, 2016); and Charles Moore, *Margaret Thatcher: The Authorized Biography: Volume One* (London: Penguin Books, 2014). Other biographies include Hugo Young, *One of Us* (London: Macmillan, 1989) and Jonathan Aiken, *Margaret Thatcher: Power and Personality* (London: Bloomsbury, 2013). Most of the literature on Thatcher as prime minister gives significant treatment of her break from the "socialist consensus" of the postwar period. For a concise biography with a section on Thatcher and the historians, see Goodlad, *Thatcher*. David Cannadine's brief biography, *Margaret Thatcher: A Life and Legacy* (Oxford: Oxford University Press, 2017), offers a guide for further reading.

Chapter 1

The Rise of Thatcher

In October 1961, when Margaret Thatcher began her first appointment in government as joint parliamentary secretary at the Ministry of Pensions and National Insurance, *The Times* wrote: "Those who know her well detect a strong will, some might say almost a ruthlessness, behind her smiling appearance."[1] The following year, Labour's John Mendleson, an active member of the socialist Tribune Group, commented on Thatcher's first major speech in the House of Commons when she provided data showing that government money for pensioners increased at a faster rate than rising prices: "My impression at the end of the hon. Lady's speech was that all she had given us was a purely academic performance." He applauded her "mastery of facts," but noted her failure to make "any reference whatsoever to her real experience" of the many British pensioners experiencing economic hardship.[2] It was a common strategy by socialists to point to the elitism of Tory politicians. But was Thatcher, the grocer's daughter, elitist?

Thatcher's modest social-economic background gave her insight into the economy that the typical privileged politician, Tory or Labour, might not appreciate or understand. Not even politicians with an academic economic background had a clear advantage on her on economic matters, especially when their championing of government intervention in the economy led to questionable results such as alarming inflation. Those who studied at the London School of Economics or elsewhere normally received a Keynesian or socialist-weighted education that ill-prepared them to solve the problem of stagflation in the 1970s. Consistently labeling her Labour opponents as socialists, Thatcher stood out in the Conservative Party as a woman whose confidence in classical economics provided direction as she faced political hurdles in a climate dominated by democratic socialist thinking that pulled many Tories to the political middle.

Initially, Thatcher's opposition to all variations of socialism and Keynesianism did not attract much attention. From their bag of tricks, politicians might adopt hyperbole and characterize their opponents as someone with destructive political ideas, but it was not until 1968 that she became a significant target of socialists. Her lecture "What's Wrong With Politics" clarified the intensity of her criticism of big government. Even most high-ranking Tories were uneasy with Thatcher's hard-nosed conservatism and during the Heath government of 1970–1974 they kept her out of economic policy. Since her entrance into the House of Commons in 1959, she mostly held an outsider status. However, by the early 1970s, Thatcher, a woman of middle-class sensibilities, secured her place as a rising political star poised for greater influence.

I

Alfred Roberts planned to be a teacher, but his family was too poor to fund his education and, thus, he left school at the age of thirteen. His early employment included food retail at a tuck shop in a private school.[3] Alfred married Beatrice Stephenson and the two devout Methodists went into business when they bought a grocery shop in 1919 located in the town of Grantham, 160 kilometers north of London. Their first child Muriel arrived in 1921 and Margaret in 1925. The Roberts lived above the shop and Margaret learned early the importance of obligation. When people knocked on the door at all hours looking for sugar, butter, or eggs, the family responded dutifully without complaint. Their job was to serve the customer.[4] The Roberts understood that most people in the community "lived on a knife-edge"; there was the real possibility that an accident or failure to practice thrift and diligence could plunge them into debt and destitution.[5] Margaret's family was never idle; there were always tasks to complete.[6]

Margaret's early years offer a contrast to the experience of politicians who had lives of privilege and wealth, one example being Labour's Anthony Benn, a cabinet minister during the 1960s and 1970s. In fact, many of the leading Labour politicians, as she did, had Oxford University degrees. Consistent with her father's thinking, her approach became more free market than the paternalism that was common among many Tory Party politicians; her modest economic upbringing, which meant not having running-hot water in her earlier years, allowed her to escape the social guilt afflicting wealthy Tories.[7]

Although her father was not a trained pastor, he occasionally delivered church sermons. However, Alfred was a staunch conservative unmoved by any Methodist clergy sympathetic to left-wing causes in an era when social gospel thinking became popular.[8] In local politics, personal responsibility and sound finance guided his course. He embraced ideas found in *On Liberty*, the influential book on the importance of liberty in society written by nineteenth-century British philosopher John Stuart Mill, and he questioned the Liberal Party's romance with "collectivism." Margaret duplicated her father's thirst for reading politics in a wide range of newspapers and magazines. She was alert to intellectuals such as English novelist J. B. Priestley who, she argued, cleverly cloaked left-wing views as practical, down-to-earth philosophy.[9] She saw the economic catastrophe of the Great Depression years as the outcome of unwise monetary policy.[10] She had the advantage of having a good instinct for free-market economics that many politicians of all stripes rejected or apparently did not understand beyond a superficial level. In the future, socialist and Keynesian ideas of increased government intervention and spending would have little appeal for her.

Margaret Roberts did not sense a division or conflict between rich and working-class people, but, in time, she learned of those who promoted the idea of class conflict for political gain. When she was young, her father read Jan Valtin's book *Out of the Night*. Because of its spine-chilling description of totalitarianism, Alfred forbade her from reading it. Without his knowledge, she read it and concluded that national socialism (Nazism) and international socialism (communism) had much in common.[11] Hitler's state control was unmistakable; he loathed free-market capitalism and liberty.[12] Another book she read was Barbara Cartland's book *Ronald Cartland*, the story of a young conservative who was one of the too few warnings that appeasement of Nazi militarism was dangerous. Sadly, Cartland lost his life at Dunkirk in 1940.[13]

At age of seventeen, Margaret prepared for examinations to get into Oxford University and was successful, becoming the first member of her family to pursue higher education. When she arrived in Oxford in Autumn 1943, she felt uncomfortable around students of privilege and wealth and the socialistic atmosphere that dominated the university.[14] There were many progressives at her Somerville College, one of the four women's colleges at Oxford. Janet Vaughan, the principal of Somerville, viewed Conservatives as people with a type of mental defect.[15] Choosing chemistry, Thatcher discovered that many scientists were on the political left, including her chemistry tutor Dorothy Hodgkin whose husband was a Marxist historian. Whereas many college students heard their professors praise socialism, Margaret rejected socialist ideology. She read left-wing books and heard progressive arguments, but she was a "true blue" conservative who never wavered.[16] For her, the democratic socialist claim of combining the best features of capitalism and socialism for a superior way to govern was naïve. Democratic socialists presented noble goals, but they failed to see or appreciate how wealth creation advanced the standard of living.

When Margaret embraced politics, the two leading political parties were the Conservative Party and the Labour Party, the latter outgrowing the once powerful Liberal Party that declined in the early twentieth century. Mostly democratic socialist, the British Labour Party drew on the intellectual traditions of Fabianism, Guild Socialism, and Marxism. The Fabian Society, created in 1884, embraced reason and a patient approach in its socialist critique of society. Its name came from the Roman General Quintus Fabius Maximus who adopted a gradual strategy in defeating Hannibal's army. George Bernard Shaw, Sidney Webb, and other Fabians sought to nibble away at the political status quo as a more effective way to achieve socialism than the violent political approach of revolutionaries. Guild Socialism was a mixture of French syndicalism and Fabianism. With French syndicalism, the "Syndicat" or trade union sought power to run industries and would do so with violence if necessary. In the British context, Guild Socialism opposed violent means, but it too saw democratic associations of workers as playing key roles in the transformation of society. These socialists valued citizen participation and they took a more decentralized approach compared to the Fabians who tended to rely on elite leaders and administrators. Marxism embraced class conflict and the eventual collapse of capitalism and the emergence of communism. Although the Labour Party refused any affiliation with the Communist Party of Great Britain, there were Marxists in the party who exerted influence, notably in the 1970s. From time to time, there were Labour Party members who were impatient with gradual and moderate approaches of political action, and they demanded more radical versions of socialism.[17] Whether moderate or radical, all self-respecting Labour politicians promised their constituents they would "soak the rich" to reduce inequality.[18]

Fascinated with politics, Margaret joined the Oxford University Conservative Association (OUCA) and learned of the influence of both democrat and radical socialists in and out of the university. As World War II concluded, the Conservative Party showed signs of complacency, unaware of a socialist landslide around the corner in the United Kingdom. She later wrote that this development should not have been a surprise since history gave evidence of war advancing people's acceptance of state control. It was not all that mysterious; voters became familiar with the command economy of the war and accepted it in peacetime.[19] Keynesianism seemed reasonable and perhaps a more rigorous application of government intervention by socialists was a good idea. Decades later, her critics linked her hardline policies to her noninvolvement in combat experience, suggesting that the social solidarity of war opened veterans to the idea of bigger government. However, this notion fails to explain the soldier-politicians who chose conservative politics.[20]

In 1945, the differences between Tory and Labour programs were not dramatic. Tories did not endorse the nationalization of industries, but they accepted the idea of extensive government spending and state control.[21] Differentiating a robust form of Keynesianism from mild socialism was not always easy. After the electoral defeat of Winston Churchill's government, the nation saw Labour, under the leadership of former social worker Clement Attlee, pull the country in a socialist direction. Discovering progressive Tories in her political circle, Margaret Roberts believed it was important to have more people with a working-class background embrace conservative politics. She argued with the "better born" Tories who supported redistribution of wealth, asking them how redistribution would work with country estates?[22] It was rare to find those with a working-class background seeking political office as a Tory. Norman Tebbit, who experienced "economic troubles" growing up, found a home in the Conservative Party, but he was one of the few who became an important Tory MP.[23]

Thatcher became president of the OUCA in 1946 as she began her research in her final year of university study. She earned a strong second-class degree in chemistry, but decided to pursue law as a more fitting avenue for her interest in politics, and, in fact, successful completion of the Bar exams did open new opportunities for her. At her first attendance at a Conservative Party conference, she lamented that party leaders were too passive to the problem of collectivism. This was the opposite of many rank-and-file Conservatives who could not reconcile themselves to any hint of socialism.[24] She witnessed firsthand how socialism was unpleasant; in 1952, socialists on her father's local counsel removed his rank of alderman from him, an act that distressed her.[25]

As had been the case for other conservatives looking for guidance, Margaret found F. A. Hayek's *The Road to Serfdom* refreshing; the controversial book warned of the dangers of state control of the economy.[26] In the chapter "The Great Utopia," Hayek wrote: "While 'progressives' in England and elsewhere were still deluding themselves that communism and fascism represented opposite poles, more and more people began to ask themselves whether these new tyrannies were not the outcome of the same tendencies."[27] More in vogue with British intellectuals were socialist thinkers or the ideas of John Maynard Keynes, who Hayek viewed as an artist and politician and less as a scholar.[28] As an opponent of big government, the Austrian Hayek encountered rejections from three publishers before the University of Chicago Press agreed to publish *The Road to Serfdom*. Socialists hated the book, but the sales were surprisingly high and additional printings were necessary to meet the demand.[29]

Years later Margaret commented on the book's influence, admitting that it was not until the mid-1970s before she fully appreciated and understood the implications of the "little masterpiece."[30] In sharp contrast to Keynesians and socialists, she wanted limited government with fewer bureaucrats. Her intellectual curiosity partly explains her desire to understand the arguments of conservative thinkers. Most of Margaret's enthusiasm for conservative, free-market ideas was due to the small-business common sense of her early years. Much of what Hayek wrote reflected her understanding of the problem with state control over the individual.

II

Leaving Oxford, Margaret Roberts had a good understanding of politics and a desire to be a member of Parliament. One of her mentors was Patricia Hornsby-Smith, "a fiery, vivacious redhead" considered by some as the leading female politician of the era.[31] In January 1949, Margaret won the Conservative candidacy for Dartford, a town on the eastern fringe of London; one year later she campaigned for the general election of February 23, 1950. Dartford was a formidable Labour seat and her first opponent was Norman Dodds, an old-fashioned, "chivalrous socialist."[32] In the *Gravesend and Dartford Reporter*, she asked readers: "Are YOU going to let this proud island race, who at one time would never accept charity, drift on from crisis to crisis under a further spell of shaky Socialist finance?"[33] She attacked socialism with passion in newspaper articles, in speeches outside factory gates, and anywhere in the constituency except drinking establishments. According to biographer Charles Moore, she presented an earlier version of Thatcherism that did not change much throughout her career.[34] Her loss to Dodds was no surprise, but she made political progress by receiving over 24,000 votes to her opponent's more than 38,000, a reduction of 6,000 votes for Dodds. In the months that followed, she learned to drive an automobile, bought her first car, met Winston Churchill, and prepared for an expected election that came in October 1951.

Churchill's election manifesto was a full attack on the British "Socialist Government"—the only one in the Empire and Commonwealth—with its "nationalization," reckless spending, and high taxation. The language was clear: "The attempt to impose a doctrinaire Socialism upon an Island which has grown great and famous by free enterprise has inflicted serious injury upon our strength and prosperity."[35] Six years of Labour government was enough, and the Conservative Party won the 1951 election with a majority of seventeen seats. However, Norman Dodds once again defeated Margaret who soon after married Denis Thatcher, a divorced businessman ten years her senior. He was a genuine Conservative and he had money to support her political ambitions to dismantle socialism and install free-enterprise policies.[36] But this would have to wait as Margaret Thatcher practiced law, became a mother in 1953 with the birth of twins Mark and Carol, and faced political disappointment when she failed to win a candidacy for a more favorable seat.

A safe Conservative seat opened in 1958 and she narrowly won the candidacy for Finchley, North London. In campaign speeches for the October 1959 general election, she maintained her attack on socialism, making the important point that the Labour Party's notion of "public ownership" or "nationalized" industries was government control rather than control by the people (nation).[37] The Tories, led by Harold Macmillan, once again were victorious and Thatcher easily won and joined the small group of 25 female MPs in a House of 630 members. There were frustrating times for conservatives suspicious of collectivist trends and Thatcher later wrote that during Macmillan's tenure as prime minister (1957–1963), the Conservative Party moved "in the direction of state intervention."[38] Macmillan was proud of his "middle way," but even his nanny concluded that "Mr. Harold is a dangerous Pink."[39] But party support was strong for Macmillan; the majority of Tory MPs had attended private schools and had upper-middle-class backgrounds.[40] The son of a lawyer, a graduate of Cambridge University, and a moderate Tory who promoted Keynesianism, Jim Prior also became an MP in 1959. He wrote that Thatcher "wasn't really one of our set."[41] Middle-way thinking was unattractive to her.

Most journalists were receptive to bigger government, and it is notable that Thatcher's maiden speech in Parliament, on February 5, 1960, defended freedom of the press. She pointed out how Labour leaders controlled the media at the local level by concealing information from journalists. Taking advantage of a loophole in the law and opposed to any check on their power, Labour-controlled councils denied reporters from committee meetings. Such socialist control was unacceptable; Thatcher wrote 250 hand-written letters to backbenchers requesting their support for her bill to make councils more accountable. She won and the *Daily Express* declared that a "new star was born in Parliament."[42]

Thatcher's so-called reactionary conservatism came with political risks. Tory Party members in the centre-left had an easier pathway to promotion whereas "reactionary" Conservatives were suspect.[43] In 1952, Prime Minister Winston Churchill had admitted the influence of Labour Party socialism on the Conservative Party: "Our complicated society would be deeply injured if we did not practice what is called in the United States the bipartisan habit of mind."[44] Thatcher knew the score and believed it was a setback for the party; there was a lack of "fire" in "Conservatism." The Labour government of the post-1964 period, Thatcher argued, caused serious economic damage, but Conservatives were also partly responsible.[45] Not wanting to be out of touch with the trend toward greater state control of the economy, many Tory politicians, she observed, became increasingly tone-deaf to the conservative instincts of ordinary people who questioned the wisdom of bigger government and subsequent higher taxes.[46]

One conservative politician bucking the trend was Conservative backbencher Nigel Birch, who argued that the government failed to control public spending. Economic Secretary to the Treasury Birch resigned as did Financial Secretary to the Treasury Enoch Powell in January 1958 in protest against the government's increased spending. Birch's speeches on economic matters offered Thatcher an excellent education on economic policy.[47] In July 1961, he stated in the House of Commons that nationalized industries in England siphoned capital from private enterprise that was necessary for economic growth. His example of the devastating impact of government intervention on the coal industry was compelling:

> Today one can import coal to South Wales coming from West Virginia more cheaply than it can be produced in South Wales. Neither Front Bench, as far as I know, is keen to import coal from West Virginia—so up goes the price of steel.

It made no economic sense for the government to continue to subsidize money-losing industries.[48] British economist Lionel Robbins, who presented important analysis on scarcity and economics, wrote: "Every act which involves time and scarce means for the achievement of one end involves the relinquishment of their use for the achievement of another."[49] In this vein, the nationalization of industries was an inefficient allocation of resources.

In the summer of 1961, Thatcher expected to receive an appointment from Prime Minister Macmillan when Patricia Hornsby-Smith left the government for the business world. The Tory leadership wanted another woman in the government and Thatcher became parliamentary secretary in the Ministry of Pensions and National Insurance (MPNI). With her new position she looked to history for answers, believing it was important to re-read the original Beveridge Report, a 1942 government statement that explained the system of pensions and benefits for a postwar Britain. The influential document paved the way for the British welfare state of family allowances, universal health care, and a commitment to full employment. Although she saw many of the report's assumptions questionable, she approved where it attempted to limit the problems of welfare dependency and declining initiative for volunteerism.[50] Her research included taking seriously the views of the average citizen. She learned much about the Social Security system through letters sent to the government and she opposed any quick replies and instead studied the issue thoroughly.

Her preparation for parliamentary questions was exhaustive. Coming up with answers was not enough; she wanted to know the "why" behind each statement.[51] In the political forum, Conservatives could not take half measures with their homework. The MPNI was an excellent place for Thatcher to learn how government worked since the department dealt with the whole population whether it was pensioners, workers, farmers, fishermen, the unemployed, and those unable to work. Perhaps not a glamorous department, its operations alerted her of the dependency culture that was an unfortunate consequence of government trying to improve society. She discovered how welfare worked and how it failed and, equally important, how expensive it was. One of her bosses was the aristocrat Richard Wood (later becoming Lord Holderness) who disliked her tough approach.[52] The horrors of the Great Depression years remained vivid, thus even Tory politicians accepted government intervention that promised full employment or near full employment. It was not a stretch for Macmillan and his "patrician" ministers to embrace "a form of social democratic settlement."[53]

Some scholars argue that Thatcher initially, for the most part, stayed in step with Tory middle-of-the road positions on the economy. But her message at one public meeting in March 1962 suggests otherwise. In her view, the spending of the nation far exceeded what the nation earned. There was too much pressure for the government to spend, which led to higher prices and a disadvantage for the British competing on the world market.[54] She understood that criticism of Keynesianism or socialism was unpopular in the eyes of many journalists. In the 1960s, it became clear to her that an "increasingly self-conscious and self-confident media class" favored the progressive ideas promoted by the left. Whereas Harold Wilson, who led the Labour Party to power in the October 1964 election, won over the press, Alec Douglas-Home, who succeeded Harold Macmillan as prime minister in 1963, received much criticism in the newspapers. Despite the media support for progressivism and the government's defeat after thirteen years in power, Thatcher held on to her seat. To her dismay, Alec Douglas-Home stepped down from the leadership even though the Tory loss was narrow.[55]

III

With the Conservatives in opposition, Thatcher became shadow spokesman on pensions and found her way in a Tory Party not sympathetic to a strong free-market approach to government, although there were some serious free marketers. One with influence in the party was Enoch Powell, a genuine Conservative intellectual. Born in Stechford, Birmingham, in 1912, the brilliant Powell won numerous academic prizes throughout school and university. Later, he spoke at least eight languages. At age of twenty-five, he received the appointment of professor at the University of Sydney, thus becoming the youngest professor in the British Empire.[56] After serving magnificently in World War II in intelligence operations (he began as a private and left the war a brigadier), he entered politics becoming a member of Parliament in

1950. His support for free-market policies was unyielding and some argue that years before "Thatcherism" there was "Powellism."[57]

However, in 1965 Thatcher did not support Powell's Conservative leadership bid against the two leading contenders. She viewed Reggie Maudling, who was chancellor of the exchequer from 1962 to 1964, as a brainy man weakened by laziness which came with someone who saw themselves as the smartest person in the room. Edward Heath lacked human warmth, according to Thatcher.[58] Despite their weaknesses, they looked better than the idiosyncratic Powell who lost support among parliamentary party members.[59] He did not play the political game properly; he spoke uncompromisingly. As Thatcher pondered whether to support Maudling or Heath, her close friend Keith Joseph and fellow MP persuaded her to support Heath, seen as the best candidate to get things done. Heath supporters viewed her support with glee and were confident of victory.[60] Heath won the leadership on the first ballot and the new leader gave Thatcher the role of shadow housing and land. Leaving pensions was a relief for Thatcher who watched helplessly as the Labour government approved large pension and benefit increases.[61]

For the snap election of early 1966, the Conservative Party pointed to its manifesto *Action not Words*, but it was not enough; Harold Wilson and the Labour Party soundly defeated the Tories, gaining a majority of ninty-seven seats. Heath made Thatcher, with her tax lawyer credentials, Treasury spokesman on tax under Shadow chancellor Ian Macleod. The Opposition Treasury team, relying on mostly unpaid experts, was at a disadvantage facing a Treasury with the best officials of the Civil Service. The government knew its proposals inside out, but Thatcher was comfortable with her new role. While lacking formal training in economic theory, she believed she had a natural understanding of the handling of public money.[62]

It was an exciting time for Thatcher to expose what she believed was the recklessness of socialist economic management. One of her major targets was a new tax introduced by the Labour Party. The Selective Employment Tax (SET) broke the Labour campaign promise of "no severe increases in taxation." Leading up to her first major Commons speech as Treasury spokesman, she studied every budget speech and finance bill since World War II. She took "great pleasure" in revealing the "absurdities" of SET.[63] As a tax lawyer and housewife, her discussion of taxation came easily. There was favorable press from the *Daily Telegraph*: she was able "to slam the faces of the Government's Treasury ministers in the mud and then stamp on them."[64] *The Times* also used attention-grabbing language: "She was in full stride, her impeccable accent beginning to hammer on Labour ears like some devilish Rodean water torture."[65] Charles Moore explains that her criticism was unique for questioning "the entire wisdom" of economic policymakers and using household economics to argue that women as workers, wives, and mothers had a better understanding of the effects of taxes and inflation "than the men who inflicted both."[66] In most cases, who did the weekly household shopping? Who was aware of rising prices on milk and eggs? Home economics was useful for getting her message across.

Thatcher's speech at the Conservative Party conference in 1966 further clarified her economic ideas, particularly the problem with Labour's "Socialist path of higher and higher taxation" that reached 34.6 percent of GNP. Each citizen saw their tax burden rise over 20 percent in the two years of Labour government and, consequently, there were workers who altered their work behavior. The lesson was obvious for Thatcher; there was less productivity because the increased personal taxation caused workers to work less. The extra effort was not worth it for the average worker in the manufacturing industry. There was also an alarming Gallup poll, published in the *Sunday Telegraph*, revealing that most British industrialists "would emigrate if they were younger men at the start of their careers." An additional problem was the Labour Party's appetite for spending. The increase was significant, and Thatcher stated: "Small wonder we have a balance of payments crisis still, small wonder that we have stagnant production."[67] Her reputation grew as someone unafraid to call out socialist economics. Even the *Sun* newspaper, generally critical of Toryism in the 1960s, gave her the admiring headline "A Fiery Blonde Warns of the Road to Ruin."[68] More so than earlier times, sixties' culture gave greater attention to women and the press often singled out Thatcher, who welcomed the political attention, to present a woman's voice on important issues.[69]

A more confident Thatcher addressing the Labour government's budget in early 1967 offered a clear critique of "Wilsonian social theory." Discussing Labour's reference to "social justice," she gave her own spin on the term, arguing that one example of social injustice was taking "away too high a proportion of anyone's income." Theories of equality sounded good, but Britain needed "practical progress," something difficult to achieve if there was high inflation and taxation and not enough appreciation for the "managerial group."[70] Weeks earlier she had visited the United States and admired its free-market culture and how its government set more reasonable tax rates than Britain.[71]

At the Conservative Party conference in 1967, Thatcher once again delivered a "textbook 'Thatcherite' assault on socialism as an economic doctrine."[72] She began with an assessment of the results of "nationalization"—a higher cost of living and industry losses. With a nationalized industry, there is no hiring and firing as in private enterprise and thus efficiency suffers which causes higher prices for products from these government-owned industries. Whereas private industries must make money to survive, there is less incentive for a nationalized industry to be cost-conscious. Thatcher referenced

Keith Joseph in explaining that competition in the market was preferable to nationalization. She warned of the "confidence trickster" who adopted "a suave smooth manner" to justify government take-over of industries that reduced the freedom of citizens: "It is good to recall how our freedom has been gained in this country—not by great abstract campaigns but through the objections of ordinary men and women to having their money take from them by the State." The argument that nationalization "put power into the hands of the people" was false; first, anyone working in a nationalized industry had less independence to oppose government and, second, ordinary men and women had no tangible way to exercise their alleged power.[73]

The Tories saw Thatcher, who became popular with the Party rank and file, as a rising star and Heath made her a member of the shadow cabinet in October with the responsibility of fuel and power.[74] What followed were her speeches in the House of Commons pointing to uneconomic coal pits where men worked in dangerous conditions "to dig up coal that no wants to buy." Responding to her data, Labour politicians drew attention to the social costs of closing mines and putting men out of work.[75] Thatcher addressed the folly of propping up failing industries and Labour pointed to unemployment; both had valid points. Among those who Thatcher faced was Barbara Castle, Labour's recently appointed secretary of state for employment and productivity. A firebrand with a talent for rabble-rousing rhetoric, Castle once declared: "I'm no feminist. Judge me as a socialist."[76]

In command of the facts, Thatcher, the *Daily Telegraph* reported in May 1968, "gave a dazzling performance, firing salvo after salvo of devastating statistics into the Labour benches like a cannon firing grapeshot into a crowd." Rejecting the Labour complaint that it had inherited the deficit from the Tories, Thatcher gave evidence of both parties running up the deficit in election years. However, the Conservative Party returned to the black whereas the Labour Party continued to run deficits. On this occasion Labour's defense was feeble, and Castle later wrote: "Never in my whole life have I been worse prepared."[77]

In 1968, Thatcher received the honor of giving the annual Conservative Political Centre lecture usually reserved for the party leader. The purpose of this annual lecture was to offer "intellectual meat" for Tory conference attendees. Heath suggested the subject of women in politics, but she thought contrarily, and, on October 11, she presented a bolder topic—"What's Wrong With Politics?" Wearing a gold dress to attract the most attention, she pointed out the unfortunate tendency of "government to provide or to legislate for almost everything," an approach that gained momentum in the early 1960s when many politicians, Keynesian or socialist, viewed state management of the economy as the best way to grow the economy. This pursuit of "economic growth" led to greater government intervention that brought "more and more officials or bureaucrats" into the system. The growth of bureaucrats, she argued, made the government remote from the people and resulted in increased authoritarianism. Less government was vital: "What we need now is a far greater degree of personal responsibility and decision, far more independence from the government, and a comparative reduction in the role of government."[78]

Perhaps most remarkable was her criticism of price and wage controls (income policies, thus hinting at Milton Friedman's monetarism that received more attention in some circles. The American Friedman was a University of Chicago economist and his focus on money supply as the cause of inflation threatened Keynesian thinking. But more than having a steady supply of money as opposed to excessive printing of money, it was essential not to distort the market economy with government-controlled prices. Later in the month, journalist Samuel Brittan wrote his long article "Money Supply: The Great Debate" for the *Financial Times*.[79] In one sense, Thatcher was ahead of her time as a politician arguing that government control of prices was an ineffective economic policy. For her, the economic record demonstrated that competition was the answer for troublesome inflation:

> There have been far more price cuts in the supermarkets than in the nationalised industries. This shows the difference between the government doing the job itself and the government creating the conditions under which prices will be kept down through effective competition.

The role of the government was not compulsion, controlling "each and every salary that is paid." No government could ever know the correct amount and a government's decision to control people's wages was "repugnant to most of us."[80]

Socialists found Thatcher's speech annoying, and they attacked it from various angles. Almost twenty years later one critic did not like her wardrobe, complaining that the photo of her accompanying the text of her speech was evidence of her being "a throwback to another, more distant age."[81] If this was when Thatcherism began, socialists argued, it was the start of difficult and dark times for Britain. Forty-one years later, the socialist *New Statesman* adopted an interesting line of attack, arguing that Thatcherism "was akin to a Bolshevik movement: a group of ideologues emerged from the margins to seize control of the very centre and effect radical change. . . . All opposition had to be crushed."[82]

As she became better known, another free-market Conservative lost influence. Enoch Powell fell out of favor with party leaders and Heath sacked him from the shadow cabinet after he gave a provocative speech in April that warned of admitting too many immigrants. Was Powell a racist as his opponents argued, or was he a realist questioning whether the nation had the resources to care for the needs of a larger number of immigrants? At the end of the month, a Gallup poll of the people showed 74 percent of respondents agreeing with Powell.[83] A powerful orator and "our finest intellect," according to Thatcher, Powell, "was disliked and probably feared by Ted Heath."[84] Immigration was a sensitive subject, but there was more to Powell who outside the shadow cabinet had greater freedom to argue for capitalism and deregulation. Thatcher hailed him for getting her and others to think more clearly about inflation. There were signs of greater opposition to the left-of-center economic policy that dominated British politics.[85] Thatcher appeared to be reading more Hayek and being influenced by the free-market ideas of the Institute of Economic Affairs (IEA). Arthur Seldon of the IEA identified the widening gap between the centrists and Conservatives such as Thatcher, Joseph, and Geoffrey Howe.[86]

Thatcher's visit to the Soviet Union in 1969 gave her further evidence of an economic system burdened by "an endless chain of non-decision-making" propped up by official propaganda. Upon her return to London, she learned of being moved from Transport to the Education portfolio, replacing Sir Edward Boyle, the shadow education secretary who supported progressive education. Thatcher's new position allowed her to criticize Labour's commitment to making the secondary school system fully comprehensive, a change she viewed as socialist. The comprehensive plan meant abolishing the division between the grammar schools that catered to bright students and the secondary moderns that educated the less academic student. As a product of grammar school, Thatcher had risen to her present position as a result of a free and good education, and she wanted the same for others. "Socialist education policies" discouraged gifted children from advancing; this was bad for society.[87] She had another reason to object to Labour; the party used the comprehensive plan to lessen the power of local education authorities and give the central government more say.[88]

In May 1970, Prime Minister Wilson saw polls favoring his party and he called for a general election on June 18. With its manifesto, *A Better Tomorrow*, the Conservative Party offered voters a contrasting message to the Labour Party and its *In Place of Strife*, the White Paper of 1969 proposing labor union reform. The outlook of intellectuals and journalists was mostly anti-Conservative as they supported government planning, greater public spending, and high taxes, but the pollsters were wrong about Labour having a lead. Enough voters were upset with the financial and economic crises of the Labour government; the election was a victorious one for the Conservatives and Thatcher.[89] With its adoption of free-market policies, evidenced by its rejection of government subsidies and prices and incomes policies, the party received a majority of thirty-one seats. Although Thatcher's appointment as education secretary was a junior post, viewed as a natural ceiling for a female when senior cabinet posts were for men only, it was a promotion signifying an important step for her political future.[90] One argument is that Heath tired of her "hectoring behaviour" and put her in education "whose business" had little connection with other departments.[91] If he hoped to corral her influence, it did not work. In time, her prominence grew, and she became a threat to Heath, the technocrat planner, who lacked the temperament to embrace new economic ideas.[92]

IV

As a first-time minister, Thatcher arrived at her office at the Department of Education and Science (DES) located on Curzon Street and discovered that her permanent secretary, Sir William Pile, was a left-wing sympathizer.[93] In Pile's eyes, Thatcher was narrow-minded with "abhorrent" passions that clashed with the thinking of the educational establishment. When she attempted to stop the reinstatement of a fired left-wing teacher who published poems written by his students, Pile told her it was not her business. At one point, she attempted to have Pile replaced suggesting he was a security risk because of his Russian wife, but Sir William Armstrong, the head of the civil service, rejected any move against Pile.[94]

Thatcher described her three-person ministerial team as "one friendly, one hostile and one neutral." Her main difficulty was not the unenthusiastic response of others to her executive style of leadership that differed from the usual consultative style of previous years. Nor did she have a problem with people on a personal level; she could cope with different personalities. The major obstacle for Thatcher was the "self-righteously socialist" ethos of central planning and social theory that dominated the department.[95] Although initially she had good relations with Toby Weaver—the deputy secretary who embodied paternalistic socialism—she gave no mention of him in her memoirs, which hurt him deeply.[96]

In a position of power, Thatcher could advance her earlier fight with Labour's comprehensive education. However, the commitment of some Tories to comprehensive education "barely distinguished them from moderate socialists." For the most part, she "was not among friends," proven almost immediately when she took a stand against the education establishment's pressuring of local authorities to go comprehensive which she believed hurt the education system. Despite her concern for the broader effects of egalitarian ideals on education and Heath's opposition to Labour's ideological tactics to turn grammar schools into comprehensives, progressivism continued at a good pace; she rejected less than 10 percent of comprehensive proposals during her stint as education minister.[97] Her most significant setback, however, came over the issue of withdrawing free school milk for students over the age of seven. The story had several twists, including initial wide support for Thatcher's attempt to protect the education budget for a school building program, but in the end many in the media portrayed her as heartless and uncaring for the welfare of young children.[98] Labour MP Willie Hamilton called her "Mrs. Scrooge with the painted face." Labour MP Edward Short declared she took "milk away from the nation's young children." *The Sun* asked: "Is Mrs. Thatcher Human?"[99] Heath considered firing her.[100]

There were also the attacks by college student protestors over Thatcher's proposal to make university student unions, usually controlled by the Left, more financially accountable with public money. She took issue with "kindergarten Marxism," recognizing that its actions were "very vicious." While participating in a ceremony at the South Bank Polytechnic, located in south London, she faced 2,000 "screaming" students upset with her attempt at reform. At various universities, students burned her in effigy and called her a "fascist pig," apparently unaware that fascism rejected the free-market capitalism and liberty she championed.[101] A common chant was "Thatcher out! Revolutionary socialism in!" It was a tough year of hostile demonstrations and mounted police were on-site for her protection. One major opponent was Jack Straw, president of the National Union of Students (NUS), who later became a lawyer and a political adviser of the Labour Party. In the end, without support from university administrators, Thatcher decided against pushing for change.[102] Overall, she held a dim view of universities and most tenured academics, notably those teaching arts and social sciences. One biographer argues that she saw these professors "as lazy, state-subsidised parasites, cynically abusing the privileged freedom which they enjoyed."[103]

More pressing was the weight of criticism from the press, but she claimed that this strengthened her. She had the support of the prime minister and, years later in his autobiography, Heath wrote of her freedom to get the job done. Deflating the notion of her being fiscally responsible, he also pointed out how the expenditure on education increased from 6.1 to 6.3 percent of GNP under her watch.[104] In early 1972, she began to experience a warmer political climate.[105] Would it be a good year? Soon problems shook the confidence of Conservatives who expected Heath to support the Selsdon Park manifesto that embraced lower taxation and minimal government intervention in industry. When Conservative leaders met at Selsdon Park Hotel in Surrey in January 1970, they sought a greater role for individual citizens, expecting them "to stand on their own feet, to accept responsibility for themselves and their families."[106] Harold Wilson coined the term the "Selsdon Man" as a characterization of the right wing of the Tory Party, but there was no apparent political gain for Labour from this label and, in fact, two years later a group of Conservative backbenchers including Nicholas Ridley, John Biffen, and Jock Bruce-Gardyne viewed the term as a badge of honor. They created the Selsdon Group to get the Tories back on track with free-market ideas. Thatcher later embraced the notion of being a "Selsdon Woman."[107]

In 1970, the signs of staying on course with a leaner government and lower taxes looked promising. Heath's dismantling of the Price and Income Board, the Industrial Reorganization Corporation, and the minister of technology had been significant moves from the government intervention of the previous Labour government. No government bailout of "lame duck" industries was a welcome position for those who wanted the Conservative Party to differentiate itself from Labour policies.[108] But to the despair of conservatives, this new approach did not last. In 1971, unemployment hit 1 million and Heath lacked confidence in the market correcting itself; he had to act. Rather than pursuing its policy of reduced public ownership, the Heath government propped up a bankrupt Rolls-Royce by issuing an emergency bill to nationalize its aero-engine division; it also reversed its decision to reduce subsidies to the Upper Clyde Shipbuilders. The government looked weak to conservatives when it failed to reduce the power of the trade unions with its Industrial Relations Act of 1971. It took 450 hours of parliamentary time for the measure to become law, but enforcing the act was problematic as various legal disputes surfaced in the wake of a coalminers' strike that demonstrated the vulnerability of the government.

A major blow to Heath was when the Amalgamated Union of Engineering Workers (AUEW) boycotted the government's Industrial Relations Court. The action of the National Union of Mineworkers (NUM) further hurt the Heath government with its coordinated pickets that slowed the distribution of coal. Thatcher was aghast that mining leaders flouted the law, rejected an 8 percent wage raise, and caused trouble for the government before agreeing to a much larger increase in 1974. The dispute had long-lasting negative effects on the government and politics.[109] In addition to the expansion of public spending in late 1971, there were two expansionary budgets in 1972. November 6, 1972, marked the day when the Tory government introduced statutory powers for income and price controls. Controlling wages and prices was a politically attractive option for governments to fight inflation as it did not require them to reduce their spending, but this represented artificial tampering of supply and demand and was not the approach recommended by free-market economists.[110] Thatcher told fellow Tory MP Cecil Parkinson that she fought against income policies in cabinet and hoped others outside cabinet would do likewise.[111]

Critics claimed that Heath lost his nerve, and this was the beginning of the government's "U turn."[112] Perhaps Heath's Keynesian convictions explain his drift from conservatism.[113] This adjustment did not alarm Tories such as Reggie Maudling whose instincts were for an interventionist economy policy.[114] Lacking a clear theory of inflation and blaming wage increases for inflation, Heath was too impatient to step back and adopt a noninterventionist economic policy, and instead saw the regulation of wages and prices as the remedy for inflation.[115] Like many others, he did not view money supply as the culprit. In August 1973, the British magazine *Management Today* compared Heath's and Milton Friedman's understanding of inflation and asked: "But is the entire phenomenon of unusually rapid and apparently ineradicable inflation new in itself?" The editors saw inflation as an ongoing component of western society. It was unwise to blame union militancy or "special-factor explanations." Perhaps "economic historians half a century hence may well not be impressed by" arguments blaming inflation on union militancy. For twenty-first-century economic historians, the editors wrote, "the inflation will probably seem a classic case of monetary inflation, engendered by the usual process of overproduction of liquid currencies."[116]

Friedman argued that Heath's imposition of wage and price controls could not solve inflation, a fact that Heath knew too. So why controls? Friedman believed Heath was a typical politician not too serious about inflation; in fact, an advantage of an "inflationary policy" was that it was a form of taxation:

> It's a form of taxation directly in the pieces of paper that are printed to pay government bills. It's a form of taxation indirectly in that, as inflation occurs, people are pushed up into higher and higher tax brackets and thus are subject to higher tax rates without any change in the law.

According to Friedman, Heath had two other reasons for price and wage controls. They were "proof" to voters that he wanted to slow inflation and they repressed "the symptoms of inflation for a time."[117] The short-term results might last to the next election. In the end, Heath was too much a Keynesian to act on anything else. Social democrat scholar Stephen Haseler argues that Heath's U-turn represented a social-democratic direction worthy of praise.[118]

V

One Thatcher biographer points out that Heath's economic policy reversals appeared to receive the support of Thatcher which, in turn, increased Enoch Powell's suspicion that Thatcher was not a genuine free marketer. Powell did not view Thatcher's position in education as a credible excuse for her lack of opposition to areas outside her field.[119] But Heath did keep Thatcher outside the circle of those making the economic decisions and she was plenty busy in the "high spending" education department attempting to keep program spending in check. Heath preferred not to hear her voice and had difficulty tolerating the sight of her.[120] Anthony Benn offered a simple reason for Heath's and Thatcher's cool relationship: "I daresay Heath doesn't like women and she probably doesn't like men who don't like women."[121] At cabinet meetings, her seat was one of the furthest from Heath; she persuaded the more senior Joseph Godber, MP for Grantham, to ask noneducation questions so that she would have an opportunity to ask supplementary questions. Reginald Maudling left meetings complaining about "that bloody woman rabbiting on."[122]

In her memoirs, Thatcher wrote that she was a "strong supporter" of Heath's Industrial Revolution Bill, but she became distrustful of parts. The bill showed significant favor to trade unionism, making it easier for workers in the key industries of gas, water, and electricity to strike. She believed that the Tories were naïve to expect their opponents would respect the bill, especially the parts viewed by labor activists as too controlling. On socialists and respect for law and order, Thatcher's assessment was overly partisan with a broad characterization of "unscrupulous people" whose primary motive was political.[123] The worst offenders were the "communists" whose strategy was to gain power in the trade union movement to advance their cause.

Thatcher was not a major cheerleader for Heath even on issues she supported. For example, she initially agreed with Heathites concerning Britain's alliance with Europe. In 1961, Prime Minister Harold Macmillan began the process of Britain joining the European Community, but entry did not take place until January 1, 1973. Some claim entry was Heath's most successful act, but by 1973 Thatcher showed just enough enthusiasm to disprove arguments that she was anti-Europe. Improving economic trade was good if there was no compromise of Britain's sovereignty. Entry was what the Tory establishment wanted and expected, reaffirming Heath's commitment from years past.[124]

The early months of 1974 were not economically promising as the Heath government initiated a three-day work week to minimize the damage caused by miner unions. The NUM had adopted "work-to-rule" in 1973 as a pressure tactic for higher wages. Could the Heath government survive a coal shortage? Reducing the consumption of electricity with the shorter work week, the government hoped to last the winter without running out of coal. With most of Britain's workforce supposedly on a three-day week, productivity varied depending on the mood of both managers and workers. Complicating the situation was a shortage of oil. *The Economist* suggested the best way to handle the demands of miner unionists was a "hardest-nosed" approach of costly penalties to unregistered unions who broke agreements and the enforcement of the "original intentions" of the Industrial Relations Act.[125] Double-figure inflation caused widespread alarm; something had to be done. The National Economic Development Council painted a "gloomy picture" of the scarcity of steel and manufacturing firms facing possible bankruptcy.[126]

Some argued for caution and not antagonizing labor leaders while others argued against appeasement as they believed there was nothing to lose since labor unions would always demand more. Thatcher understood that NUM, consisting of many militants, was a powerful organization, able to cut off the electricity supply if negotiations were unsatisfactory. She believed that NUM wanted to bring down the Conservatives as much as it wanted to increase miners' earnings.[127] *The Economist* warned of the trade unions infiltrated by communists whose focus was on power rather than increased wages. Despite the Communist Party's small membership of approximately 30,000, its influence in trade unions increased each year because it saw the opportunity for greater power in the economic chaos of the 1970s. The militancy of the Socialist Labour League and other leftist groups motivated the communists to act more forcefully. It helped socialists that most ordinary union members showed no interest in running their unions and were usually unaware of the politics of union candidates. *The Economist* noted the communist power of shop stewards at major companies such as Dick Etheridge at British Leyland Longbridge, Jock Gibson at Chrysler's Ryton plant, Jimmy Reid at Govan Shipbuilders, and Bernie Steer at the London docks. Of the thirty-five-man executive of the Transport and General Workers' Union, ten were card-carrying communists. Even further to the left was the AUEW with its Marxist president Hugh Scanlon. Its fifty-two-man national committee was responsible for policy-making and it consisted of twelve communists and fifteen Marxist allies. The National Union of Teachers had a communist president and many of the officials of the National Union of Public Employees were Marxists. NUM was one of the most militant unions, with thirteen militant leftists on its twenty-seven-man executive. In many industries and workplaces, communists were usually articulate and influential candidates who demanded action.[128]

In January 1974, the miners took the next step of a full-blown strike and the Tories were in trouble. Labour leaders sensed victory, but with the combination of a poor economy and growing labor militancy could the Labour Party and its "Back-to-work with Labour" program be the answer? The proposed program introduced in January would cost 2.5 billion pounds a year and thus bring much higher taxation. *The Economist* was not hopeful:

> Ordinary mortals would need to be saints if they did not respond to higher taxes and to a giveaway to the miners by demanding higher wages themselves. Otherwise virtually every working man in the country would have to take a sizeable cut in his living standards.[129]

In the following month, Heath called an election and campaigned on the question of "Who Governs Britain?" The issue of labor leaders defying the authority of the government was important, but was it enough to give the Tories victory? Voters had their say and while the Conservative Party won more popular votes it received fewer seats than the Labour Party. With less than half of the seats in the House of Commons, it was Labour's turn to get the nation in economic order.

When the Labour Party returned to power in March 1974, Denis Healey, as chancellor of the exchequer, continued much of Heath's economic approach to state-managed capitalism.[130] The Tory government of 1970–1974 had failed to control its borrowing and spending and inflation took its toll.[131] Thatcher won her seat easily, but she was unhappy with Heath's economic direction and frustrated with the lack of alternative approaches.[132] In her mind, she served British workers by championing the taxpayer against government spenders and by opposing the trade unions that in her view did not have the best interests of workers.[133] The grocer's daughter embraced the values of hard work and individual responsibility, but the Tory Party favored policy with a progressive flavor. Tory Keynesianism was often too close to socialism. She argued that Heath's U-turn was a failure; it brought more inflation and tarnished the Conservative Party.[134] If there was any chance of her playing a major role in leading the Tory Party in another direction, she would need to gain more credibility on what Britain required to rise above its economic difficulties.

NOTES

1. *The Times*, 11 October 1961.

2. Hansard, HC, 13 March 1962, Volume 655, columns 1161 and 1281, https://hansard.parliament.uk/Commons/1962-03-13/debates/0b7f180e-7ca5-48df-af80-b70ad6d7e82c/NationalInsuranceAndNationalAssistanceBenefits. For additional information on Mendleson, see John Mendleson, M.P., http://discovery.nationalarchives.gov.uk/details/r/7a34baf9-b936-4e8f-bdc4-0a7304d494b5. Mendleson was born in Poland.

3. Margaret Thatcher, *Margaret Thatcher: The Autobiography* (New York: HarperPerennial, 2010), 1.

4. Thatcher, *Margaret Thatcher*, 2.

5. Thatcher, *Margaret Thatcher*, 3–4. Mark Garnett, "Banality in Politics: Margaret Thatcher and the Biographers," *Political Studies Review* 5 (2007), 174.

6. Thatcher, *Margaret Thatcher*, 8.

7. Harris, *Not for Turning*, 13, 15, 17.

8. David W. Bebbington, *Evangelicalism in Modern Britain: A History from the 1730s to the 1980s* (London: Routlege, 1993), 212. The so-called social gospel refers

to the emphasis on social and political reform to transform society rather than a focus on individual sin and salvation.

9. Thatcher, *Margaret Thatcher*, 17.
10. Thatcher, *Margaret Thatcher*, 18.
11. Thatcher, *Margaret Thatcher*, 19, 24.
12. Severe price and wage controls were the norm as was National Socialist control of what businesses could produce. Nazi propagandists might claim Germany had a free-market economy, but in truth companies were expected to do the bidding of the state. William Shirer, *The Rise and Fall of the Third Reich* (New York: Simon & Schuster, 2011), 261. Richard J. Evans, *The Third Reich in Power* (New York: Penguin Books, 2005), 335, 347, 351.
13. Thatcher, *Margaret Thatcher*, 24.
14. Goodlad, *Thatcher*, 18–19.
15. Moore, *Margaret Thatcher*, 45.
16. Thatcher, *Margaret Thatcher*, 23.
17. David Regan, "The Local Left and Its National Pretensions," in *Policies of Thatcherism: Thoughts from a London Thinktank*, eds. Richard Haas and Oliver Knox (Lanham, MD: University Press of America, 1991), 3–5, 9–11, 12, 25–26. Also see, Eric Heffer, "Communists and the Labour Party," *New Statesman*, 8 February 1974, 171–72. For more on the socialist theory of moderates (those opposing any major transformation of capitalism), see Patrick Diamond, *The Crosland Legacy: The Future of British Social Democracy* (Bristol: Bristol University Press, 2016).
18. "Mr Healey's Half-Measures," *New Statesman*, 16 August 1974, 205.
19. Harris, *Not for Turning*, 30–31. Thatcher, *Margaret Thatcher*, 27, 36.
20. Harris, *Not for Turning*, 25.
21. Shirley Letwin, *The Anatomy of Thatcherism* (London: Fontana, 1992), 56. One dissident conservative voice was A.G. Erskine-Hill.
22. Moore, *Margaret Thatcher*, 55.
23. Norman Tebbit, *Upwardly Mobile* (London: Futura, 1989), 3.
24. Thatcher, *Margaret Thatcher*, 39–40.
25. Goodlad, *Thatcher*, 16.
26. Thatcher, *Margaret Thatcher*, 40.
27. Caldwell, ed., *The Collected Works of F.A. Hayek Volume II*, 78.
28. Friedrich A. Hayek, *A Tiger by the Tail: The Keynesian Legacy of Inflation* (San Francisco: Cato Institute, 1979), 97–98.
29. Caldwell, ed., *The Collected Works of F.A. Hayek Volume II*, 15–18.
30. Thatcher, *Margaret Thatcher*, 41.
31. Thatcher, *Margaret Thatcher*, 43, 50.
32. Thatcher, *Margaret Thatcher*, 51. In her political career, she had good rapport with other left-wing politicians, including Charlie Pannel, Eric Heffer, and Dennis Skinner. See Harris, *Not for Turning*, 39.
33. Margaret Thatcher Foundation (MTF), *Gravesend and Dartford Reporter*, 28 January 1950, https://www.margaretthatcher.org/document/100856.
34. Moore, *Margaret Thatcher*, 98.

35. 1951 Conservative Party General Election Manifesto, http://www.conservativemanifesto.com/1951/1951-conservative-manifesto.shtml.

36. Harris, *Not for Turning*, 43–44. Thatcher, *Margaret Thatcher*, 49, 59.

37. Harris, *Not for Turning*, 40.

38. Thatcher, *Margaret Thatcher*, 62.

39. Letwin, *The Anatomy of Thatcherism*, 59.

40. Goodlad, *Thatcher*, 26.

41. Jim Prior, *A Balance of Power* (London: Hamish Hamilton, 1986), 21.

42. Thatcher, *Margaret Thatcher*, 73–75. Also, see Moore, *Margaret Thatcher*, 147–48.

43. Thatcher, *Margaret Thatcher*, 76.

44. John Ramsden, "'A Party for Owners or a Party for Earners?' How Far Did the British Conservative Party Really Change after 1945?," *Transactions of the Royal Historical Society* 37 (1987), 52.

45. Thatcher, *Margaret Thatcher*, 76.

46. Thatcher, *Margaret Thatcher*, 76.

47. Thatcher, *Margaret Thatcher*, 77.

48. Hansard, 1803-2005 – People (B), Mr Nigel Birch, Economic Situation, HC Deb, 26 July 1961 vol 645 cc558-560, https://api.parliament.uk/historic-hansard/commons/1961/jul/26/economic-situation#S5CV0645P0_19610726_HOC_263.

49. In his book *An Essay on the Nature & Significance of Economic Science* (1932), Robbins wrote: "Economics is the science which studies human behaviour as a relationship between ends and scarce means which have alternative uses." https://milescorak.files.wordpress.com/2020/02/robbins-essay-nature-significance-economic-science.pdf.

50. Thatcher, *Margaret Thatcher*, 78–79.

51. Thatcher, *Margaret Thatcher*, 80.

52. Moore, *Margaret Thatcher*, 160. Campbell, *Margaret Thatcher*, 143, 146.

53. Daniel Stedman Jones, *Masters of the Universe: Hayek, Friedman, and the Birth of Neoliberal Politics* (Princeton University Press, 2012), 191, 197.

54. MTF, Speech to Finchley Conservatives, 19 March 1962, https://www.margaretthatcher.org/document/100958.

55. Thatcher, *Margaret Thatcher*, 84–87.

56. Philip Norton, "The Oratory of Enoch Powell," in *Conservative Orators: From Baldwin to Cameron*, ed. Hayton Richard and Andrew S. Crines (Manchester: Manchester University Press, 2015), 74.

57. Harris, *Not for Turning*, 66–67. However, Philip Norton argues that there were Powellites, but not Powellism. See Norton, "The Oratory of Enoch Powell," 81.

58. Thatcher, *Margaret Thatcher*, 87–89.

59. Robert Blake, *The Conservative Party from Peel to Thatcher* (London: Methuen, 1985), 306.

60. Thatcher, *Margaret Thatcher*, 88–89. Edward Heath, *The Course of My Life: My Autobiography* (London: Hodder & Stoughton, 1998), 268. Also, Moore, *Margaret Thatcher*, 178.

61. Thatcher, *Margaret Thatcher*, 89.

62. Harris, *Not for Turning*, 63. Thatcher, *Margaret Thatcher*, 89–90.

63. Thatcher, *Margaret Thatcher*, 90.

64. Quoted in Thatcher, *Margaret Thatcher*, 91.

65. Quoted in Campbell, *Margaret Thatcher*, 171.

66. Moore, *Margaret Thatcher*, 182–83.

67. MTF, Speech to Conservative Party Conference (1966), 12 October 1966, https://www.margaretthatcher.org/document/101520.

68. Goodlad, *Thatcher*, 31.

69. Moore, *Margaret Thatcher*, 183.

70. MTF, HC S [Budget Resolutions and Economic Situation], 17 April 1967, https://www.margaretthatcher.org/document/101551.

71. Moore, *Margaret Thatcher*, 200.

72. Harris, *Not for Turning*, 64.

73. MTF, Speech to Conservative Party Conference (1967), 20 October 1967, https://www.margaretthatcher.org/document/101586.

74. Moore, *Margaret Thatcher*, 189.

75. MTF, HC S 2R [Coal Industry Bill], 28 November 1967, https://www.margaretthatcher.org/document/101594.

76. On Castle's rhetoric, see David S. Moon, "The Oratory of Barbara Castle," in *Labour Orators from Bevan to Miliband*, eds. Andrew S. Crines and Richard Hayton (Manchester; New York: Manchester University Press, 2014), 62–75.

77. Campbell, *Margaret Thatcher*, 188.

78. MTF, Conservative Political Centre Lecture ("What's wrong with politics?"), 11 October 1968, https://www.margaretthatcher.org/document/101632. Also, see Moore, *Margaret Thatcher*, 192–93.

79. Edward Nelson, "Milton Friedman and U.K. Economic Policy: 1938-1979," *Federal Reserve Bank of St. Louis Review* 91, no. 5, Part 2 (September/October 2009), 486.

80. Conservative Political Centre Lecture ("What's wrong with politics?"), 11 October 1968. Also, see Moore, *Margaret Thatcher*, 192–93.

81. Bill Swartz, "The Thatcher Years," *Socialist Register 1987: Conservatism in Britain and America. Rhetoric and Reality* 23 (March 1987), 119.

82. *New Statesman*, 2 March 2009, 4.

83. Dominic Sandbrooke, "'Enoch Powell Speaks for Britain': The Press, the Public and the Speech," *The Political Quarterly* 89, no. 3 (July–September 2018), 393.

84. Thatcher, *Margaret Thatcher*, 93. Also see, Moore, *Margaret Thatcher*, 194–95.

85. Thatcher, *Margaret Thatcher*, 92, 96. Moore, *Margaret Thatcher*, 194.

86. Campbell, *Margaret Thatcher*, 179, 181.

87. Thatcher, *Margaret Thatcher*, 99–100.

88. Moore, *Margaret Thatcher*, 202–4.

89. Blake, *The Conservative Party from Peel to Thatcher,* 307–8, 311.

90. Goodlad, *Thatcher*, 35.

91. Hugo Young, *One of Us* (London: Macmillan, 1989), 67.

92. Harris, *Not for Turning*, 73.

93. Young, *One of Us*, 72.

94. Campbell, *Margaret Thatcher*, 216.

95. Thatcher, *Margaret Thatcher*, 105.

96. Campbell, *Margaret Thatcher*, 219–20.

97. Thatcher, *Margaret Thatcher*, 106–9. On Heath's criticism of Labour's policy, see Heath, *The Course of My Life*, 448.

98. Thatcher, *Margaret Thatcher*, 111–12.

99. Harris, *Not for Turning*, 81.

100. Moore, *Margaret Thatcher*, 223.

101. Thatcher, *Margaret Thatcher*, 114–15. Goodlad, *Thatcher*, 37. On fascism, see Wolfgang Schivelbusch, *Three New Deals: Reflections on Roosevelt's America, Mussolini's Italy and Hitler's Germany, 1933-1939* (New York: Picador, 2006).

102. Campbell, *Margaret Thatcher*, 234.

103. Campbell, *Margaret Thatcher*, 369–70.

104. In what can be read as a jab, Heath writes that Thatcher proved "very proficient at spending taxpayers' money." See Heath, *The Course of My Life*, 447–48.

105. Thatcher, *Margaret Thatcher*, 116.

106. F.T. Blackaby, ed., *British Economic Policy, 1960-74* (London: Cambridge University Press, 1978), 53.

107. Thatcher, *Margaret Thatcher*, 102. Campbell, *Margaret Thatcher*, 201, 262.

108. Andrew Gamble, *The Free Economy and the Strong State: The Politics of Thatcherism*, Second Edition (London: The Macmillan Press Ltd., 1994), 82.

109. "Miners in Britain End Their Strike; Get Raise of 35%," *New York Times*, 7 March 1974. Thatcher, *Margaret Thatcher*, 136.

110. Thomas Sowell, *Basic Economics: A Common Sense Guide to the Economy, Fifth Edition* (New York: Basic Books, 2016), 60.

111. Moore, *Margaret Thatcher*, 236.

112. Blake, *The Conservative Party from Peel to Thatcher,* 312–14; Keegan, *Mrs Thatcher's Economic Experiment*, 29–30, 55. Also Peter Jenkins, *Mrs Thatcher's Revolution: The End pf the Socialist Era* (London: Jonathan Cape Ltd, 1987), 50 and Andrew Denham and Mark Garnett, *Keith Joseph* (Chesham Bucks: Acumen, 2001), 227–29.

113. Denham and Garnett, *Keith Joseph*, 245.

114. Jenkins, *Mrs Thatcher's Revolution*, 60. Thatcher, *Margaret Thatcher*, 123.

115. Thatcher, *Margaret Thatcher*, 121.

116. Nelson, "Milton Friedman and U.K. Economic Policy: 1938-1979," 489.

117. Milton Friedman, "Is Inflation a Curable Disease?" 6, 14.

118. Stephen Haseler, *The Grand Delusion: Britain After Sixty Years of Elizabeth II* (London: I.B. Taurus, 2012), 67.

119. Harris, *Not for Turning*, 74; Blake, *The Conservative Party from Peel to Thatcher,* 320.

120. Thatcher, *Margaret Thatcher*, 124. Harris, *Not for Turning*, 85.

121. Tony Benn, *Conflicts of Interest: Diaries 1977-80*, ed. Ruth Winstone (London: Hutchinson, 1990), 182.

122. Nicholas Wapshott and George Brock, *Thatcher* (London: Macdonald & Co, 1983), 97–98.

123. Thatcher, *Margaret Thatcher*, 127.

124. Campbell, *Margaret Thatcher*, 246.

125. "The Thee-day Test," *The Economist*, 5 January 1974, 11–12. Also see "A Cold, Dark, Three-day Week," *The Economist*, 5 January 1974, 63–64.

126. "Oh, Oh, Nedo," *The Economist*, 12 January 1974, 84.

127. Thatcher, *Margaret Thatcher*, 133–34.

128. "Who Runs the Unions," *The Economist*, 19 January 1974, 62–63.

129. "Labour's L21/2 Billion Bill," *The Economist*, 19 January 1974, 65.

130. Samuel Brittan, *The Economic Consequences of Democracy* (London: Temple Smith, 1977), 77.

131. Harris, *Not for Turning,* 89.

132. Thatcher, *Margaret Thatcher*, 137.

133. Jenkins, *Mrs Thatcher's Revolution*, 53.

134. Thatcher, *Margaret Thatcher*, 128.

Chapter 2

A New Direction

Margaret Thatcher's close friend Keith Joseph gave a remarkable speech on June 22, 1974, in East London that was an important step in the reshaping of the Tory Party. Although Joseph's warning about excessive public spending was not unusual, what was remarkable was his declaration that both the Labour and Conservative parties were guilty of accepting "too much Socialism" since World War II. Conservative governments returning to power had failed to reverse much of Labour's socialist policies that caused British economic decline. Joseph declared he too was guilty of being a "statist" within the Tory Party for over thirty years. This bold criticism of his own party was more than a curious rant of a maverick. Months after Labour took power in March 1974, the economy showed no signs of improvement despite Harold Wilson's praise that his cabinet "was richer in previous experience than perhaps any incoming Government this century."[1]

Few believed that Keynesian economics was the problem. Still popular, it held that government intervention and management of the economy was essential for the economic well-being of a nation. Higher taxes, comprehensive regulation, and price controls were components of Keynesian macroeconomic management. Keynesianism and socialism shared the idea of using central planning to correct the imperfections of the free-market system; all-knowing "government knowledge" was superior to "market knowledge." To guarantee economic growth, equity, opportunity, and a better standard of living, the government favored a "mixed economy" that did not smother the market mechanism of capitalism.[2] Labour politicians found all this reasonable and some Tories found parts agreeable.

Becoming more vocal against the Keynesian economics of middle-of-the road Toryism, Thatcher was someone to watch in 1974. Favoring Keynesianism with a touch of socialism, the Labour Party leaders were wary too. Denis Healey became aware of her in 1960 when Labour MP Charlie Pannell told him to keep an eye on the "exceptionally able" Conservative. Healey did watch her, but did not find her to be anything special, at least in the early years. When she became part of the Conservative Shadow's chancellor's team, his opinion of her rose; her tax lawyer background helped make her "a formidable opponent." Her brain power was superior to Edward Heath's, but Healey was unaware of "her vaulting ambition or her iron determination."[3]

The future of Tory leader Edward Heath was less secure. Shortly after the Tory loss to Labour, Heath gave Joseph permission to establish a fund to do research on the private enterprise success of various European countries. Heath had no idea that his support and the money raised would result in the Centre of Policy Studies (CPS), an organization that stood against most of his economic policies. Heath's closest supporters were bitter that the CPS had become a power base for Thatcher who wanted to see the Conservative Party take another economic direction. When the party lost again in the general election of October 1974, Heath refused to resign as leader or agree to a leadership vote. There was pressure within the party for change, but the best possible successors were loyal to Heath and unwilling to stand against him. This bought Thatcher time to pursue the leadership of a party not generally enthusiastic with free-market ideas.

I

It was Labour's turn to get the economy back on track, but the party needed to trade a minority government for a majority one.[4] The Labour victory in February 1974 was slim and in fact the Conservative popular vote was almost 1 percent higher (37.8 to 37.1). The seat count was Labour 310, Conservatives 296, and others 34; many expected another election within the year. In Labour Party circles there was much discussion of greater equality and extension of democratic rights for the British people. But how far would leaders take the big government bus? Author Patrick Diamond provides a helpful list of the key groups within the Labour coalition: "trade unionism, syndicalism, Christian socialism, municipal socialism, radical liberalism, humanitarianism, and a cadre of middle-class intellectuals all of whom had 'different ideologies and interests.'"[5] The composure of the party was diverse and contradictory. Throughout the 1960s and into the early 1970s there was a significant split between Labour Party members who favored the nostalgic past of socialist commitment and the preservation of traditional industries and those party leaders who sought labor union reform and greater attention to economic realities.[6]

After the Labour defeat of 1970, the *New Statesman* had commented on Labour's lack of commitment to socialist principles. There was no mistaking its point that the Labour Party had lost its way. Had the party won in 1970, it "could only too easily have become a Conservative government in all but name."[7] Founded in 1913 by socialist (Fabian) intellectuals Sidney and Beatrice Webb, the leftist *New Statesman* magazine is known for its high quality of political and cultural analysis. The four editors in the seventies were Paul Johnson (1965–1970), Richard Crossman (1970–1972), Anthony Howard (1972–1978), and Bruce Page (1978–1982). Years after his editorial tenure, Paul Johnson watched the faltering economy with increasing concern and changed his economic thinking to become a free marketer. Richard Crossman was a Labour MP from 1945 to 1972, serving in Harold Wilson's cabinet in the 1960s. He was one of three Labour leaders who committed perjury in a libel case against *Spectator* magazine.[8] The tenure of Anthony Howard, the son of a Church of England clergyman, at the helm of the *New Statesman* covered the challenging years for the Labour Party as it dealt with economic crises. Bruce Page and the other *New Statesman* editors faced the task of dealing with the publication's operating losses.[9]

In the early weeks of Labour taking power, the *New Statesman* presented articles favorable of a socialist reset. Its March 1974 editorial "A Step Towards Socialism" welcomed the Labour Party's budget, introduced in March by the chancellor of exchequer Denis Healey. His 1974 budget went "straight to the core of the doctrine that must be at the centre of any socialist's faith"—proper distribution of wealth. Labour pledges included increases in pensions, subsidies for basic foods, and a steep increase in taxation for the rich. The *New Statesman* reassured readers that Labour victory was proof "that it really is possible to change society for the better through the political process."[10]

Change comes slowly and in June the economy continued to be in serious trouble with "almost total gloom" predictions from the National Institute of Economic and Social Research.[11] There were problems everywhere. The miners' previous three-day work week was a self-inflicted wound that had long-term consequences and Heath's failed policies in recent years also guaranteed poor performance numbers for economic growth, unemployment, and inflation.[12] In a June issue, former *New Statesman* editor Paul Johnson mused about the inevitable poverty predicted by pundits by giving his account of worker productivity. In a "slow-motion exercise" on the street outside his home, the Gas Board dug a huge hole and then refilled it. Two men did most of the work while other workers assembled in a tea-making hut.[13]

Four months after the election, the *New Statesman* prodded the Labour government to reveal the "unvarnished truth" on the state of the economy and begin using socialist principles to solve economic problems.[14] In another article, Christopher Price viewed the poor economy as an opportunity for bold socialism including additional taxing of wealth and gifts, the elimination of private beds from National Health Service (NHS) hospitals, and a new industrial model of greater public ownership. A key step was a Labour Party manifesto with specific pledges for "holding the minister to his socialist duty and providing him with crucial ammunition to compel his reluctant bureaucrats to do what they were told."[15] *New Statesman* letters to the editor painted a bleak picture of NHS hospitals starved of necessary funds. One socialist writer pointed to the lower salaries of hospital workers, the lack of modern equipment, and the reality of obsolete buildings. Another assessment came from J. W. Jones, aged seventy-four, who praised hospital workers who were not properly valued for their work. Jones waited three weeks in intense pain for his appointment, but once in the hospital the entire staff—despite "miserable wages and bad conditions"—demonstrated medical skill and kindness to get him healthy.[16]

Better and more public ownership was the rallying call of the *New Statesman*; the increase of business failures was evidence that more nationalization was "a good idea" to reverse this trend.[17] But was this the answer for the high inflation burdening the British? One thing was clear: the magazine strongly opposed Keith Joseph's argument that an increasing money supply was responsible for the inflation problem. Socialist Roger Opie, for example, wrote that anyone who had experienced unemployment was unlikely to find Joseph's program attractive.[18] But, in truth, many in the Tory Party thought no differently about Joseph's economic ideas. With their Keynesian thinking, centrist Tories rejected Joseph's ideas.

II

As the Labour Party struggled to find effective answers on the failing economy, most of the Heath team plodded along with little notice of new economic developments. In 1974, several key American economists gathered at a New York City restaurant to discuss supply-side economics. Professor Arthur B. Laffer became the main spokesman for a tax-cutting approach expected to solve the problem of stagflation, the term used to describe the combination of a stagnant economy and high inflation. What became known as the Laffer curve showed how rising tax rates caused people to lose the incentive to earn a higher income.[19] When the government took a progressively larger portion of a person's rising income, why bother working harder?

The Laffer curve—composed of a graph of tax rate percentages on a vertical axis and revenues on a horizontal axis—also made the point that high tax rates resulted in less revenue for the government. If profits were small due to high taxation, why would anyone take the financial risk of starting or enlarging a business? Fewer businesses meant fewer employees and less tax money for the government. The novelty of supply-side thinking is that lower taxes could result in more revenue for the government. Although the tax rate was lower, the government received more taxation revenue because the economic pie was much bigger. Supply-side theory illustrated how high taxes diminished productivity and wealth creation and it eventually gained momentum in America; however, its impact in Britain was small even though it offered conservatives a platform to attack the high taxation of the Labour government.

Not even Thatcher gave any evidence of studying Laffer's ideas. Since the 1960s she talked about the relationship between high taxation and low productivity, but she was no supply-sider expecting lower taxes to pay for themselves and cover government borrowing.[20] It was Milton Friedman's monetarism that intrigued Thatcher.[21] Money management made sense to the grocer's daughter who was an "old-fashioned fiscal conservative." A housekeeper or storekeeper should not spend more money than what came in and a government should not print excessive money that was out of proportion to the nation's productivity.[22] Monetarism corresponded with her ideas of limited borrowing and self-discipline. When the government allowed the market to operate freely, there was less government spending and thus less printing of money that caused inflation. Centrist Tories did not share Thatcher's intellectual interest in monetarism. Heath saw no value in Friedman's arguments for tighter money supply to control inflation.

Heath lost the election, but his dominance of the Tory Party continued. Most understood it was unwise to change leadership when there was a distinct possibility of another general election within a year. Taking the loss badly, Heath calculated his hold on power by joining forces with the Liberal party. In addition, Thatcher believed Heath saw coalition as a way to tame conservativism.[23] In the end, his plan failed when the Liberals, led by Jeremy Thorpe, rejected the coalition scheme of Heath as prime minister. William Whitelaw and Lord Carrington suggested he put his leadership to a vote to quash the complainers who were unhappy; they understood that it was unlikely anyone would challenge Heath while another general election loomed. However, Heath refused, believing he and the Tory Party would soon be back in power when the economy worsened, and voters realized they had made a mistake. When he formed his new shadow cabinet, he suppressed critical voices and surrounded himself with moderate Tories.[24] He chose Robert Carr as shadow chancellor rather than giving the post to Keith Joseph. Not incorporating dissenting views was unwise in the long term, but Heath still had the support of many, especially those comfortable with his economic approach. At the Conservative Research Department (CRD), Ian Gilmour became chairman and Chris Patten director, both opposing the free-market ideas of Joseph and Thatcher. An economic and social liberal, Gilmour disputed many of Thatcher's future policies.

In a May shadow cabinet meeting, Joseph pitched his monetarist analysis to defeat inflation, but only Thatcher and Geoffrey Howe were open to his argument. The Tory leadership feared that new economic ideas would bring higher unemployment with a troubling social cost; this was conventional wisdom. But Joseph and Thatcher were about to shake up their party.[25] Joseph had played a major role in Thatcher's economic education; he was, in her words, the one who "really began to turn the intellectual tide back against socialism."[26]

Joseph was born on January 17, 1918, the only child of Samuel and Edna Joseph, a well-to-do Jewish couple. His father's wealth allowed Keith to live a comfortable life and attend Oxford University where he received first-class honors in jurisprudence. During World War II he served in the army for over six years, fighting in the Middle East and Italy. In 1946, Joseph successfully read for the Bar examination, but he never practiced law, opting to work in the family building business until turning to politics.[27] Sir Joseph, the hereditary baronetcy due to his father's title of Lord Mayor of London, became a Tory MP in 1956 when he won a by-election in Leeds North-East, Yorkshire. Displaying integrity and sincerity, he stood out for his courteous and competent rational arguments in the House of Commons; his achievements included having cabinet appointments under prime ministers Harold Macmillan, Sir Alex Douglas-Home, and Edward Heath.[28] Thatcher had high praise for Joseph's intellect, his many years of experience in politics, his interest in economic and social policy, and, especially, his humility to listen to differing viewpoints. When he consulted others, he candidly probed arguments and took notes to ponder later. He was probably "too good a man for politics."[29]

In early 1974, Joseph began an intense education process that included consulting the Institute of Economic Affairs (IEA), a research organization established in 1957 with a focus on the merits of the free market. Joseph asked its director Ralph Harris, whose mustache gave him the appearance of a Battle of Britain escapee, if the IEA could assist his quest to better understand economics. Joseph's appetite for economic literature was insatiable and his study of contrasting economic views was an impressive exercise of integrity. He also paid a visit to Alan Walters at the London School of Economics (LSE) who did not receive him kindly, questioning Joseph's judgment for not speaking out against the nonsense of Heath's economic policies.[30] The LSE economics professor was a key source for those Tories open to new thinking.

Walters was born in Leicester in 1926. He grew up in a working-class family and his father was a communist during Alan's early years. As a young boy, he romanticized those who fought against "the capitalist exploitation of the working class." At age seventeen, Walters volunteered for the army and fought to the end of the war. The University College of Leicester prepared him well and he scored high with the London BSc (economics) examinations of 1951. After an academic year at Oxford University, he began teaching statistics at the University of Birmingham where he "discovered the efficacy of free markets first in 'getting prices right' and in allocating resources efficiently." At Birmingham, Walters's research and writing were on transportation economics, but he left the university for a visiting professorship at the Massachusetts Institute of Technology and then to a chair position at the LSE. In 1968, he was the only economist appointed on the Commission on London's Third Airport (Roskill Commission). Believing that he did his best work when he challenged "conventional wisdom," he saw himself as "a natural candidate for the vanguard of the monetarist revolution in the United Kingdom."[31]

Walters's closer contact with London was beneficial and he wrote that "a factious House of Commons and socialist government were providing endless opportunities for illustrating the fallacies of ideas and the follies of policy." Involved with the IEA, he was hopeful that the Conservative victory in 1970 meant sensible economic policies were forthcoming. He accepted the job of part-time adviser on macro-politics for the Heath government. When the government pushed for huge fiscal stimulus and monetary growth, Walters sent a memorandum entitled "Inflation, Devaluation and More Inflation" that warned of a serious rise in inflation, which indeed occurred. The government ignored the advice and his job as an adviser came to an end. The leadership option of Wilson or Heath in the 1974 election was, Walters concluded, "a choice between the devil and shallow blue sea." However, the rise of Thatcher gave him hope, writing that she was not like Heath "who disliked ideas and hated people who went on about them." More importantly, she was passionate to see "the permanent demise of socialism in our land."[32]

Given Walters's strong free-market views, his cool response to the visit of Joseph, a long-standing Tory MP, is not surprising. Interestingly, Joseph's encounter with Alfred Sherman, a fellow Jew, was similar; Sherman refused to shake his hand.[33] Son of a Labour councilor, Sherman was from East End London where it was natural, according to Sherman, to be a socialist. After fighting in the Spanish Civil War with the communists, he returned to get his degree at LSE. Years later he developed a disdain for Labour politicians, and he converted to free-market theory with a vengeance. However, he remained contemptuous of the elitism of the Tory old-boy network and wondered if there was any hope for the Conservative Party and its weakness for Keynesianism. Sherman visited Joseph's house and told him "Keynes is dead." Appreciating Sherman's keen mind and his journalistic skills for targeting many Labour politicians, Joseph found a thinker whose clarity of thought was intoxicating.[34] Whereas Joseph, a shy man, was courteous in debates, Sherman was a brilliant and "ruthless polemicist" who enjoyed ripping apart poor economic arguments and the ideology behind such thinking. His hard approach made enemies, but Thatcher valued him as "a formidable complement and contrast to Keith."[35] Certainly, Sherman's knowledge of monetarism helped Joseph with his critique of British politics, particularly the persistence of failing economic policies that suggested most politicians were economically illiterate or blind to the flaws of Keynesian and socialist thinking.

With the assistance of Sherman, Joseph took another important step that helped change British politics: the creation of CPS. His shadow cabinet responsibility was research on policy, and he wanted to do research on European economies with a focus on West Germany's promising "social market economy." His plan for a research body required Heath's approval before he could proceed. Claiming that a study of European economies would benefit the party, Joseph got his approval from Heath who typically saw the conservative wing of the party as misguided and not to have any important positions of power.[36] There are hints that Heath was suspicious of Joseph and one interpretation is that it was Heath's idea for Joseph to take charge of the research group, viewing the episode as "a chemistry set with which he would hopefully blow himself up."[37] Sara Morrison, a Heathite, declared: "We were a bit one-eyed about what was going on in the party."[38] James Prior suggested deceit: The CPS "was envisaged as being broadly based and was never presented to us at the outset as some new pressure group for monetarism, which is what it soon became."[39] Other commentators believed that Joseph was clever to get Heath's approval and the subsequent financial support from Tory donations, but some argue that Joseph was sincere and not guilty of deceit.[40] Thatcher viewed the matter as evidence of Joseph's concern for the Conservative Party; emerging from the "wreckage" of Heath policies, he saw the need for significant change.[41] Heath placed Adam Ridley (distant cousin to conservative Nicholas Ridley), as his spy, on the board of directors, and in return Joseph could use Heath's name for fundraising.[42]

On June 22, 1974, Joseph announced the formation of the CPS. It was small, but its leadership was impressive with Joseph as chairman, Sherman as director of studies, Nigel Vinson as treasurer, and Thatcher as vice chairman who was aware of the risk of angering Heath and encountering the scorn of socialist commentators. An IEA trustee since 1970, Vinson was a successful entrepreneur known for his creativity in improving techniques and tools. Philosophically he was an excellent fit for the CPS; he declared Britain needed "fewer faint hearts" and more creative and courageous entrepreneurs.[43] From the perspective of democrat socialists, the CPS was home to the radical right, ideological insurgents determined to dismantle the "post-war social-democratic consensus."[44]

The rise of the CPS was a key component of an economic revolution that bode poorly for Heath, but was good news for Thatcher who, apparently, was the only Tory invited by Joseph to join. The CPS emboldened her conservatism and thus greater exposure to Hayek, Friedman, and other free-market economists gave her the necessary arguments to build her credibility as a serious politician reaching the next tier of political life.[45] Sherman remembered that he loaned her many books which she failed to return.[46] Her voracious appetite for economic literature was unusual for a politician, an observation borne out in the reading of political memoirs. Joseph admitted that Thatcher had an instinct for free-market thinking whereas he needed "laborious analysis" to find his way.[47] Getting the free-market message out did take time, however. Eventually, the economic ideas discussed at the CPS began to reach a broader audience through several speeches by Joseph in the summer and autumn that exposed "the follies and self-defeating consequences of government intervention." Centrist Tories steeped in Keynesianism increasingly became uncomfortable.[48]

Written mostly by Alfred Sherman, Joseph's Upminster speech of June 22, which also introduced the launching of the "small policy studies centre," angered the Tory establishment not happy with his assessment of the Conservative Party being guilty of accepting "socialistic fashions." In the previous month, Heath gave a lecture rejecting both Marxism and "laisser-faire" doctrine and now Joseph pointed to Tory's role in the previous three decades of allowing socialism to take hold in the nation.[49] As Joseph declared, the economic results were dismal: "The reality is that for 30 years the private sector of our economy has been forced to work with one hand tied behind its back by government and unions. Socialist measures and Socialist legacies have weakened free enterprise." Britain was "more socialistic in many ways than any other developed country outside the Communist bloc, in the size of the public sector, the range of controls and the telescoping of net income."[50] Compared to Germany, Sweden, Holland, and France, Britain had the largest nationalized sector, longer working hours, lowest pay, highest taxes, lowest investments, and the worst production per head. The poor economy and revenue not only hampered the caring treatment of the disabled and others in need, but also failed to properly pay teachers and nurses. Joseph had empirical data to support his points and he had an answer for criticism of his comparisons. He admitted that some of the countries doing better than Britain were democratic socialist, but the reason for their better economic performance was that "Social-Democratic" politicians abroad were "far more realistic in relation to private enterprise, to the essentials of economic policy, to the limits on government's power to intervene for good." Stating that never in British history had "so many good intentions by so many people created so many disappointments," Joseph listed four reasons for British failure: too much faith in the power of government ("shortcuts to Utopia"), the burdening of the private sector, unreasonable action by trade union leaders and workers, and antagonistic socialist doctrine.[51]

Joseph's speech was the start of a more concerted effort arguing it was time for Conservatives to promote free enterprise and see a higher standard of living for the British people. Even if the Selsdon Man was a myth, as some scholars argue, and there was no serious policy commitment to change economic course in 1970, there were Tories who did not need events of recent history to convince them of the correct path to follow. As free enterprise Conservatives understood since the 1940s, an economy dominated by social-democrat thinking did not always work well and a better model was having a stronger private sector. The required adjustments were for both the individual and industry levels: reduce the welfare state, lower direct personal taxation, encourage wider property-ownership, curb the powers of trade unions, reduce obstacles for businesses, and favor policies of lower inflation rather than full employment.[52]

Heath disagreed with Joseph's push for a re-evaluation of the party's economic policies, but there was no stopping Joseph's enthusiasm and conviction that action was necessary for the party and for the nation. To the annoyance of Heath and most of the shadow cabinet, Joseph alerted the party of his intention of giving a major speech in September that went further than his Upminster speech. James Prior enlisted Thatcher's assistance to stop Joseph: "You know this is a disastrous speech—can't you stop him giving it?"[53] Her response was that she did not think she could influence the determined Joseph, and, moreover, she trusted Alfred Sherman, who had written the speech. Having read an early draft, she judged it to be "powerful and persuasive," and she made no suggestions to Joseph for any changes. The problem for Heath, Prior, and other Keynesian Tories was that Joseph undermined Heath's economic record when a general election was on the horizon. He also threatened Heath's idea of forming a coalition government with the Liberal party, a party equally guilty in the eyes of conservatives of promoting failed economic policies over the last three decades.[54]

On September 5, Joseph delivered his speech "Inflation is Caused by Government" at Preston. The 7,000-word speech, according to Thatcher, "fundamentally affected a political generation's way of thinking."[55] The first sentence was blunt: "Inflation is threatening to destroy our society." Much of the remaining speech was equally hard-hitting, offering a combination of historical examples and economic lessons. Without effective policies, inflation would cause "catastrophic" damage to people's savings, the job market, business investment, economic growth, social services, and open the door for solutions that denied people's freedom. Rejecting the common belief that inflation was mostly due to "rocketing world prices" linked to international events and decisions, Joseph placed greater blame on the domestic policies of both the Labour and Tory parties. Inflation was the result of excessive growth of the money supply that occurred with all governments. It was difficult to see the dire consequences of loose monetary policy due to a time lag of "many months, or even as much as a year or two." However, inflation was inevitable.[56]

Politicians expected mild inflation, which was a reasonable trade-off for full employment, but Joseph argued that the creation of new money and deficit financing guaranteed economic distress. Unemployment numbers, rather than inflation, frightened politicians even though the accuracy of unemployment statistics was suspect. Joseph understood that some people fell in the category of "frictional unemployment"—workers without employment as they moved from job to job. He argued that others were simply unemployable for various reasons or were not on job sites because they fraudulently received unemployment benefits. The problem, as he saw it, was labor shortage rather than labor surplus. Curbing monetary growth was not a perfect solution since it increased unemployment. However, the rise of unemployment would be temporary whereas inflation would continue to destroy jobs. Joseph referred to John Maynard Keynes several times to support his points. In fact, he believed Keynes "would have disowned most of the allegedly Keynesian remedies urged on us in his name and which have caused so much harm."[57] Although a recent study takes the opposite position and makes the case that Keynes wanted more socialism, most economists do not see Keynes as a kind of radical.[58]

Joseph scorned government attempts to control prices with incomes policies; they had a poor record. It was "like trying to stop water coming out of a leaky hose without turning off the tap; if you stop one hole it will find two others."[59] It might take three to four years to see success, but an anti-inflation policy of controlling money growth was the right thing to do in the long term. Courage and commitment were essential, something missing with the Labour Party. Joseph asked:

> Can we expect the socialists to do this even if they think it to be necessary? No! In the first place, for them, economic policy is a perpetual popularity contest. Promise today, disappoint tomorrow, and then blame industry, finance, the banks, anyone but their own exaggerated promises and spendthrift policies.[60]

Many Tories did not understand monetarist arguments, but they knew status quo economic thinking had a poor record in solving a troubled British economy.[61] Although Joseph's speech angered Tory establishment leaders, it was a pioneering move that gave Thatcher room to maneuver as she staked out her place in the future of the party.

III

In March 1974, Thatcher received the shadow environment portfolio, a better choice than shadowing the Labour member doing Thatcher's old job at Education. Without the luxury of having a staff, she kept plenty busy with her environment duties. As she explained to the *Liverpool Daily Post*, "If you want to look up a reference to something, you have to go to a library and do it yourself."[62] As in the past, she did her homework when challenging Labour's environment secretary Anthony Crosland, who wrote the influential book *The Future of Socialism* in the 1950s. Others experienced her sharp tongue. In an April House of Commons debate on the topic of London, Thatcher demonstrated her confidence in discussing urban problems. In response to John Silkin, minister for planning and local government, who suggested patience as the new government sought to solve all problems, Thatcher gave a clear message on the record of socialism:

> In the difficult London boroughs Socialism has been in power all the time. In fact, the worse those boroughs are the more Socialism they have had. The prosperous boroughs have been Conservative all the time and the medium boroughs have been part Conservative and part Socialist.[63]

The main environment task for Thatcher was to formulate new housing policies that could win the confidence of voters and return the Conservatives to power. When she chaired a committee on mortgage policies, some conservatives doubted she had the strength to break away from the government interventionism of Heath. Pledging a fixed interest rate went against the free play of market forces as did the plan to give tenants some advantages to buy their council houses.[64] Her housing policy committee wanted to see more homeownership for tenants, but she opposed any plan of subsidizing mortgages or selling council houses at bargain prices. Selling council houses at discounted prices was unfair to other houseowners who had no such government handout when they saved and bought their own homes. Pressured by Heath to settle on an interest rate as low as possible, she stated that 9.5 percent was as low as she could go.[65]

Soon influential journalists gave more attention to Thatcher as a serious contender for the Conservative leadership.[66] One of the earliest champions was Patrick Cosgrave who became the political editor of *The Spectator* in 1971. Cosgrave was born in 1941 and was only ten years old when his father died. Life was difficult and he experienced a life of poverty in Dublin. With his impressive intellect, Cosgrave took a first in history at University College Dublin and wrote a doctoral thesis on World War I British foreign policy at Cambridge University.[67] His criticism of Heath and praise for Thatcher led to a greater awareness of her potential. Even as late as 1974, Thatcher was doubtful of Britain being ready for a female leader, informing a Liverpool *Daily Post* reporter that "it will be years before a woman either leads the Party or becomes Prime Minister. I don't see it happening in my time."[68] But the admiration of Cosgrave and others grew, and in July she received encouraging news from David James, the MP for Dorset West, that a private straw poll viewed her as a promising candidate for party leadership.[69] Although she was not stirring the political pot with bold economic speeches like Joseph's, she spent many hours throughout the summer reading classic economic theory and attending lunches at the IEA. Her ability to point out the problems with socialism became stronger as she learned much from Ralph Harris, Alan Walters, and Douglas Hague, an economist at Manchester Business School and the author of *A Textbook of Economic Theory* (1953), a book that had a significant impact on her.

Thatcher was fully supportive of Joseph's September 5 speech, and she later wrote that the Conservative Party might have had a winning hand with its warnings about socialism and reforms on mortgages. The problem was party division. There was no way Heath would embrace the economic thinking of Joseph and other like-minded free marketers and, consequently, she had little hope of a Tory victory in the next election.[70] Days after the Preston speech, the Conservative Party released its manifesto which did not offer anything new. In mid-September, the Labour Party announced October 10 as the date of the election and there was much action as the parties jockeyed for position. On September 24, Thatcher defended Tory's housing and rates proposal, described by Anthony Crosland as "a pack of lies." In the lackluster Tory campaign, she stood out and her promise of a reduction of the mortgage rates to 9.5 percent by Christmas led the press to refer to her as "Santa Thatcher" which improved her national profile.[71] Her pledge was not consistent with a free-market approach, but there was no turning back on the promise.

Thatcher was not receptive to Heath's push for a national unity approach and when she met with him at his home, on October 1, to hear his pitch for a Government of National Unity she left "extremely angry." Her campaign focus was defending housing policies and attacking the problem of "creeping socialism," but Heath, who earlier insisted on specific numbers, believed his best chance to return to Downing Street was to avoid detailed pledges on housing and rates policies.[72] Keeping policies vague would make Heath's goal of national unity, and perhaps a coalition, more promising.[73] While her relations with Heath grew cooler, her electoral prospects looked favorable as she performed well in the election campaign. Except for two trips, she remained in London enjoying greater press attention than ever before with her promise of lower mortgage rates.[74] Labour took special effort to unseat this rising star, including Harold Wilson's visit to her constituency where he attempted to bolster the confidence of the Labour candidate by saying "I gather you have dear Margaret on the run."[75] This claim was implausible, but the fortunes of the Tories were up in the air. Heath remained receptive to a national government which made Conservative campaign promises suspect. Would members of other parties who might support Heath allow Tory policies to proceed as planned? Was the Conservative Party offering anything new to sway the voters?

On October 10 election day, the Labour Party won a slim majority of three seats. It was Heath's third defeat in four elections, yet he did not retire, a decision that hurt potential moderates seeking leadership. By not releasing the loyalty of his high-ranking supporters, Heath allowed conservatives to proceed without having to compete with other formidable Tories.[76] One shadow minister declared: "Look, he threw it all away . . . [and] created the opportunity for Margaret and Keith and now he is undermining the position of moderates."[77] A group of Conservative MPs met on October 13 at the flat of free-marketer Nicholas Ridley to consider suitable candidates to challenge Heath for the leadership. Joseph was their first choice, and he informed the group by telephone of his willingness to be a candidate. Another influential group of Conservatives was the 1922 Committee and its chairman Edward du Cann. In a unanimous vote by the eighteen-member executive, the group insisted on a leadership race. Du Cann relayed the news to Heath in a brief and angry meeting.[78]

Thatcher knew Heath, unable to change and "too defensive of his past record," had to go if the Tories were ever to adopt new economic policies. She looked to Joseph as the one to lead the party and she became virtually, in her words, "Keith's informal campaign manager." This did not last. On October 19, Joseph gave a speech at Edgbaston in Birmingham that hurt his prospects as a leader. Going against the advice of Alfred Sherman, Joseph told his audience that too many women in poverty were foolishly having children they were unable to care for. He imprudently used the phrase "human stock." Was the front runner for leadership among conservatives hinting of eugenics? It did not look good. Was there more to the story? Thatcher explained that "the most incendiary phrases" were from the writings of "two left-wing sociologists." In subsequent speeches, the CPS staff carefully deleted unwise language that was open to misunderstanding. However, the damage was done, and socialists denounced him as "a mad eugenicist." Newspapers had headlines such as "Sir Keith in 'Stop Babies' Sensation." A sensitive man not able to adjust to the hostility and distortions of his critics, Joseph marred his cause by "constantly explaining, qualifying and apologizing."[79] Biographer Morrison Halcrow claims that a different type of politician would have said little and waited for the storm to blow over. On the day after the speech, Terry

Coleman of the *Daily Mail* asked Joseph about a possible candidacy for the Tory leadership. Joseph replied: "I think I may have damaged—things which I rather deeply believed. I hope not." The *Economist*, which supported Heath, commented that "a political sage must be clever as well as holy."[80]

IV

Thatcher's prospects improved after Heath reshuffled the shadow cabinet that appointed her as Robert Carr's deputy with special responsibility for the Finance Bill. This was an excellent position to demonstrate her talents, which she did in the subsequent weeks. Part of the preparation for her new role was attendance at the Economic Dining Group with key members Nicholas Ridley, John Biffen, Jock Bruce-Gardyne, and John Nott. Her first challenge was Denis Healey's quarterly budget introduced on November 12, a budget that included cuts in business taxes. In the Budget Debate, Thatcher scored points with Tory backbenchers when she debated Harold Lever, chancellor of the Duchy of Lancaster who came from a wealthy family:

> I always felt that I could never rival him at the Treasury because there are four ways of acquiring money. To make it. To earn it. To marry it. And to borrow it. He seems to have experience of all four.

Later in the debate she spoke of the suffering of small businesses and admitted both parties were guilty of harmful policies. When economist and Labour MP of Nuneaton Leslie Huckfield noted Thatcher's "interesting admission," she replied: "I never flinch from accepting responsibility for my part in any situation."[81]

Thatcher showed leadership qualities and appeared ready for battle. She may have got the best of Denis Healey when she quoted a newspaper report of him saying, "I never save. If I get any money I go out and buy something for the house." When Healy claimed he said no such thing, she took the opportunity to explain that he was one more socialist politician with his own country house: "I am delighted that we have got on record the fact that the Chancellor is a jolly good saver. I know that he believes in buying houses in good Tory areas."[82] Thatcher's attack on the Labour's Capital Transfer Tax won her a growing number of Tory supporters tired of their half-hearted leaders. What seemed impossible was now possible for Tories willing to take a second look at Thatcher. For example, Geoffrey Finsberg, MP for Hampstead, told her: "If you contest the leadership you will almost certainly win."[83]

On November 21, Keith Joseph tracked Thatcher down for a serious discussion; he told her of his withdrawal from the leadership election.[84] As he explained: "I am sorry, I just can't run. Ever since I made that speech the press have been outside the house. They have been merciless. Helen [his wife] can't take it and I have decided that I just can't stand." With Joseph officially out, Thatcher decided to run and arranged to see and inform Heath. In her version of the brief meeting of November 25, she said: "I must tell you that I have decided to stand for the leadership." Heath looked coldly at her, turned away, and stated: "If you must."[85] While visiting the Conservative Research Department, R. A. Butler, a former high-ranking Tory MP and key promoter of consensus politics, asked Christ Patten: "We don't need to take this Thatcher business seriously, do we?"[86]

The Heath team struck first two days later when newspapers printed stories depicting Thatcher as a hoarder of tinned food. It was a tough blow by Heath supporters, but they overplayed their hand with the claim that a witness caught Thatcher buying large quantities of sugar from a local shop. The story stopped when news came that the alleged shop did not exist. An angry Thatcher told fellow Tory Bill Shelton: "I saw how they destroyed Keith. Well, they're not going to destroy me."[87] When the *New Statesman*'s Alan Watkins provided analysis of the key candidates to unseat Heath from the leadership, he devoted one sentence to Thatcher: "Let them eat Spam."[88] Her continued good performances in the House were timely, but Thatcher was not the first choice of many Conservative MPs; they turned to Edward du Cann as the strongest leadership candidate. A successful businessman, an experienced politician, and chairman of the 1922 Committee, he had the respect of backbenchers. However, he withdrew from the field and invited Thatcher and her husband Denis to his house to inform her. She did not try to persuade him to stay in the run for the leadership, an omission that made him "a bit miffed."[89]

With Du Cann out, MP Airey Neave transferred his support to Thatcher, a development that was a major boost. A war hero and a man of impressive political skills, Neave took charge of her campaign. His advice was for her to focus on parliamentary duties, and he would take care of campaign details. Her performance in the Commons, notably her exchanges with Denis Healey, improved her prospects. In a January 31 speech to her constituency, she pointed to her leadership in opposing the "socialist Capital Transfer Tax proposals" and the socialist thinking that weakened the nation:

> There is a widespread feeling in the country that the Conservative Party had not defended [Conservative] ideals explicitly and toughly enough, so that Britain is set on a course towards inevitable socialist mediocrity. That course must not only be halted, it must be reversed.[90]

In mid-October 1974, the bookmakers' odds had Thatcher at 50/1 for being the new leader.[91] However, much changed in the following months. The vote for leadership was by Conservative MPs only and to win on the first ballet a successful candidate needed a majority plus 15 percent of votes. The MPs gathered on February 4 for the first ballot and the results shocked establishment Tories. Heath received the bad news from Sir Timothy Kitson: "I am sorry Ted, but it's all up." With tears streaming down his cheeks, Hugh Fraser told Heath that he was "terribly sorry" for the turn of events. Reggie Maudling declared: "The party's taken leave of its senses. This is a black day."[92] James Prior, who missed the vote due to a late train, said it was "one of the most miserable days" of his life.[93] There were 130 votes for Thatcher and 119 for Heath, who announced his resignation as leader. The winner needed 139 and consequently a second ballet was necessary. On the day of the vote, Thatcher went to Rothschild's Bank for a lunch appointment and experienced a hostile reception. To the young Tory who had taken her there, she declared: "Never take me to that red bank again."[94] The second ballot results gave Thatcher a more dominant victory of 146 votes to 79 for Willie Whitelaw, 19 votes each for Jim Prior and Geoffrey Howe, and 11 for John Peyton. Biographer Robin Harris writes that the leadership election "was a raw and ruthless struggle."[95] Other than Joseph, no member of the shadow cabinet voted for Thatcher on the first ballot.

Behind Tory opposition to Thatcher were issues of personality, style, and ideology. But one clear shortcoming for centrist Tories was her free-market views that allowed room for monetarism. What some introduced in the 1960s and what Keith Joseph pushed in 1974 did not go away. In his memoirs, James Prior wrote:

> What began to stick in the gullet was the growing belief during our years in opposition that the only thing that really mattered was control of the money supply and Professor Milton Friedman and Hayek, as the high priests of monetarism, stood above all others as our prophets and gurus.[96]

Prior was wrong to imply that Friedman and Hayek agreed on the issue of monetarism and that Thatcher and others believed that monetarism was all that was necessary for solving inflation, but his complaint reveals the serious threat that Thatcher posed with her economic criticism of the postwar settlement. Slow to see that inflation could be a bigger enemy than unemployment, centrist Tories rejected what they believed was a misguided panacea to solve all economic problems. As a member of the Economic Reconstruction Group, Prior witnessed monetarists such as Joseph "sprouting the most dreadful nonsense."[97]

For some, there was something appealing about Thatcher's economic approach. The dominant narrative was that British economic decline was mostly the result of global factors such as destabilized world currencies and

Middle East oil spikes rather than flawed domestic economic policies.[98] Could it be possible that this explanation was wrong? As a response to inflation, perhaps a variation of monetarism was better than Keynesianism. However, it was not Thatcher's free-market views alone that made her the first female leader of a British political party. She received support from Tory politicians disappointed with Heath for his poor record of winning elections, his lack of warmth, or his reversal of conservative policies. Some simply believed it was time for change.[99]

At her post-victory press conference, Thatcher told the press her leadership would embrace a "distinctive Conservative philosophy." As she explained: "Oh, you don't win by just being against things, you only win by being *for* things and making your message perfectly clear." She planned to stand for

> a free society with power well distributed amongst the citizens and *not* concentrated in the hands of the state. And the power supported by a wide distribution of private property amongst citizens and subjects and not in the hands of the state.[100]

The next step was to learn how to stay true to her old-fashioned conservative principles in a divided party where establishment Tories, favoring Keynesianism, wielded significant influence.

NOTES

1. Harold Wilson, *Final Turn: The Labour Government 1974-1976* (London: Weidenfeld and Nicolson, 1979), 17.
2. Daniel Yergin and Joseph Stanislaw, *The Commanding Heights: The Battle Between Government and the Marketplace That Is Remaking the Modern World* (New York: Simon & Schuster, 1998), 10–12.
3. Denis Healey, *The Time of My Life* (London: Michael Joseph, 1989).
4. Wapshott and Brock, *Thatcher*, 108–9. Thatcher, *Margaret Thatcher*, 149. Goodlad, *Thatcher*, 41–42.
5. Diamond, *The Crosland Legacy*, 191.
6. Richard Jobson, *Nostalgia and the Post-war Labour Party: Prisoners of the past* (Manchester: Manchester University Press, 2018).
7. Stuart Middleton, "'Affluence' and the Left in Britain, C. 1958—1974," *The English Historical Review* 129, no. 536 (2014), 133.
8. Mihir Bose, "Britain's Libel Laws: Malice Aforethought," *History Today* 63, no. 5 (May 2013), 7. The *Spectator* lost in court, but Crossman later admitted that journalist Jenny Nicholson was accurate in her report of the drunkenness of the three Labour politicians.

9. "Letter: Myth of the New Statesman's 'golden age,'" *The Independent*, 5 October 1995.

10. "A Step Towards Socialism," *New Statesman*, 29 March 1974, 429.

11. Paul Johnson, "Whom the Gods Wish to Destroy," *New Statesman*, 14 June 1974, 823.

12. "Government and Truth," *New Statesman*, 5 July 1974, 1.

13. Paul Johnson, "Land of Hope and—What?," *New Statesman*, 28 June 1974, 907. Johnson argues for a hopeful future.

14. "Government and Truth," *New Statesman*, 5 July 1974, 1.

15. Christopher Price, "The October Manifesto," *New Statesman*, 19 July 1974, 74–75.

16. "Private Beds and Public Hospitals," *New Statesman*, 19 July 1974, 83.

17. "The Courage of Conviction," *New Statesman*, 6 September 1974, 301.

18. For example, see Roger Opie, "Sir Keith's Dole Queue," *New Statesman*, 13 September 1974, 336.

19. Brian Domitrovic, *Econoclasts: The Rebels Who Sparked the Supply-Side Revolution and Restored American Prosperity* (Wilmington, DE: ISI Books, 2009), 9–10.

20. Jenkins, *Mrs. Thatcher's Revolution*, xii.

21. One theory is that Enoch Powell generated the British interest in monetarism. See Wapshott and Brock, *Thatcher*, 187.

22. Jenkins, *Mrs. Thatcher's Revolution*, xii.

23. Thatcher, *Margaret Thatcher*, 149.

24. Moore, *Margaret Thatcher*, 253.

25. Campbell, *Margaret Thatcher*, 265–67.

26. Morrison Halcrow, *Keith Joseph: A Single Mind* (London: Macmillan, 1989), x.

27. Halcrow, *Keith Joseph*, 8.

28. Halcrow, *Keith Joseph*, 22.

29. Thatcher, *Margaret Thatcher*, 156.

30. Halcrow, *Keith Joseph*, 59, 64.

31. A. Walters, "A Life Philosophy," *The American Economist* 33, no. 2 (1989), 18–21.

32. Walters, "A Life Philosophy," 22–23.

33. Campbell, *Margaret Thatcher*, 263.

34. Halcrow, *Keith Joseph*, 61–63.

35. Thatcher, *Margaret Thatcher*, 156.

36. Wapshott and Brock, *Thatcher*, 109.

37. Denham and Garnett, *Keith Joseph*, 239. For Thatcher's account see Thatcher, *Margaret Thatcher*, 157.

38. Moore, *Margaret Thatcher*, 253.

39. Prior, *A Balance of Power*, 97.

40. Denham and Garnett, *Keith Joseph*, 240–41.

41. Thatcher, *Margaret Thatcher*, 156.

42. Halcrow, *Keith Joseph*, 65; Thatcher, *Margaret Thatcher*, 157. On Ridley as spy, see Moore, *Margaret Thatcher*, 253.

43. Thatcher, *Margaret Thatcher*, 157. Campbell, *Margaret Thatcher*, 266. Halcrow, *Keith Joseph*, 66.

44. Haseler, *The Grand Delusion*, 88–89. In 1981, Andrew Gamble wrote of the rise of "right-wing pressure groups" in the late 1960s, "germinating like dragons' teeth." See, Andrew Gamble, *Britain in Decline: Economic Policy, Political Strategy and the British State* (London: The Macmillan Press Limited, 1981), 145.

45. Moore, *Margaret Thatcher*, 253–54. Harris, *Not for Turning*, 99–100.

46. Moore, *Margaret Thatcher*, 254.

47. Campbell, *Margaret Thatcher*, 264.

48. Thatcher, *Margaret Thatcher*, 157.

49. Heath, *The Course of My Life*, 524.

50. MTF, Keith Joseph, Speech at Upminster ("This is not the Time to be Mealy-Mouthed: Intervention is Destroying us"), 22 June 1974, https://www.margaretthatcher.org/document/110604.

51. Joseph, Speech at Upminster, 22 June 1974.

52. E. H. H. Green, "Thatcherism: An Historical Perspective," *Transactions of the Royal Historical Society* 9 (1999): 19–20, 35.

53. Prior, *A Balance of Power*, 97.

54. Thatcher, *Margaret Thatcher*, 158–59. Young, *One of Us*, 88–89.

55. Thatcher, *Margaret Thatcher*, 159.

56. MTF, Keith Joseph, Speech at Preston ("Inflation is Caused by Government"), 5 September 1974, https://www.margaretthatcher.org/document/110607.

57. Joseph, Speech at Preston, 5 September 1974.

58. See Crotty, *Keynes Against Capitalism*, 4.

59. Joseph, Speech at Preston, 5 September 1974.

60. Joseph, Speech at Preston, 5 September 1974.

61. Moore, *Margaret Thatcher*, 258.

62. Quoted in Campbell, *Margaret Thatcher*, 270.

63. Hansard, HC Deb 29 April 1974 vol 872 cc787-906, https://api.parliament.uk/historic-hansard/commons/1974/apr/29/london.

64. Wapshott and Brock, *Thatcher*, 111. Young, *One of Us*, 82–83.

65. Campbell, *Margaret Thatcher*, 271–72.

66. Wapshott and Brock, *Thatcher*, 110.

67. "First rate brain that loved to provoke," *The Irish Times*, 22 September 2001.

68. Quoted in Wapshott and Brock, *Thatcher*, 110.

69. Denham and Garnett, *Keith Joseph*, 276.

70. Thatcher, *Margaret Thatcher*, 160.

71. Aiken, *Margaret Thatcher*, 146–47.

72. Thatcher, *Margaret Thatcher*, 161.

73. Moore, *Margaret Thatcher*, 263.

74. Campbell, *Margaret Thatcher*, 276.

75. Quoted in Campbell, *Margaret Thatcher*, 278.

76. Young, *One of Us*, 91.

77. David Butler and Dennis Kavanagh, *The British General Election of 1979* (London: The Macmillan Press Ltd., 1980), 64.

78. Wapshott and Brock, *Thatcher*, 114–15.

79. Thatcher, *Margaret Thatcher*, 162–63; Halcrow, *Keith Joseph*, 84.

80. Halcrow, *Keith Joseph*, 86–87.

81. Hansard, Budget Resolutions and Economic Situation, Vol. 881, 14 November 1974, https://hansard.parliament.uk/Commons/1974-11-14/debates/7b2e7262-d47a-4e9b-bb97-6930de16b9f5/BudgetResolutionsAndEconomicSituation.

82. Hansard, Orders of the Day, Vol. 881, 14 November 1974, https://hansard.parliament.uk/Commons/1974-11-14/debates/4dde9703-2139-4911-8ed9-536c9fdff719/OrdersOfTheDay.

83. Thatcher, *Margaret Thatcher*, 165.

84. Denham and Garnett, *Keith Joseph*, 268.

85. Thatcher, *Margaret Thatcher*, 165–66.

86. Moore, *Margaret Thatcher*, 275.

87. Thatcher, *Margaret Thatcher*, 166–67.

88. Alan Watkins, "Mr Du Cann's Bandwagon," *New Statesman*, 13 December 1974, 850.

89. Campbell, *Margaret Thatcher*, 286, 291.

90. MTF, Speech in Finchley (Conservative leadership election), 31 January 1975, https://www.margaretthatcher.org/document/102605.

91. Denham and Garnett, *Keith Joseph*, 278.

92. Heath, *The Course of My Life*, 534.

93. Prior, *A Balance of Power*, 100.

94. Quoted in Moore, *Margaret Thatcher*, 292.

95. Harris, *Not for Turning*, 94.

96. Prior, *A Balance of Power*, 104.

97. Prior, *A Balance of Power*, 104, 108.

98. For example, see Wilson, *Final Turn*, 16, 22.

99. Butler and Kavanagh, *The British General Election of 1979*, 62–63.

100. MTF, Press Conference after winning Conservative leadership (Conservative Central Office), 11 February 1974, https://www.margaretthatcher.org/document/102487.

Chapter 3

Thatcher as Leader

Anthony Benn of the Labour Party gave Thatcher credit, writing in his diary that "politics is a brutal business, and I think we would be foolish to suppose that Mrs. Thatcher won't be a formidable leader; and Harold couldn't pour scorn on a woman because people wouldn't have it."[1] With Thatcher as leader, Benn expected the Conservative Party to move to the right, thus giving voters a clearer option of what political direction was best for British society. Others agreed that Thatcher was no establishment Tory ready to accommodate left ideas. One young man remembered how Thatcher offered "a combative sort of ideology that said *we aren't defeated, we don't have to surrender, it doesn't have to be like this, it can be different.*" Socialist ideas had permeated university life and there seemed to be an expectation of an inevitable slide "towards a Soviet style of economy" and a declining standard of living. There was the question of whether the Conservative establishment could prevent this since many Tories accepted the postwar consensus of a growing modern welfare state. Any serious Conservative economic correction was futile; a Labour government would only renationalize industries. But Thatcher, if ever so slowly, wanted to build on something different—an alternative of Friedman, Hayek, and Edmund Burke, all packaged in a "more pugnacious style of Conservatism."[2]

Thatcher read F. A. Hayek, who wrote: "Once the free working of the market is impeded beyond a certain degree, the planner will be forced to extend his controls until they become all-comprehensive."[3] Could Thatcher influence the party to be more forceful against government intervention?[4] Her first two years as the Conservative leader represented a period of adjustment with two forces at play: her desire to transform establishment Toryism and the resistance of moderate Tories unwilling to turn from Keynesianism. On the first front, there was not much evidence of her transforming the party. There were more demands on her time, and she also moved cautiously. Economics partly explains the resistance of moderate Tories to her free-market thinking. The difficulty was that many politicians, of all political parties, apparently lacked an understanding of wealth creation and if they were curious of basic economics, it rarely went beyond the confines of Keynesianism and socialism. Except for Keith Joseph and his supporters, new economic ideas did not generate enthusiasm within the party. His speeches did expand economic discussion to include monetarism, but Keynesian ideas persisted. Any headway on winning economic arguments and demonstrating the problem with Keynesian intervention could easily be squashed by discussion of high unemployment and the daily suffering of the jobless trying to make ends meet. Divided on economic policy, the Tory Party struggled to capitalize on the shortcomings of Labour's economic decisions.

I

Some Labour members recognized Thatcher would be formidable, but the Labour Party was also confident: "No need to worry about the next election. It's a foregone conclusion."[5] Many critics saw her as too humourless and dogmatic to gain enough popular support to defeat the Labour Party. She was politically out of her league. Sandy Mutch, former president of the Scottish Conservative Party, told Anthony Benn: "Even if she wins an Election, there will be a coup d'état between the Election and the formation of the Government and someone else will be Prime Minister."[6] Simply put, she was not popular with the Tory establishment. Edward Heath's supporters had little faith that she could ever be prime minister. Of the twenty-three in Heath's shadow cabinet, only three likely voted for her as leader. Not even Geoffrey Howe, much to her disappointment, voted for her on the first vote. Thatcher's first meeting with high-ranking Tories was not a pleasant experience for moderates who believed that their party had suffered "a calamitous fate." One man wrote of "the long faces and people stumbling into the room."[7] It was awkward since formal reappointments of the shadow cabinet had yet to take place and some members would be dropped. Thatcher wrote that the formalities of the meeting suggested "a kind of armed truce between the competing views and personalities."[8]

Heath made no conciliatory gestures and refused Thatcher's offer to join the shadow cabinet. He contradicted her version: "She offered me nothing!"[9] When she planned her front-bench team there were few conservatives to find among the many progressive Tories. If some expected Keith Joseph to be shadow chancellor of the exchequer, they were wrong since Thatcher chose Sir Geoffrey Howe instead, a recent convert to free-market thinking. Born in

Wales in 1926, Howe followed the career footsteps of his father and became a lawyer, studying at Cambridge University. He began his law practice in 1952 and twelve years later he became a Conservative MP only to lose it in the General Election of 1966. He was back in the House of Commons in 1970, receiving the appointment of solicitor general in Heath's government. He was a key supporter of Heath's corporatism, a blend of government interventionism and business that fit Howe's idea of government as a force for good, able to direct the world of business to improve economic conditions and provide social reform. Thatcher's criticism of progressive Toryism took the flexible Howe down another path. He took Joseph's ideas and formulated economic policies, but cautiously since Thatcher could not move too quickly due to the resistance of progressive Tories who still outnumbered the converts.[10]

Keith Joseph was responsible for policy formation, more in line with his talents, and Lord Peter Thorneycroft took on the duties of party chairman—a wise choice by Thatcher. Out of active politics for nine years, Thorneycroft was a principled man who had resigned as chancellor of exchequer in 1958 to protest government overspending. His presence "signalled a continuity with the Conservative past."[11] There was discussion on whether Enoch Powell would receive a position, but Thatcher could not forgive his advice to voters to support the Labour Party in 1974 over the issue of Britain joining the Common Market, which he opposed.[12]

Key progressives receiving positions included Willie Whitelaw, James Prior, Francis Pym, Lord Carrington, and Ian Gilmour. Her most serious leadership rival had been Whitelaw who failed to stop her momentum. With Thatcher as leader, Whitelaw chose to be a good loser and show his loyalty, but when she selected him as deputy leader his wife told him to avoid any social engagements with the leader. He received no special treatment from Thatcher, and he complained to friends of the "the awful woman" who was merciless with her criticism of those failing to meet her high expectations.[13] There were a handful of progressives who did not stay. Geoffrey Rippon and Peter Thomas chose to step down and Thatcher dumped Robert Carr and Peter Walker. Carr stipulated that he wanted foreign affairs or nothing and his departure shocked Heath. Walker was an influential member of Heath's inner circle who was an unrepentant Keynesian with grave concern for "extreme monetarist policies." He feared that the rise of "the Right" meant a long period of diminished influence for those with "liberal views." Another opponent of monetarism was Ian Gilmour, chairman of the Conservative Research Department (CRD), but Thatcher moved him from the CRD and made him first shadow home secretary.[14]

At the first party conference with Thatcher as leader, there was no public reconciliation between Heath and Thatcher. He found his seat without going near her and later he walked by her dinner table without acknowledging her.[15] The larger issue went beyond this poor relationship and the abilities of any one leader; the Tory Party was far from ready for a full assault on socialism either domestic or foreign. The progressives expected to tone down Thatcher's conservatism.[16] For James Prior, the lesson of Heath's demise was not that his policies failed; his economic management policies were successful until the misfortune of the miners' strike. He believed that the Thatcherites were ignorant about trade union activity and too confrontational with union leaders. Educated at Cambridge University with a degree in estate management, Prior was also a clever politician seeking a way to keep progressive ideas alive under Thatcher's leadership. He sniped behind her back, but Thatcher needed him and she was in no position to push many senior Tories aside.[17] On trade union policy, there were three main groups within the Conservative Party: those who favored close dialogue and relations with trade union leaders; those who pushed for trade union reform that did not cause labor militancy; and those who took a hardnosed approach such as Thatcher. The new Conservative leader chose the moderate Prior as shadow secretary of state for employment, a decision suggesting she had to bide her time before any articulation of forceful labor union reforms. Nicholas Ridley never understood why she chose Prior, declaring "he was a landowner and farmer, a patrician Tory, very much on the left side of the Party and not at all in sympathy with her views."[18]

With these political realities, Thatcher spent only modest energy on winning moderates to her free-market thinking which in essence lacked clarity. She made no significant changes to the CRD, seen by conservatives as representative of a consensus-oriented approach that made the Conservative Party directionless and "stranded in the middle." Its director, Chris Patten, was "on the Left of the Party."[19] He mostly opposed Thatcher's vision and apparently called Joseph "the Mad Monk."[20] The CRD and Joseph's CPS competed, but Joseph's zeal for writing, publishing, and lecturing made him formidable. In pursuing the goals of restricting labor powers, rejecting incomes policy, and tightening money supply, Thatcher had the support of Joseph and Alfred Sherman, and she could also count on Norman Tebbit, Nigel Lawson, George Gardiner, and Nicholas Ridley.

Raised in a working-class family, Norman Tebbit landed a job in 1947 at the *Financial Times* at the young age of sixteen. As a price-room hand, he rejected what he saw as the labor union authoritarianism of the printing press union that could easily expel any member who questioned the power of union leaders. For him, it was a noble goal to "to break the power of the closed shop."[21] In the early 1950s, he flew jets for the Royal Air Force. Political office came in 1970 when he became MP for Epping. Tebbit's most notable confrontation with socialism was his assessment of the "Ferrybridge Six," the men who had lost their jobs and ability to collect unemployment. Michael

Foot, secretary of state for employment, backed the union, explaining that anyone who "declines to fall in with new conditions of employment which result from a collective agreement may well be considered to have brought about his own dismissal." According to Tebbet, Foot was guilty of "pure undiluted fascism."[22] In addition to using strong language to get attention, Tebbit developed tactical ideas on how Thatcher could effectively debate socialist policies in the House of Commons. The tactic was for backbenchers to ask questions that allowed Thatcher to dispense with any preamble and go to a limited number of direct questions which usually put even the "wily" Harold Wilson "on the defensive." [23]

Both Nigel Lawson and George Gardiner became MPs in 1974. Lawson, born in 1932, was from a well-to-down Jewish family, and Gardiner, born in 1935, lived with his mother in a shoddy rental home after his parents' divorce. Lawson and Gardiner attended Oxford University where they each earned a first-class honors degree in Philosophy, Politics, and Economics. Born in 1929, Nicholas Ridley also attended Oxford University and after working as a civil engineer, he became MP for Cirencester and Tewkesbury in 1959. A champion of free-market economics, he formed the Economic Dining Group whose attenders included Thatcher. Tebbet, Lawson, Gardiner, and Ridley were important voices to support Thatcher as she prudently contemplated free-market policies that incorporated new approaches to employment and inflation. Their assistance was significant as she faced intense pressure to adopt consensual policies that moderates believed were the answer for uniting the party and nation. However, it was not clear how much she would fight trade union power and make the argument for monetarism.

Along the way she gained the support of influential journalists such as Samuel Brittan, a friend of Nigel Lawson and the chief economic commentator of the *Financial Times*. Lawson viewed Brittan, author of many important publications, as having more influence than most academic economists. Brittan published with the think tank Institute of Economic Affairs, had ties with the Selsdon Group, assisted Keith Joseph with speeches, and met with Thatcher on many occasions. Brittan's effectiveness as a "self-appointed educator of the influential classes" at a time of stimulating economic debate was his ability to articulate economic jargon in plain language. Although he was more an "iconoclastic libertarian" than an actual conservative, his skepticism of Keynesianism made him an attractive resource for conservatives.[24]

II

Early in Thatcher's leadership both Harold Macmillan and Edward Heath delivered speeches warning Tories not to take the party to the right. Another setback for Thatcher was the party's confused economic policy; there were too many contradictions as new ideas clashed with entrenched ones. As it was, the new ideas were at an early stage of development when Thatcher and Joseph sought Alan Walters's understanding of inflation.[25] Keynesianism dominated and there was much resistance to change. On April 11, the shadow cabinet discussed a recent paper by Joseph, and Quintin Hailsham, taking his own notes, wrote: "There was hardly a dull moment." Reggie Maudling, the Shadow foreign secretary and major opponent of monetarism, found nothing in the paper he could agree with. Francis Pym stated that the paper was "a recipe for disaster" since British society was moving to the left. Progressives wanted the party to consider continuity and articulate a broad policy. Turning to Gilmour, Thatcher asked: "Ian you do believe in capitalism?" He responded: "That is almost blasphemy. I don't believe in Socialism."[26] There were separate meetings, composed of different leaders and members, each tackling a specific policy issue and other meetings attempting to find a synthesis of ideas. In mid-May, 1975, David Howell, John Mott, Michael Niblock, and Anne Bullock, the secretary, gathered for a full day at Howe's home for an economic discussion of floating exchange rates, the housing mortgage market, and reducing the Public Service Borrowing Requirement (budget deficit). There was no mention of monetarism and talk of trade unionism was incomplete due to the meeting running late.[27]

Thatcher was not ready to present specific economic policy. While she clearly opposed socialism, much of her message was a general presentation of traditional conservatism. On May 21 to the Conservative Women's Conference at Central Hall, Westminster, she explained the importance of personal ownership, enterprise, opportunity, protection, law, and liberty. The dream of homeownership was important to a vast number of British people who were willing to save money to achieve it. With hard work, people could own homes, giving them "a sense of independence, of self-reliance, of individuality." Recognition of these values, according to Thatcher, was key to building a proper policy superior to "the discredited theories of Karl Marx" and the "thoughts of Chairman Mao." Those who believed that ownership was inferior to a "pure socialist morality" were incapable of appreciating the practice of self-denial and hard work.[28]

Whether at the individual, small-business, or corporate level, enterprise not "harried by taxation" was essential for a prosperous nation. Better off without state intervention, this activity brought jobs, goods, and services and contributed to the building of "national character." Thatcher found it unfortunate that the socialist approach burdened wealth creators, small and large, with taxation, regulations, forms, and surveys. The influence of "socialist propaganda" made it acceptable to disincentivize enterprise, investment, and saving. It appeared that politicians had lost faith and confidence in the British people and the signs were troubling. Thatcher explained: "I venture to doubt if enterprise, as we have known it in this country for many generations, can possibly survive the piecemeal destruction of the private sector which is now proceeding." It was time for Conservatives to respond and restore enterprise "to its rightful place in our society" and protect the flame of individual freedom: "It will be our care, our mission, to see that it never is extinguished, that it will continue to burn here clear and bright, to illuminate the way ahead, for all peoples."[29] It was difficult to measure the sentiment of the British people. Her supporters cheered the hopeful message of action against socialism while opponents saw her rhetoric as conservative platitudes lacking facts and authority.

Thatcher recognized that the Tory Party was far from having a clear free-market message and this was obvious when she faced Harold Wilson in the House of Commons on May 22. The easy part was pointing to Labour's economic shortcoming. On the economy, Thatcher moved:

> That this House, being gravely disturbed by the total failure of the policies of Her Majesty's Government to curb the accelerating rate of inflation, calls upon Her Majesty's Government to abandon their damaging plans for further nationalisation, to take immediate action to cut public expenditure and to secure a reduction in the level of pay settlements, as essential parts of a programme designed to restore confidence and promote the economic recovery of the nation.[30]

To begin, she referred to Wilson's own assessment that the nation faced the gravest economic crisis since the Great Depression. In addressing Britain's problem of inflation, graver than many other countries, she quoted German novelist Thomas Mann: "severe inflation is the worst kind of revolution . . . only the most powerful, the most resourceful and unscrupulous, the hyenas of economic life, can come through unscathed." The common people suffered, notably the elderly who depended on their savings. She identified government spending and borrowing as the primary cause of inflation; however, also problematic was the failure of Labour leaders to act compared to politicians elsewhere.[31]

The response of Sydney Bidwell, Labour MP of Ealing, Southall, was that employers had mostly failed to look after their employees and thus the lack of a "spirit of co-operation" explained Britain's economic performance relative to other nations. When Thatcher turned to the public sector borrowing requirement, raised to £9 billion from £2.7 billion 15 months earlier, John Pardoe, Labour MP of Cornwall, North reminded Thatcher that while she was secretary of state for education she had contributed to an increased borrowing requirement of the Conservative government and that the Tories neglected to raise taxes to cover "their profligate schemes." Thatcher argued that if a government had to spend, it was better to do so during good economic times than when the economy was stagnant. As it was, increasing public expenditure and "nationalisation" represented a redistribution of the "nation's income from the people to the public sector," something unfair to "the people" and "the private sector." When she stated her desire to list areas for cuts, Ioan Evans, Labour MP of Aberdare, suggested the Tory Party was in no position to speak of cuts given its demands for an increase in spending in social services and defense. Of course, everyone present knew Evans would not oppose more money for social services. To Thatcher's earlier suggestion that the Labour Party opposed the idea of personal property, Evans explained it was "the duty of Socialists to try to enable more people to take a share of that personal property" contrast to a Tory society where there are those with "great wealth and possessions" and the many others who are "denied access to cars, houses and other possessions." The Labour Party sought to see "a system of fair shares."[32]

In the debate, Labour gave little attention to economic theory or to the specific issues of productivity, investment, and a more favorable business climate. Instead, Labour MPs, including Harold Wilson, usually pointed to the failure of the previous Tory government to do the conservative things it wanted the Labour Party to do. Baiting the opposition made little difference as when Thatcher stated: "It would, perhaps, be too much to hope for tax reductions or real tax incentives to create wealth. That is not the way of a Socialist Government." Out-of-control borrowing and spending were "the results of Socialist measures and the Socialist administration led by the present Prime Minister for which he must take responsibility." To this, Wilson praised the Labour's better performance with overseas trade than what the Tories achieved in the last quarter of 1973. The prime minister also shared the good news of signing trade agreements with the Soviets, creating new opportunities for British exporters.[33]

Another response by Wilson was to remind the Conservative Party that the world was experiencing "the deepest recession since the 1930s" and that there were countries with a worse record of unemployment and economic decline. When he did address economic theory, he pointed to Keynes's argument that the government must step in when there is insufficient investment to maintain employment. According to Wilson, the Labour Party's National Enterprise Board (NEB), which gave the state more control of an industry, was simply an updated concept that all British politicians agreed to in 1944. The Labour Party saw no problem with the NEB, as opposed to a private merchant bank, involving itself in a business. The advantage of state intervention was that part of the profits went "from private owners to the community as a whole."[34]

Thatcher rejected robust Keynesianism and socialism, but there were limitations on how hard she could drive any free-market analysis. There was no economic policy consensus among Tories, thus Labour could refer to Tory inconsistencies, including Thatcher's. In late 1974, she promised a mortgage cut to 9.5 percent, a mortgage subsidy that would have, according to Wilson, increased government expenditure by at least "£180 million net of tax." Certainly, he scored a major point when he declared: "It is significant that we have heard nothing this afternoon about the Conservative Party's basic economic philosophy. We have heard nothing about monetarism or about unemployment." It did not matter that Labour members were unlikely to enter a serious discussion of Milton Friedman ideas; their focus was on Tory weakness. Unlike the Tory Party, Wilson declared, the Labour Party made its economic argument "clear in successive Budget speeches and debates." He reminded Thatcher that "one of the functions of the Opposition is that they should have an alternative policy to put before the country." With Joseph being absent, Wilson spoke of Thatcher's "Rasputin, who has been kennelled up for this debate so that we are unable to ask him about his policy." Wilson viewed the Tory's confused proposals as "a recipe for a permanently weakened Britain in a divided and unjust society." He asked the House to reject the Tory motion as did Denis Healey who called "upon all thinking Members to join the Labour Government in rejecting the motion with the contempt that it deserves." After many hours of debate, the House defeated the motion 278 votes to 244.[35]

In 1970, Milton Friedman had argued that "inflation is always and everywhere a monetary phenomenon in the sense that it is and can be produced only by a more rapid increase in the quantity of money than in output."[36] Even if Thatcher had a convincing economic policy with a significant monetarism component, any acceptance of monetarism pointed to the shortcomings of the previous Tory government. If an increase in the money supply took about a year and a half "to work through in the form of higher taxes," the Conservative Party and not the Labour Party was mostly responsible for the high inflation. To head off any trouble from Heath and progressive Conservatives, Thatcher had to be prudent with public statements on monetarism. In addition, Heath pressured her publicly to support policy that controlled prices and incomes, a position favored by many Tories and the Labour Party.[37]

Even though Nicholas Ridley met with Christopher Dow, senior economist of the Bank of England, and heard how inflation worried Dow, the timing of any future "informal" meeting between the governor and Thatcher would need to be carefully planned to avoid the optics of partisanship.[38] Of course, conducting studies on inflation, as the bank did, was easier than deciding what was the proper approach for defeating inflationary trends. When it came to defending free-market or progressive ideas it was no contest. There was no political will to defend monetarist ideas with any force, and despite the lack of evidence of incomes policy solving inflation, it was politically more palatable to the ear. Even Joseph's enthusiasm for innovative economic ideas failed to interest the media in early summer 1975. When he hired the ballroom of a hotel to present his message to journalists, only nine showed up.[39] In her first year as leader, Thatcher made no significant progress on advancing new economic thinking that could dislodge entrenched Keynesian and socialist policy ideas.

III

Political adviser Gordon Reece advised Thatcher that "impressions" rather than issues had greater influence on many voters. He explained the importance of the question: "Do I like or admire or respect one of the candidates more than another?"[40] Following traditional political wisdom, she continued to press the issue of socialism, but she also was more aware of creating the right impression. In the early stage of her leadership, she made headway against socialism with her commentary on international socialism and her visits to foreign nations, especially the United States. Her criticism of socialism abroad stretched back many decades. Years before she took public office, she wrote of Karl Marx's flawed theory of class hatred that led to Russia's "Totalitarian Communism."[41] In many other speeches, throughout the early Cold War period she made reference to Russian "propaganda." On several occasions in the House of Commons, she raised the issue of the Soviet imprisonment of Gerald Brooke, a British teacher arrested in 1965 by KGB agents for possessing anti-Soviet documents; Brooke's freedom came four years later when there was an exchange of Soviet spies. Someone who highly valued liberty and market competition, Thatcher, while visiting Moscow in 1969, learned from young university students of the reality of KGB scrutiny in a socialist state.[42]

As leader of the Conservative Party, her first major speech on the dangers of the Soviet Union came on July 26, 1975. To the Chelsea Conservative Association, she listed communist hotspots in Portugal, Vietnam, and Cambodia, and pointed to the threat of Soviet fleets striking key shipping lanes. It was unfortunate that protestors, who opposed American involvement in southeast Asia, downplayed revolutionary socialist expansion, thus remaining mostly silent about the "open savagery of the Khmer Rouge" in Cambodia. Thatcher declared that while western Europe was as economically strong as the Soviet Union, militarily it fell short of the Soviets who outspent the United States on weapons. The Soviet navy, for example, had more nuclear submarines than all the other navies put together. America led in curbing "Russian opportunism," but Britain and the rest of Europe needed to share a greater burden of defence or else the Americans would have less enthusiasm to protect Europe.[43]

Thatcher suggested that détente, the diplomatic attempt by Americans to lessen tensions with communists, was unsuccessful in countering Soviet expansion:

> Detente sounds a fine word. And, to the extent that there really has been a relaxation in international tension, it is a fine thing. But the fact remains that throughout this decade of detente, the armed forces of the Soviet Union have increased, are increasing, and show no signs of diminishing.

In addition to the issue of military power was the loss of liberty due to Soviet repression of dissenters in Russia such as Alexander Solzhenitsyn. Better than politicians or diplomats, dissenters in the fields of literature and science presented a clear picture of the "real attitudes and intentions" of Soviet leaders. Thatcher argued that the best lesson was to stand strong against Soviet leaders, who viewed western attempts of reconciliation as weakness, and pay less attention to western "gullible" western disarmers. Their ridicule of anti-communists fearful of "Communists under every bed" did not alter the facts that there were Soviet spies and others who were sympathetic to the Soviet Union.[44] Within her own party, there were those who opposed her tough warnings about international socialism. It became clear to Thatcher that the appointment of Reggie Maudling as shadow foreign secretary was a mistake. It was not helpful that the former chancellor of the exchequer was a staunch Keynesian and a lazy man who complained about her, but worse was his softness toward the Soviet Union.[45]

Never much of a traveler, Thatcher needed a crash course in foreign affairs, and in her first year as leader she visited the United States, France, Germany, Romania and Turkey.[46] Before her trip to America, she met with Ronald Reagan when he visited London. Their scheduled 45-minute meeting went two times longer as they found their worldviews were very similar. Reagan wrote that "it was evident from our first words that we were soul mates when it came to reducing government and expanding economic freedom."[47] Thatcher's interest in the United States grew and it was during interactions with Americans when she improved her foreign relations credentials. As a Cold Warrior who sought to defeat socialism at home and abroad, she had much in common with many American politicians. Eight years earlier during the presidency of Lyndon B. Johnson, she experienced an exciting first trip to the United States when she travelled from coast to coast for six weeks, marvelling the nation's free-enterprise economy. One meeting was with one of her Finchley constituents who escaped the "over-regulated, high-taxed Britain" to work at NASA.[48]

As opposition leader, Thatcher had her most important foreign trip in September 1975 when she returned to the United States. Her appearance generated much excitement, especially with those wanting to know more about the declining British economy. The Institute of Socio-Economic Studies in New York was the venue of her first speech, and she won the audience immediately with her first statement:

> Only a week or two ago, Vermont Royster wrote that—and I quote—"Britain today offers a textbook case on how to ruin a country." I do take some consolation that there's only one small vowel sound between "ruin" and "run" a country. The small vowel sound is "I."

She welcomed debate on whether the "progressive consensus" of the previous thirty years was successful. What effect did the redistribution of wealth and income have on the economy? What does it mean to put "social" in front of justice? Her starting point was the Labour axiom: "It's just because market forces tend towards growing inequality in incomes and property that massive redistribution is necessary if political freedom and other civilised values are to be preserved." Drawing on a major study by the Royal Commission on the Distribution of Income and Wealth, Thatcher stated that Britain's redistribution of incomes in 1972 was similar to Poland's in which there was no wide range of income between the top 1 percent of earners and the bottom 50 percent of earners. Wealth ownership numbers, with pension rights included, showed that the top 1 percent of the population owned 28 percent of British wealth compared to the year 1938 when the 1 percent owned 50 percent of the wealth. Her point was that government taxation led to the rich "getting poorer" which reduced the effectiveness of more taxation. Taxing the rich further neither paid "for much more government spending" nor made "a significant difference to the wealth of the bulk of the population." She was no supply-side theorist, but her thinking hinted of the Laffer curve that there was a point in taxation where government revenue decreased.[49]

Thatcher also used the 1975 survey by the Political and Economic Planning Group to show that people saw steady economic growth rather than massive redistribution as "the chief requirement for maintaining general satisfaction with incomes and earnings." She noted a significant divide in the views of ordinary people and socialist thinkers. The motivation of those pressing for equality by state invention was twofold: envy and bourgeois guilt. However, the resentment and guilt of egalitarians and subsequent socialist policy brought "happiness to no one, except to those who impose it." The British economy, Thatcher argued, was not improving with the government controlling more than half of the Gross National Product. The state took 25 percent of the industrial earnings of the typical worker, who in turn pressed for a higher salary to compensate for the higher taxes. The cycle resulted in price increases. In the end, "Government expenditure is private taxation or borrowing for which the citizen has to pay." Another difficulty was the distorting effect on the labor market caused by the movement of workers from private to public sector employment. She pointed out that with the growth of government jobs, there was a smaller pool of workers employed in productive industry.[50]

Companies were also hurt by burdensome taxes and the loss of profits which discouraged entrepreneurial investment. Thatcher explained that the strategy of wage and price controls to combat inflation was problematic:

> If you put restraint on profits, you found, in fact, that you were not making sufficient profits properly to invest for the future. If you put restraint on prices, as we have also done, the prices were not high enough to enable the companies to make enough profit. And so you consequently come up against the position whereby our companies have not been able to get the prices, because of price control, to make the profits which are necessary to make the investment which is necessary to provide the growth and the jobs tomorrow.[51]

Weaker companies and a decline in productivity resulted in less government revenue so politicians resorted to borrowing which caused a rise in interest rates and the relentless cycle of inflation. Looking for a good return on their investments, people opted for government stock, but this deprived the private sector of necessary money for its development. She told her American audience that the taxation rate for Britain's highest earners was 83 percent on earned income and 98 percent on unearned or savings income. These tax rates put companies in Britain at a disadvantage since the best talent could earn a better gross salary by taking middle and upper management positions in other countries.

Thatcher argued that socialist government policies of expanding the state and pursuing equality were at the heart of the "British sickness." The lesson of the previous decades was that the pursuit of equality was a mirage, certainly less practicable than the "pursuit of equality of opportunity." Her understanding of opportunity allowed "the right to be unequal and the freedom to be different." With more emphasis on the value of an individual, a society became stronger; if citizens developed their full potential and received rewards for their originality, skill, energy, and thrift, the greater community benefited. To drive home her point, she noted the words of reformist Alexander Dubcek, the socialist leader of Czechoslovakia in the late sixties: The pursuit of equality "has developed in an unprecedented manner and this fact has become one of the most important obstacles to intensive economic development and higher living standards." Too many "lazy people, passive individuals, and irresponsible employees" profited at the expense of dedicated employees, skilled workers, and "those with initiative and talent." To counter retorts that she was heartless, Thatcher stated the importance of caring for those with physical and social handicaps. In fact, incentive and opportunity through private enterprise increased the wealth of the nation and allowed more resources for social programs.[52]

Thatcher continued to generate significant nationwide media attention and she gave a long interview with Barbara Walters on NBC's "Today" show, watched by 7 million households. Sitting in front of a large mural of the British Isles, Thatcher explained that governments only spend people's money: "There is no such thing as a Government grant. There is only a tax-payers' grant." For the government to do more for citizens, it had to take more from the people, but if it took too much, people lost incentive to work more. She saw there was a serious flaw to "propaganda campaigns" that began saying "Look, let's tax the rich." In the long run, ordinary people suffered because eventually there would be fewer wealthy people to tax and thus the government raised taxes on the average person.[53] A luncheon guest remarked: "Here is this little blonde, blue-eyed woman in this pale peach dress with baby blonde hair. She is a flower among thorns. But it's no little girl act either. She is just plain well-informed and extremely articulate."[54] Giving a traditional conservative economic message came natural for Thatcher; when she was on point, she believed everything she said.

The Labour Party found Thatcher's criticism of its policies offensive and reporter Michael Brunson asked her if she was guilty of transgressing the unwritten rule of British politicians speaking in foreign nations not to discuss internal politics. She was unapologetic:

> I think that people would not expect me to say that a state in which we have 25%; inflation, 1¼ million unemployment, unprecedented public expenditure is one in which we think everything is all right, and I have in fact been showing that we are tackling these problems and we are able to tackle them, but of course, as you would know, it's no part of my job to be a propagandist for a socialist society.[55]

Keeping a busy schedule of meetings in New York, Washington, and Chicago, Thatcher clarified her belief in Britain and the British people while also pointing out the failings of a socialist political vision. To the National Press Club, she said, "I reject Marxism because its doctrines seem to me false. It is the negation of human dignity. Wherever you have Marxist Government you have tyranny, oppression and drabness." Perhaps strategically she made no effort to differentiate between democratic socialism and the revolutionary socialism of the Soviet Union, China, Cuba and others.[56]

In Chicago, Thatcher gave the "Walter Heller International Finance Lecture," devoting a significant component to economics. She praised the "remarkable" Adam Smith and his *Inquiry into the Nature and Causes of the Wealth of Nations* that ushered in an economic revolution, ending feudalism and releasing "all the innate energy of private initiative and enterprise which enabled wealth to be created on a scale never before contemplated." The genius of Smith was his recognition of unchangeable "economic, physical, and also moral laws" which no authoritarian leader could repeal. However, Thatcher lamented that economic teaching had become too mathematical and theoretical for those outside academic circles and explained, in part, why many politicians failed to learn and understand basic economic principles. Many economists did not do themselves any favors when they ignored the political consequences of their economic "solutions." One exception of relevant teaching was the Chicago School of Economics that provided "realistic and thorough" ideas. Without specifically identifying its name, Thatcher noted its deserved "worldwide reputation," despite promoting ideas not yet popular.[57]

The western thinking class continued to rely heavily on John Maynard Keynes, particularly on the issue of unemployment, but Thatcher questioned whether his disciples got it right when they tolerated government borrowing "year in, year out." Politicians desired to smooth the extremes of the business cycle, but their efforts were rarely successful as they escalated government control: "In the economic sphere it has resulted in growing frustrations for both the people (because of the disincentives to be enterprising and responsible) and politicians (because their efforts have not borne the results they expected)." Not understanding the effects of their decisions, politicians watched inflation spoil their best-laid plans. Echoing F. A. Hayek and Keith Joseph, Thatcher argued that had Keynes lived longer "he would have become one of the leaders in the fight against inflation." Inflation was a "pernicious evil," but what to do? Although she declared the importance of "getting the money supply broadly right," she provided no specifics. She repeated the old view of reining in peoples' income expectations and being aware of worldwide effects such as Middle Eastern oil policies. Her idea of a "Declaration of Interdependence" for solving international economic problems was mostly aspirational and absent of economic theory.[58]

Thatcher agreed to most speaking engagement suggestions, but she rejected the idea of having lunch at the Brookings Institute, a "liberal-left" think tank.[59] In her memoirs she only mentions four of the many people she met: President Gerald Ford, Secretary of State Henry Kissinger, Defense Secretary James Schlesinger, and Treasury Secretary William Simon, who likely offered her the most stimulating analysis on economic matters. Simon discarded President Richard Nixon's wage and price controls. He was arguably the most important and fearless free-market thinker in the Gerald Ford administration, a notable contrast to Ford who, according to Thatcher, was not likely "to challenge accepted orthodoxies."[60] They were kindred spirits on the critical role of markets. In contrast to Thatcher's appraisal, Labour's Denis Healey put Simon "far to the right of Genghis Khan" due to his devotion "to the freedom of the financial markets."[61] A month after their meeting, Simon wrote to Thatcher commending her courage to pursue "the policies necessary to bring inflation under control."[62] Although she made no outstanding statements on economic theory during her visit, she said enough for people to recognize she was a politician who consistently exposed the economic problems of socialist thinking. She championed free enterprise unapologetically.

When she returned to Britain, the *Guardian* concluded that "the Tories have been taken over by the extremists."[63] The Labour Party hit her with much criticism, which appeared to raise her profile with the British people and "the upper echelons of the Conservative Party."[64] Her economic message received greater attention; the nation had a better economic future if it avoided big government and socialist ideas. In her first speech to her constituents, she said private enterprise was responsible for 97 percent of Britain's exports and she wanted to "build it up—not do a Benn on it," referring to the socialist thinking of Labour's Tony Benn.[65] Perhaps her case against socialism in general also hit too close to the Keynesian economics that welcomed greater government intervention and control.

IV

In the past, the Conservative Party failed to stay true to free-market principles when unemployment numbers increased, and it was not clear whether Thatcher could break free from the Keynesianism of her party. Could there be an economic path acceptable to both the progressive and more free-market wing of the party? Pessimism continued in establishment circles and Harold Macmillan lamented in early October: "The Tory Party is not regarded as a national party now. We tried—Churchill, Eden, myself—to make it a sort of jolly for everyone. It was a party for the nation. Now I'm afraid they've lost that."[66] Thatcher's faith in private enterprise and markets was unsettling.

As the Party Conference of October 10, 1975, approached, she consulted with Chris Patten and others of the CRD to find the proper tone for her speech. Unfortunately, the collaboration was unsatisfactory. She spent the weekend writing sixty pages when she received a call from a friend and former Labour MP who agreed to read it and help with revisions on Sunday evening. The combination of the weekend effort and new material from the

CRD underwent additional revision by the playwright Ronnie Millar, who gave it wordsmith flair. Thatcher needed a good performance, especially since Heath showed no desire to bury the hatchet, despite requests by his friends. When it was obvious Heath's pride prevented him from seeing Thatcher, Willie Whitelaw asked her to make the first move. She agreed and waited for confirmation of the meeting and details. However, Heath had second thoughts and the reconciliation two days before her speech did not happen.[67]

In her speech, Thatcher identified two challenges: overcoming a stagnant economy and regaining "our confidence in Britain and ourselves." Her criticism of the Labour Party was straightforward. It was her intention to "go on criticising Socialism, and opposing Socialism because it is bad for Britain—and Britain and Socialism are not the same thing." The problem with Labour politicians was having "the usual Socialist disease—they've run out of other people's money." She argued that some Labour MPs wanted to replace free enterprise with a "Marxist system" and Harold Wilson himself worried that they might capture key positions in the party. Her attacks generated regular and enthusiastic applause as did her general statements concerning economics that were appealing to all Tories. It was the standard Tory line of having a free economy, good profits, and high investment, all of which generated "well-paid jobs and a better standard of living tomorrow."[68] Charles Moore argues that the subsequent standing ovation was "genuine, the reaction of long-disheartened troops hearing their own inner beliefs expressed with vigour and optimism." Even Chris Patten, years later, admitted: "She cheered up the troops more than any party leader since Churchill."[69]

In early 1976, Thatcher did some modest reshuffling of the shadow cabinet. One addition was Energy spokesman John Biffen, a farmer's son who had graduated with a first-class Cambridge honors history degree. A free marketer, he had connections with leading free-market economists. Thatcher's first speech of the year was a spirited assault on the Labour Party, but her target was Labour's defense policy rather than its economic policies. In her January speech at Kensington Hall, Chelsea, she suggested the Labour Party was not fulfilling its duty to keep Britain safe against the Soviets "bent on world dominance." The Soviets' weak economy had yet to hamper their military buildup on land and sea, and this was not the time for the Labour government to take a passive approach and cut military spending: "If there are further cuts, perhaps the Defence Secretary should change his title, for the sake of accuracy, to the Secretary for Insecurity." According to Thatcher, the root of Britain's weak defense was due to the "disastrous economic legacy of Socialism."[70] Politically, the best reaction to her speech came from the Soviet newspaper *Red Star* that referred to her as "The Iron Lady."[71] She wore this label proudly.

As the Labour government faced an economic crisis in 1976, the Conservative Party spent months crafting *The Right Approach*. The collaboration range was broad; Keith Joseph, Geoffrey Howe, Chris Patten, Angus Maude, and Jim Prior produced what might be best called a "truce" document. In the period leading to its publication in October, there was much activity within the party to find a common voice to clearly illustrate the economic difference between the opposition and governing parties. The British people needed to know how the Conservatives would approach the economic chaos differently.

In a January 7 three-page memorandum to Patten, Joseph wrote how Labour in 1974 "stamped on the public sector acceleration while nearly throttling the private sector to death," causing much of the present high unemployment. However, he suggested that the party avoid calling for or supporting any increase of the money supply. In his letter he included an analysis showing the unreliability of the monthly unemployment statistics by the Department of Employment and requested the CRD review them carefully.[72] Accurate data mattered. On the plus side, having a better understanding of the labor market would benefit the Conservatives once they regained power. On the negative side, Joseph's analysis of unemployment put Thatcher on the spot in the House of Commons. At the end of the month, Denis Healey taunted her on whether she accepted Joseph's numbers:

> The right hon. Lady, as so often, has refused to answer a very relevant question. She is a director of the research organisation [CPS] to which I have referred. Her Rasputin or Malvolio, the right hon. Member for Leeds, North-East [Joseph], is another director and, we are told, manages its studies. What we want to know is whether the right hon. Lady will tell us what her view is.

If she disagreed with the CPS, Healey suggested she abolish it and replace Joseph with a new economic adviser.[73] Some Tories probably agreed with this suggestion. Not yet a Conservative insider, political analyst John Hoskyns expressed concern that the CPS could not influence the "Conservative Party machine."[74] Thinking politically and thinking economically did not always align.

The intellectual activity at the CPS was vibrant and free marketers like Joseph and Alfred Sherman were willing to debate economic ideas and even meet and find "common ground with thinking people in and associated with the Labour movement."[75] There were risks to sharing ideas when the goal of gaining political advantage over the opposing party persisted, but free marketers were typically confident that their economic ideas, if given a fair reading, would win. When Joseph heard of the BBC inviting popular Canadian-American economist John Kenneth Galbraith to do a lecture series, he discussed with Willie Whitelaw getting Frank McFadzean, a successful businessman and economist, to respond to Galbraith's socialist ideas. Although Galbraith's books were "half-baked and dependent upon bold and inaccurate over-simplification," they were influential. His popularity with many university students, his backing of the Labour Party, and his support for a permanent price and income policy made him a "dangerous political opponent."[76] For "proper balance," Geoffrey Howe suggested talks by Hayek or Friedman.[77] It was essential to contrast free-market and socialist ideas.

Joseph had the most success in clarifying varied economic approaches. On April 5, he delivered a major paper entitled "Monetarism is Not Enough." In the foreword, Thatcher argued that inflationary measures introduced by the government to abate unemployment had the opposite effect and that both parties acknowledged this fact, in large part due to Joseph's "forceful expositions." However, there was fear of the old errors creeping back "in new form." Joseph sought to disarm critics by suggesting that every economist is a monetarist in the sense that they accept a relationship between the supply of money and price levels. It was useful to define monetarism as "the policy of trying to move towards and then maintain a stable growth in money supply closely related to the probable growth in output capacity, as most likely to create the conditions for prosperity and high employment in freedom." There was no reason for "some so-called Keynesians" to distrust monetarism, especially if monetarists did not see monetarism as the magical answer to solve all economic problems. If there were monetarists guilty of "wondercures," so too were the "pseudo-Keynesians" who believed their Keynesian focus on stimulating demand could solve "specific non-monetary" problems. Joseph exposed how the Labour Party misrepresented monetarism:

> The monetarist thesis has been caricatured as implying that if we get the flow of money spending right, everything will be right. This is not—repeat not—my belief. What I believe is that if we get the money supply wrong—too high or too low—nothing will come right.[78]

Joseph argued that part of the problem was learning the wrong lessons from history, something hard to avoid given that "socialists and Keynesians" wrote revisionist economic history. For the most part, Britain experienced economic progress "well before" Keynes's *General Theory*. It was incorrect for politicians to believe that state intervention assured full employment, stability, and a high growth rate. For decades, there were also the counterproductive effects of a "socialist anti-enterprise climate," embraced by politicians, civil servants, union leaders, and intellectuals who were distasteful of "the makers of wealth—whether self-employed, small, medium or large." Politicians were confident in the ability of government to manage the economy and when high inflation hit, they did what came naturally—they acted. But price controls, for example, "imposed a heavy toll of losses." The arrival of "stagflation" began to cast doubt on whether interventionist policies could correct high inflation and high unemployment occurring simultaneously. There was a better way. As Joseph saw it, monetarism was not enough, but it was an important part of a package that included "substantial cuts in tax and public spending and bold incentives and encouragements to the wealth creators."[79]

Joseph returned to the issue of monetarism many times throughout 1976, urging the party to state a clear message on incomes policy. For example, one month after his Stockton speech, he sent Geoffrey Howe, Jim Prior, Ian Gilmour, Chris Patten, Angus Maude, and Nicholas Ridley a twenty-six-page draft explaining that governments caused inflation and an incomes policy had no chance of abating inflation. If Tories remained silent and gave the impression that they believed an incomes policy could defeat inflation, they would give Labour the advantage.[80]

Although Joseph's efforts were commendable, traditional thinking persisted; it was a slow process to have his Tory colleagues be more receptive to monetarism and less enthusiastic with an incomes policy. Throughout the summer, the party discussed ways to tackle inflation without necessarily discounting some form of an incomes policy. In June, the Economic Reconstruction Group, attended by Chairman Geoffrey Howe and three MPs Prior, Gilmour, and David Howell, deliberated on the possibility of abolishing "overall price control" and introducing "a code of practice, voluntarily agreed with the food manufacturers."[81] This was a softer version of control, deemed necessary given the seriousness of rising food prices. In another meeting, the group agreed that "wage-restraint was a crucial part of economic policy," a position similar to Labour's.[82] Meanwhile, talks continued between free-market MPs seeking to influence "informed opinion in the right direction" and one plan was to have key people, including people from the Bank of England and the Treasury Department, join a private meeting with Milton Friedman during his planned visit to London at the end of summer.[83] If Joseph's progress in influencing Tories was modest, his enthusiasm for economic theory grew as he met with free-market thinkers outside of government who shared their insights on economics and socialists. Greek financier Minos Zombanakis, born in Crete and educated at Harvard (MA), told Joseph that Healey was a tough, "determined and shrewd Socialist intent on demonstrating the failure of the private sector."[84]

In a party strategy paper, Howe argued that the party's policy objectives lacked "a convincing clarity," a problem that the Labour Party once had and overcame. Young people especially found the Conservatives unlikable, and the party needed to convince them that Conservative policies offered them more enjoyment, jobs, spending power, and freedom. Howe's strategy appeared sound: "We need to find ways of differentiating ourselves clearly from Labour, of choosing our own ground, of creating our own language for the issues."[85] Simply reacting to Labour policies was not enough. But could the party deliver clarity? After months of discussion, the Conservatives were close to publishing *The Right Approach*. One late revision was to delete all phrases in the economic section that made "it look like a manifesto, such as 'we will.'"[86] This revision, however, did not communicate strength.

On October 4, the Tories released *The Right Approach*, a seventy-one-page document on "Conservative aims." The tone was balanced with no new and bold language of free-market thinking. On the issue of individual enterprise, Tories favored "an economic system predominantly based on private enterprise," but added "this does not make us a *laissez-faire* party." The Tories approved the role the state played in balancing different interests that arise from "conflicting groups." Much of the economic content was in the large sections "the right economic strategy" and "bringing the economy into balance" which pointed to Labour's excessive public spending, state control of industries, and over-optimistic assumptions of economic growth at the very time of declining productivity. The socialist "obsession" with increasing the power of the state meant the stifling of private enterprise, rising taxes and demand, distortions in the economy, and inflation. According to the Tories, the Labour Party failed to see what Britain needed— "a genuine attempt to increase profits substantially." The Tories went with traditional conservative points and in fact they declared they did not "expect salvation to come from any sudden new initiative." The only hint of monetarism was one sentence: "To this end [conquering inflation], a steady and disciplined monetary policy is vital."[87] But first the state had to put its finances in order. *The Right Approach* simply came down to the government living within its means, allowing its citizens individual freedom, and taking the tax and regulation shackles off private enterprise thus allowing initiative and industry to blossom. *The Right Approach* sought consensus and revealed the resistance Thatcher faced for her economic ideas on inflation. Her study of economics gave her an advantage over Tory critics who were weak on economics, but too many of them were political heavyweights still holding to Heathite economic solutions.[88] In James Prior's assessment, Thatcher's commitment to monetarism in her first two years as leader was weak.[89]

David Wood, political writer for *The Times*, also from Thatcher's hometown Grantham, told Anthony Benn in February 1977 that Thatcher was "bold in thought," but in action "very cautious." He suggested she was no different than most Tory politicians who understood the power of trade unions and who saw the importance of broadening the base of the Tory Party. Other people who shared comments on Thatcher with Benn included television journalist Robin Day who argued that Thatcher was a "radical," but there was no right-ward shift of the Tories.[90] Others were less confident. In a March 1977 cabinet meeting, Shirley Williams feared that Thatcher as prime minister would result in a confrontation with the trade union movement and an undermining of democracy.[91] Her Labour critics usually said little about her economic thinking, but they understood that her animosity for socialism represented a serious threat to their policy ideas for a better Britain.

After not quite two years as leader of the Conservative Party, Thatcher provided steady but unexciting economic guidance. While Joseph and other free marketers generated stimulating work, she proceeded with restraint understanding the progressive wing of the Conservative Party barely tolerated her leadership. They looked at monetarism with suspicion and they believed successful management of the economy depended on an incomes policy, otherwise there would be a devastatingly high number of jobless people. For decades, Keynesians had been wary of the threat of soaring unemployment numbers. Heath himself did not hide his criticism of Thatcher at party conferences, in Parliament, and in the media.[92] In this climate, the Tories could not capitalize on Labour's troubles, but if the free marketers like Joseph were correct, Labour would be unable to escape difficult economic times in the months ahead. Besides, there was also plenty of drama within the Labour Party as various expressions of socialism gave evidence of significant division among Labour MPs.

NOTES

1. Tony Benn, *Against the Tide*: *Diaries 1973-76* (London: Hutchinson, 1989), 311.
2. John Shepherd, *Crisis? What Crisis?: The Callaghan Government and the British 'Winter of Discontent'* (Manchester: Manchester University Press, 2013), 136.
3. Caldwell, ed., *The Collected Works of F.A. Hayek Volume II*, 137.
4. For a discussion of the postwar consensus, see Richard Toye, "From 'Consensus' to 'Common Ground': The Rhetoric of the Postwar Settlement and Its Collapse," *Journal of Contemporary History* 48, no. 1 (2013), 3–23.
5. Campbell, *Margaret Thatcher*, 309.
6. Benn, *Against the Tide*, 420.
7. Wapshott and Brock, *Thatcher*, 141.
8. Thatcher, *Margaret Thatcher*, 177.
9. Moore, *Margaret Thatcher*, 297.
10. Young, *One of Us*, 104–7.
11. Alan Howarth, "Obituary: Lord Thorneycroft," *The Independent*, 5 June 1994.
12. On Thatcher's assessment of Powell's betrayal of his constituency workers, see Thatcher, *Margaret Thatcher*, 146.
13. Campbell, *Margaret Thatcher*, 313–14, 325.

14. Campbell, *Margaret Thatcher*, 320. For Thatcher's assessment, see Thatcher, *Margaret Thatcher*, 179–80.
15. Wapshott and Brock, *Thatcher*, 145, 149–50.
16. Goodlad, *Thatcher*, 47.
17. Young, *One of Us*, 109–10.
18. Shepherd, *Crisis? What Crisis?*, 135.
19. Thatcher, *Margaret Thatcher*, 181.
20. Harris, *Not for Turning*, 119–20.
21. David Kynaston, *Austerity Britain, 1945-51* (New York: Walker and Company, 2008), 466.
22. Tebbits, *Upwardly Mobile*, 192.
23. Tebbits, *Upwardly Mobile*, 183.
24. Roger Middleton, "Brittan on Britain: 'The Economic Contradictions of Democracy' Redux," *The Historical Journal* 54, no. 4 (2011), 1143, 1148, 1161–62.
25. MTF, Sir Keith Joseph to MT, 25 February 1975, https://www.margaret thatcher.org/document/111215.
26. MTF, Hailsham diary (Shadow Cabinet squabbles over Keith Joseph paper), 11 April 1975, https://www.margaretthatcher.org/document/111134.
27. In a letter to Thatcher, Geoffrey Howe wrote it was crucial to discuss changing the balance of power of the government and trade unionism. See MTF, Economy: Fentiman Road seminar, 18 May 1975, https://www.margaretthatcher.org/document /109968.
28. MTF, Speech to Conservative Women's Conference, https://www.margaret thatcher.org/document/102694.
29. Speech to Conservative Women's Conference.
30. Hansard, HC Deb 22 May 1975 vol 892 cc1637-768, https://api.parliament.uk /historic-hansard/commons/1975/may/22/the-economy.
31. HC Deb 22 May 1975.
32. HC Deb 22 May 1975.
33. HC Deb 22 May 1975.
34. HC Deb 22 May 1975.
35. HC Deb 22 May 1975.
36. https://miltonfriedman.hoover.org/friedman_images/Collections/2016c21/IEA _1970.pdf.
37. Thatcher, *Margaret Thatcher*, 185.
38. MTF, Economy: Adam Ridley note for MT, 5 March 1975, https://www. margaretthatcher.org/document/109954.
39. Denham and Garnett, *Keith Joseph*, 298.
40. Moore, *Margaret Thatcher*, 307.
41. MTF, Article for *Young Kent Forum*, 1 October 1949. https://www. margaretthatcher.org/document/109511.
42. MTF, HC PQ, 6 November 1967, https://www.margaretthatcher.org/document /101590. Thatcher, *Margaret Thatcher*, 99.
43. MTF, Speech to Chelsea Conservative Association, 26 July 1975, https://www .margaretthatcher.org/document/102750.

44. Speech to Chelsea Conservative Association, 26 July 1975.

45. Less than two years later Thatcher fired Maudling. See Campbell, *Margaret Thatcher*, 321.

46. Young, *One of Us*, 119.

47. Ronald Reagan, *An American Life: The Autobiography* (New York: Simon & Schuster, 1990), 204.

48. Thatcher, *Margaret Thatcher*, 98–99.

49. MTF, Speech to the Institute of SocioEconomic Studies ("Let Our Children Grow Tall"), 15 September 1975, https://www.margaretthatcher.org/document/102769.

50. Speech to the Institute of SocioEconomic Studies, 15 September 1975.

51. Speech to the Institute of SocioEconomic Studies, 15 September 1975.

52. Speech to the Institute of SocioEconomic Studies, 15 September 1975.

53. MTF, TV Interview for NBC *Today,* 16 September 1975, https://www.margaretthatcher.org/document/102565.

54. Quoted in Moore, *Margaret Thatcher*, 317.

55. MTF, Press Conference after meeting President Ford, 18 September 1975, https://www.margaretthatcher.org/document/102464. Also, see Moore, *Margaret Thatcher*, 317.

56. MTF, Speech to the National Press Club, 19 September 1975, https://www.margaretthatcher.org/document/102770.

57. Thatcher declared: "I know my comments on economists will not be taken amiss in this particular city. It deservedly has a world-wide reputation for a school of economic thought which has consistently been realistic and thorough, though not always very popular." MTF, Speech at Roosevelt University, 22 September 1975, https://www.margaretthatcher.org/document/102465.

58. Speech at Roosevelt University, 22 September 1975.

59. Moore, *Margaret Thatcher*, 315.

60. Thatcher, *Margaret Thatcher*, 208–9.

61. Healey, *The Time of My Life*, 419.

62. Moore, *Margaret Thatcher*, 319.

63. Moore, *Margaret Thatcher*, 321.

64. Thatcher, *Margaret Thatcher*, 209.

65. MTF, Speech to Finchley Conservatives, 1 October 1975, https://www.margaretthatcher.org/document/102774.

66. Quoted in Gamble, *The Free Economy and the Strong State*, 92.

67. Thatcher, *Margaret Thatcher*, 189–90.

68. MTF, Speech to Conservative Party Conference, 10 October 1975, https://www.margaretthatcher.org/document/102777.

69. Moore, *Margaret Thatcher*, 326.

70. MTF, Speech at Kensington Town Hall, 19 January 1976, https://www.margaretthatcher.org/document/102939.

71. Thatcher, *Margaret Thatcher*, 210.

72. MTF, Keith Joseph memorandum to Chris Patten, 7 January 1976, https://www.margaretthatcher.org/document/111971.

73. MTF, HC I, 29 January 1976, https://www.margaretthatcher.org/document/102946.

74. MTF, John Hoskyns letter to Sherman, 24 February 1976, https://www.margaretthatcher.org/document/111926.

75. MTF, Sherman memorandum to Keith Joseph, 17 February 1976, https://www.margaretthatcher.org/document/111925.

76. MTF, Keith Joseph to Willie Whitelaw, 17 March 1976, https://www.margaretthatcher.org/document/111226.

77. MTF, Geoffrey Howe to Sir Keith Joseph, 22 March 1976, https://www.margaretthatcher.org/document/110039.

78. MTF, Stockton Lecture, 5 April 1976, https://www.margaretthatcher.org/document/110796.

79. Stockton Lecture, 5 April 1976.

80. MTF, Keith Joseph to various colleagues, 4 May 1976, https://www.margaretthatcher.org/document/111230.

81. MTF, Economic Reconstruction Group—Minutes of Meeting 16, 10 June 1976, https://www.margaretthatcher.org/document/110235.

82. MTF, Economic Reconstruction Group—Minutes of Meeting 18, 24 June 1976, https://www.margaretthatcher.org/document/110237.

83. MTF, Geoffrey Howe to Sir Keith Joseph, 2 July 1976, https://www.margaretthatcher.org/document/110067.

84. MTF, Keith Joseph to Geoffrey Howe, 19 July 1976, https://www.margaretthatcher.org/document/111232.

85. MTF, Geoffrey Howe paper, 1 August 1976, https://www.margaretthatcher.org/document/110078; also, Norman Strauss notes, 3 August 1976, https://www.margaretthatcher.org/document/220210.

86. MTF, Geoffrey Howe to MT, 30 July 1976, https://www.margaretthatcher.org/document/110076.

87. MTF, *The Right Approach,* 4 October 1976, https://www.margaretthatcher.org/document/109439.

88. Moore, *Margaret Thatcher*, 340.

89. Prior, *A Balance of Power*, 109.

90. Tony Benn, *Conflicts of Interest: Diaries 1977-80* (London: Hutchinson, 1990), 25, 39.

91. Benn, *Conflicts of Interest*, 88.

92. Gamble, *The Free Economy and the Strong State*, 94, 102.

Chapter 4

Labour and Inflation

Anthony Benn wrote in his diary on February 21, 1977, about his lunch with other Labour MPs. There were jokes and serious discussion. Dickson Mabon, a Labour Co-operative MP, introduced the topic of the "legitimate left" and Benn asked him, "Am I a member of the legitimate left?" Mabon replied: "Oh yes, but the legitimate left has got to be careful it doesn't pave the way for others to come in." As a hardline socialist, Benn often traveled a lonely road. Harold Wilson, Denis Healey, James Callaghan, and many high-ranking MPs leaned toward a middle-of-the road socialist position that encompassed Keynesianism. Benn commented to his lunch colleagues of the rift in the Labour Party and the "harsh choice to be made between monetarism and the Labour manifesto." Audrey Wise, MP for Coventry South, spoke of the "terrible deterioration of morale in the Government." Benn saw the need to win the argument for socialism and work for a united party.[1] They were ambitious goals. The Labour Party could score points from the divisions in the Tory Party and Thatcher's inability to present a unified and clear economic philosophy; however, Labour was no better off.

For decades, there was a tug of war between moderate socialists and those taking a less practical and more ideological approach. There were always a fair number of Labour MPs who were unenthusiastic with the cautious approach of their leaders. A Labour prime minister with socialist instincts was not enough; he had to act boldly on his socialism. When rising inflation became a major focus, the rift of different socialist visions became more obvious even if there was confusion over economic policy. For example, Benn's reference to the "monetarism" of other Labour politicians was puzzling because there was no Milton Friedman monetarism within the Labour Party. Few really talked about money supply and no one, including the Keynesians, could possibly agree with Friedman's opposition to state intervention in the economy. One example of Friedman's anti-state position was his disapproval of the British/French Concorde project and the injection of government money to fund supersonic air service. It was a mistake, "a step toward socialism and away from free enterprise."[2] The closest Labour got to monetarism—which was not very close—was cutting back planned spending, pursuing the "Social Contract" which was an incomes policy, and accepting a loan from the International Monetary Fund as part of the strategy to confront high inflation and the fall of the sterling pound. In the end, what mattered the most for politicians, so they claimed, was having government policies bring a healthy economy of good jobs and wages for British voters. The years 1975 to 1977 did not give Labour much to cheer about.

I

The long-lasting tension within the Labour Party between those desiring a moderate socialist approach of Keynesianism and those demanding greater socialist action was no less obvious in the second half of the 1970s. For Labour moderates, the leading revisionist theorist was Anthony Crosland, author of *The Future of Socialism* (1956).[3] Crosland was born in 1918 and grew up in North London. He attended Oxford University before and after the war. Denis Healey claimed Crosland lacked the nerve to join the Communist Party even though as a student he considered himself a Marxist.[4] James Callaghan relished Crosland's "reckless devil-may-care attitude" that was a camouflage for "a deeply serious intellect."[5] During the war, Crosland experienced combat and reached the rank of captain. His return to Oxford led to a first-class honors degree in Philosophy, Politics and Economics, and the presidency of the Oxford Union. When Thatcher was the president of the Oxford University Conservative Association, she was aware of Crosland who "could condescend to a Duchess."[6] From 1950, he served many years as a Labour MP, holding key cabinet positions including economic secretary to the treasurer and minister of state for economic affairs in the 1960s. Crosland and Anthony Benn were old political friends, but while appreciating Crosland's "heart of gold" Benn saw him as "arrogant" and "difficult," someone on the opposite side of the party who wrote an influential book that "misread the underlying crisis in a capitalist economy."[7]

Gordon Brown writes that *The Future of Socialism* "marked a decisive moment in post-war Labour history." Crosland's "wake-up call" had a greater impact on Labour thinking than the writing of any other Labour author.[8] Crosland wrote that prewar socialists sought the end of poverty by creating a social service state and instituting economic planning. But to ensure equalization of wealth and full employment, the forcible overthrow of capitalism was necessary; "a merely *ad hoc* reformist approach" was not enough. Earning the title "revisionist," Crosland strongly disagreed with key socialist assumptions of the 1930s; throughout his book, he clarified that Marx had "little or nothing to offer the contemporary socialist, either in respect of practical policy, or of the correct analysis of our society, or even of the right conceptual tools or framework."[9] Equally provocative were his arguments that after World War II, capitalist "ruthlessness" mostly disappeared, "aggressive 'free enterprise' propaganda" lessened, and the key to improved standard of living was by "higher production per head." Nationalization of industry was not necessarily the best policy, and it was time for a rethinking of the "strong tendency within the Labour Party towards a suspicious, militant, class-conscious Leftism." Crosland maintained that more practical was a socio-democratic approach to reach the goals of equality and quality of life.[10] His brief mention of Keynes, notably in the last two paragraphs of the book, is positive.

Hugh Gaitskell was also a revisionist socialist. Born in a well-to-do family in 1906, Gaitskell attended Oxford University where he graduated with a first-class degree in Philosophy, Politics and Economics. On his thirty-first birthday, he married Anna Frost, born in Russia but raised in Britain. He had a long-term affair with the wife of James Bond creator, Ian Fleming. In politics, Gaitskell embraced a "moderate labourist" position and battled with other Labour leaders on effective strategies to win a general election. However, Anthony Benn found it interesting that Gaitskell gave a good socialist speech in the House of Commons on December 5, 1945: "Capitalism is inefficient, it creates insecurity, it is unjust, and the Labour Party is united by a single philosophy." Gaitskell was leader of the Labour Party from 1955 to 1963. Thatcher recognized that he won the respect of much of the Labour Party, but Marxist historian John Saville, writing in the *Socialist Register*, lamented the "disastrous" results of Gaitskell's accommodating approach.[11] His unexpected death in 1963 opened the door for Harold Wilson.

Thatcher acknowledged Wilson's skill in the House of Commons, writing that she "usually scored nothing better than a draw against him in the House."[12] Born in 1916, Harold Wilson had a middle-class upbringing; his father James Herbert Wilson was an industrial chemist who lost his job during the economic slump of the post-World War I period. It was a life lesson for Harold: "Unemployment more than anything else made me politically conscious." After winning a scholarship, he attended Royds Hall secondary school, Huddersfield, and then transferred to Wirral grammar school where his academic progress led to a history scholarship at Oxford. At Oxford University he was a serious student who avoided distractions, and his hard work earned him the Webb Medley economics prize and the Gladstone history prize. His first-class honors degree was an impressive achievement as was his election to a junior fellowship at University College where he did research on unemployment and business cycles.[13]

Like Gaitskell, Wilson's views aligned closer to moderate rather than hard-line socialism. He joined the Oxford Labour Club mostly due to the influence of socialist economist G. D. H. Cole. During the war, he served as director of economics and statistics at the Ministry of Fuel and Power. Wilson became a Labour MP in 1945 and his political rise was fast, entering cabinet in 1947 as president of the board of trade. In 1951, he resigned from the government as a protest of Gaitskell's budget. As the chancellor of the exchequer, Gaitskell included the addition of National Health Service charges. Wilson's coauthorship of the *Tribune* pamphlet "One Way Only" marked his identification with those socialists opposed to moderate, revisionist policies. Labour lost the general election of 1951, but Wilson did not enter the shadow cabinet until 1954 when he replaced Aneurin Bevan, a hardline socialist who resigned his position due to a policy disagreement. Key socialists became suspicious of Wilson, especially after 1956 when he supported Gaitskell rather than Bevan for the leadership. When Gaitskell died suddenly, potential candidates for the leadership had limited time to advance their arguments. Wilson, George Brown, and James Callaghan fought for the leadership with Wilson winning by the second ballot, 144 votes to 103 for Brown.[14]

With Wilson as leader, Labour won the October 1964 general election by a slim margin of five seats. A return to the polls two years later gave Labour a majority of ninety-seven, but the Wilson government faced several bouts of economic crisis and it lost to the Tories in 1970—the only election won by Edward Heath as leader. Wilson provided steady opposition while keeping the party mostly united and ready to return to power. Moderates rejected the class conflict approach of radicals and instead found revisionist thinking more practical for creating wealth and raising the standard of living. Labour MP George Howarth called Wilson a "Keynesian Social Democrat"; he moderated the radicalism that some MPs demanded. But there were no guarantees and Wilson himself did not expect to win in February 1974. He often drifted as someone without a compass. Even Denis Healey viewed him as having neither "political principle" nor a "sense of direction." However, Wilson led Labour to victory in February and eight months later, despite the grumblings of radicals within the party, notably Anthony Benn, who were unenthusiastic with Wilson's leadership over the summer months.[15] His criticism of Wilson was blunt, writing that he did not arouse "affection in most people."[16]

Anthony Wedgwood Benn was born in Westminster, London in 1925. He was from a prominent family; his father was a Labour MP who entered the House of Lords as Viscount Stansgate. At age of nineteen, Benn served in the war as a Royal Air Force pilot. After the war, Oxford University beckoned and he studied Philosophy, Politics, and Economics and became president of the Oxford Union. Thatcher knew him at Oxford as a socialist star who was an effective debater.[17] Someone burdened with "class guilt," he was a Fabian centrist who later adopted a more radical socialist position. In a 1971 address to the Engineering Worker Union, he argued that when one speaks of industrial democracy, it "means that the people ultimately control their managers. Just that, no more, no less."[18] He wanted Wilson to be more courageous with socialist ideas; here was someone who was "capable of being Prime Minister four times without doing anything to change the structure of power in society."[19] Benn was bitter that Wilson pushed aside a radical economic strategy, notably the plan of greater public ownership of industry. In his eyes, Wilson was a sell-out.[20] Benn had no affection for the "bully" Denis Healey and cared little for former Labour leader candidate George Brown. When Brown resigned from the Labour Party, Benn wrote: "Most people thought he had left years ago but he finally resigned and was on the radio tonight—drunk as ever, giving the most muddled reason why he resigned."[21] Despite his feistiness, Benn was secretary of state for industry in 1974 and 1975 and secretary of state for energy from 1975 to 1979. He kept a comprehensive diary that provides fascinating insights on his socialism and many others in the Labour Party and trade union movement. On the death of Mao, he wrote of the leader's "tremendous achievements," a school teacher who transformed China into a "new society."[22]

Did Wilson deserve more credit than what he received from Benn? Wilson sided with Michael Foot and opposed a statutory incomes policy, but Wilson, despite Foot's plea, also shifted Benn's position from Industry to Energy.[23] Michael Foot was born in 1913 and educated at Oxford University where he studied Politics, Philosophy, and Economics. Due to his chronic asthma, his attempt to volunteer for military service was unsuccessful. He worked for the *New Statesman* and the more socialist *Tribune* where he was editor in the late 1940s and 1950s. In 1945, he began political life as a Labour MP, but lost his seat ten years later. He returned in 1960 and later declined Wilson's offer to join the cabinet. Although his political alignment was not moderate Labourism, he served in Wilson's shadow cabinet in the early 1970s and became secretary of state for employment when the Labour Party took power in 1974.

Unlike Benn and Foot, Denis Healey and James Callaghan were receptive to the revisionism of the Gaitskellites. Denis Winston Healey was born in Mottingham, Kent in 1917. He went to Oxford University where he demonstrated his socialist credentials by joining the Communist Party. This decision did not alarm his parents since his mother was a socialist and his father, Healey writes, "took the familiar line that if I was not a Communist at twenty, there was something wrong with my heart; if I was still a Communist at thirty, there was something wrong with my head." However, Healey's intellectual foundation of socialism was less Karl Marx and more Nikolai Berdyaev and Reinhold Niebuhr.[24] The Russian Berdyaev and American Niebuhr were bold opponents of socialist totalitarianism. Healey left the Communists, served in the war, and joined the Labour Party, ready to play his "part in building a new Britain based on social justice."[25] In the late 1940s, he wanted the Labour Party to aid the "socialist revolution" unfolding in Europe.[26] A frequent writer for the socialist *Tribune*, he occasionally wrote for *The Economist* before deciding it was not worth it since the paper offered little pay and did not publish a writer's name. He won a by-election in 1952 to enter the House of Commons where he discovered that many Labour politicians, and the labor movement itself, had a utopian view of Stalin's Russia as a "workers' paradise." His initial MP salary was £1,000 a year with no additional funds for expenses such as postage and telephone calls; his constituents appreciated his hand-written responses unaware that it was due to penury rather than principle.[27] In 1972, Wilson appointed Healey shadow chancellor and he became the chancellor of the exchequer in the Wilson government. Having not studied economics in university, he was skeptical of economics which he viewed as "a branch of social psychology"; economics made the "absurd assumption," without proper study of culture, of being able to understand why people made, sold, and bought things. He claimed that he abandoned Keynesianism in 1975.[28] Gordon McLennan, the new general secretary of the Communist Party concluded that Benn was the only credible alternative leader and Healy was his only credible rival.[29]

James Callaghan's working-class origins set him apart from the many Oxford-educated politicians. He was born in 1912, but before he reached his teenage years his father died of a heart attack. Unable to afford university, Callaghan worked various office jobs, including as a senior tax inspector. During the war, he served in the navy. In 1945, he entered the House of Commons as Labour MP of Cardiff South. He held several important shadow cabinet and cabinet positions. He was shadow chancellor of the exchequer, first under the leadership of Gaitskell and later under Wilson. He disagreed with Gaitskell's attempt to purge the clause in the Labour Constitution calling for public ownership of industry, but he was all for socialist planning to see a restructuring of British industry with new technology.[30] From 1964 to 1967, he was chancellor of the exchequer and from 1967 to 1970 as home secretary. During the Heath government, he had three different shadow appointments. When the Labour Party took power in 1974, he became secretary of state for foreign and Commonwealth affairs. Ambitious to be prime minister since the 1960s, he often clashed with Harold Wilson and, according to Denis Healey, he was anxious to replace Wilson.[31] Callaghan had no patience for the "extreme left-wing" who joined the Labour Party in the 1970s and accepted the tactic of militant action. As he wrote in his memoirs, "The rancour between them and traditional Labour Party activists was well-publicised and there were doubts as to whether Labour could win an election with such an encumbrance."[32] Although Callaghan had policy disagreements with Benn, the latter found his avuncular persona likable.[33]

As the minister for prices and consumer protection from 1974 to 1976, Shirley Williams participated in many inflation discussions, taking a moderate socialist position. She was born in Chelsea, London, in 1930 and her father was a political scientist, and her mother wrote novels. She graduated from Oxford University with a degree in Philosophy, Politics, and Economics and did post-graduate work at Columbia University in New York. In 1964, she entered the House of Commons as Labour MP for Hitchin. Williams saw the hardline socialism of Anthony Benn as out of touch.[34] The rise of radicalism in the Labour Party disturbed some MPs enough to consider crossing the floor to the Tories. In May 1975, Brian Walden discussed joining the Tory Party with six other Labour MPs, but the plan went nowhere.[35]

II

Harold Wilson's leadership kept the party together, but there were Labour MPs and many within the labor unions who were unhappy with him. As for Thatcher, she portrayed all Labour politicians as socialist and made no distinction of whether one was revisionist such as Gaitskell or radical such as Benn. But it is important to point out that Wilson and others cared about the threat of inflation. In early 1973, the Labour Party and the Trades Union Congress (TUC) agreed to a "Social Contract" in which the government supported various trade union policies and, in return, trade unions agreed to restrain wage hikes. The crucial battleground for old socialist and new conservative ideas was inflation. However, the reality of destructive inflation also divided the Labour Party between those who favored or rejected an incomes policy. Perhaps a voluntary Social Contract could diminish Labour divisiveness; there was something to the argument that only Labour could negotiate with the trade union movement.[36]

When Labour became the government in 1974, Denis Healey viewed Wilson as more relaxed and "no longer plagued by the demons of jealously and suspicion which had tormented him in his first two Governments." The primary task for Labour was to "manage the economy" and have high growth, low inflation, and "a fairer distribution" of wealth.[37] Healey needed Wilson's support as he prepared a budget while the nation experienced both high inflation and high unemployment, something the *Economist* in its March 30 headline called "Slumpflation." On short notice and at a time of unpredictability, Healey worked on a budget that increased pensions and food and housing subsidies, encouraged public utilities to restrain increasing their prices, cut defence expenditure, scrapped projects approved by the previous Tory government, and increased taxes. Describing Healey's budget proposals, Wilson wrote later of the necessity of "a massive increase in taxation." Predictably, the Conservative Party denounced Labour's management of the economy, but there was also unease within the Labour Party as radicals demanded additional state ownership of industry. Wilson warned that inflation in the modern world was "father to unemployment" and that it was not the time for "grandiose proposals for nationalizing anything and pretty nearly everything."[38] While some in the National Executive Committee of the Labour Party wanted more socialism, Wilson surveyed how many international leaders, economic policymakers, and bankers "canonized" Milton Friedman and downplayed Keynesianism.[39] The prime minister had limited room to maneuver. To complicate matters, the Finance Bill that received the Royal Assent at the end of July was not enough; almost immediately it became obvious that inflation demanded "further measures" which led to policy changes described as Healey's "mini-Budget.[40] At the time of the Labour budget of autumn 1974, inflation was 17 percent; Healey blamed the economic policies of the previous Tory government and the Middle East oil crisis. Despite the high inflation, Labour honored its Social Contract by repealing the Tories "anti-union legislation" and increasing various benefits, including old-age pensions.[41]

It became obvious that Labour's management of the economy in 1974 was not a success. In early 1975, Wilson's message to trade unionists was pessimistic; he and others stressed an unwelcome truth: "existing living standards would be impossible to maintain."[42] Healey's budget speech of April 15 included an equally grim message that a statutory policy for incomes was unlikely to produce good results. If strictly obeyed, a volunteer policy was preferable. However, if trade unions disregarded restraint, Healey warned, "the consequence can only be rising unemployment, cuts in public expenditure, lower living standards for the country as a whole, and growing tension throughout society."[43]

Anthony Benn disagreed with the tough language by Wilson and Healey. While attending the Commonwealth Prime Ministers' Conference in Jamaica in late April and early May, Wilson planted a story of Benn's soon removal from secretary of state of industry. He secretly met with Harry Boyne of the *Daily Telegraph* to see the story run. When Wilson reshuffled Benn to Energy, the fiery MP "took it extremely hard" and Wilson expected him "to retire to the back-benches," something Wilson hoped against. The appointment of Eric Varley did not begin smoothly since Varley told Wilson he would not accept the position if Benn resigned. In the end, the bitter Benn decided to accept Energy and stay in the cabinet.[44] On the reshuffling of the government, he wrote in his diary that Wilson made a "fatal error," and he predicted he would not be the leader at the end of the year.[45]

Wilson's focus was on the steady rise of inflation, but he never did enough in the eyes of the Tories who pointed to the slow response of the government. Despite Tory criticism, there were many deliberations within the Labour Party on how inflation hurt millions of citizens and on the question of a statutory incomes policy. In the House of Commons on July 1, 1975, Healey reported Labour's discussions with the TUC and the Confederation of British Industry (CBI) to find an agreeable path for reducing the rate of domestic inflation to 10 percent in 1975 and to single figures before January 1977. If there were no action, high unemployment and low investment would continue, as would the suffering of housewives and pensioners. However, Healey demanded action be "fair and just"; any early wage settlements could "not be left behind by later settlements at an excessive level." [46]

Healey explained that the government plan was to control public sector wage increases (by fixing cash limits for wage bills) and use the price code to see "compliance by private employers." His focus was on the CBI and TUC honoring a volunteer policy work that satisfied agreed-upon targets. Geoffrey Howe pointed out there was no mention of reducing nationalization or public spending, but Healey also experienced pressure from his own party. According to Norman Atkinson, Labour MP for Tottenham, Healey's "minimum voluntary conditions" were in essence the "introduction of compulsory wage control." Furthermore, his targets represented "a severe cut in wages" unacceptable to the TUC and the annual conference of the Labour Party. Atkinson argued that the proposed reduction in inflation from 25 percent to 8 percent meant a reduction of at least 6 percent in real living standards, "and that a cut of such brutality will be totally unacceptable to the trade union movement." [47]

In the following ten days, Harold Wilson gave two important speeches: one to the National Union of Mineworkers Conference on July 7 and the other to the House of Commons on July 11. For the sake of the mining industry and Britain, it was clear he needed a good response from the miners: "Never, in thirty years in Parliament, had I prepared a speech with such care—dictating, writing, amending, inserting, discarding and drafting again." He viewed mineworkers as among the "warmest-hearted of Her Majesty's subjects," but miner delegates were "dour" and immovable." Certainly, there was no rousing message for either workers or union leaders. Although the coal industry had "an insured long-term future," the problem of inflation called for sacrifice: "*your* decisions and *your* actions, will decide whether coal is to retain the competitive price advantage which above all guarantees firm employment prospects and good wages." Wilson also argued that Britain faced a crisis and neither government borrowing nor subsidies were enough to pay for wage increases; in essence, any continuation of the wage awards of recent months "would be to eat the seed corn." After Wilson sat down, Mick McGahey, vice president of the union, told him that he did not agree with anything that Wilson had said.[48] The day before, Anthony Benn wrote of the *Observer*'s coverage of the "Government U-turn," corroborated by labor leader Jack Jones's support for Wilson and Michael Foot's view that Healey would make a good leader: "It was confirmation that the Foot-Healey-Jones-Wilson group is running the Government, and that explains why I am on the outside."[49]

Wilson's speech to a packed House of Commons four days later gave additional information on the government's incomes policy of a "limit of £6 per week for pay settlements." Wilson assured the compliance of the Civil Service, the National Health Service, the Armed Forces, and nationalized industries. He had a clear message for those considering noncompliance: they "must face the certain consequence that there will be an inescapable cut-back in the current expenditure of the board or corporation concerned." For cases of noncompliance at the local level, the government could restrict grants, control borrowing, and reduce capital programs. For the private sector, the Labour government would respond forcefully against employers who negotiated wages above the government's limit.[50]

Wilson argued that such policies were better than a "general price freeze" which depressed investment and worsened employment opportunities. The government also ensured that prices for essential family items were to "be held to about the 10 per cent target." According to Wilson, all the government measures sought to restore confidence, stimulate investment, and make British industry more competitive. If there was no reduction of the "present disastrous rate of inflation," British citizens "will be engulfed in a general economic catastrophe of incalculable proportions," he warned.[51] During the press conference that followed, Wilson, Healey, Michael Foot, and Shirley Williams took numerous questions from journalists alert to any party fallout from the "toughest statement" on pay restraint of any British government during peacetime. The *Guardian* reported Wilson's "squaring the circle" in which he kept both Foot and the Treasury satisfied. Exhausted, discouraged, and conflicted, Anthony Benn contemplated getting out but decided it was better to stay inside the government and fight for "Labour policy." Later in the month, the government's policy carried in Parliament 327 votes to 269.[52]

There were heroics elsewhere. At the Winter Gardens' ballroom at Blackpool, Jack Jones, the general secretary of the Transport & General Workers Union (TGWU), told 1,000 conference delegates that the Labour Party was in trouble and needed the support of the trade unions. It was high drama as journalists covered the conference, wondering whether Jones's speech could win support for Wilson. A hot-tempered man of "great self-confidence," Jones was a "towering" figure in the TGWC, but the £6 a week pay rise limit was a hard pill for delegates to swallow. Throughout its history, the TGWU opposed any wage restraint. A friend of the Labour Party, Geoffrey Goodman wrote that Jones "was insisting that something as dramatic, indeed unique, as this was now inescapable if the unions were to rescue the Wilson Government from disaster." Remarkably, Jones gained the approval of the delegates.[53] Since 1973, Benn believed that Jones, a communist earlier in his life, was "far from being a left-wing radical."[54] These were strange days.

July was also the month when Labour began an additional program intended to defeat inflation. Wilson appointed Geoffrey Goodman, who unknown to Wilson had been a secret Communist agent, to start and run the Head of the Counter-Inflation Publicity Unit (CIPU).[55] Given free rein to select his own staff and an annual budget of £2.5 million, Goodman began with research on how people viewed the British economy. From a sample of over 2,400 adults, 75 percent viewed the economy as "extremely serious" or "very serious," 17 percent as "fairly serious," and only 5 percent answering "not particularly serious."[56] As important as this research was, the most crucial task of the CIPU was the articulation, in plain language, of the Social Contract. It was vital to clarify the danger of out-of-control inflation and win the trust of trade union leaders and employers. The success of the anti-inflation advertisement campaign depended on both sides of industry working together. Thatcher opposed the scheme and, according to Goodman, she compared his role "with that of Dr Josef Goebbels." More receptive was Tory centrist Willie Whitelaw who met with Goodman privately to discuss the unit's advertisement campaign. Goodman had less success with the Treasury since the top bureaucrats showed little interest in a voluntary system of restraint; they demanded a statutory incomes policy to keep the International Monetary Fund at bay.[57]

Healey sided with Treasury and was supportive of a statutory incomes policy, but Michael Foot won this battle at the last hour before Wilson's July 11 speech. The cabinet debate the day before lasted five hours and the key moment was Foot's threat of resigning if the cabinet agreed to a statutory policy. According to Goodman, Healey never forgave Wilson for this outcome and other flawed policies, "which he regarded as symptomatic of Wilson's weakness and lack of direction."[58] Healey offered little assistance to Goodman's anti-inflation work; he declined Goodman's suggestion of visiting various factories to build better relations between workers and the party. The gamble was too risky, claimed Healey: "We would become exposed to attacks from the militants, the Trots and all that lot; and the press would pick it up. It would do the Government no good at all." Goodman claimed that Healey's reluctance to assist him was partly due to the "deep personal hostility between Wilson and Healey." While "very few members of that Cabinet actually liked each other," the Wilson-Healey antipathy was on another level.[59]

Another important player who supported an incomes policy was James Callaghan who made this clear in a speech to the Woolwich Labour Party in January 1976. Privy to inside information on the timing of Wilson's retirement, Callaghan wanted to show his commitment to fight inflation "in the event of a leadership contest."[60] Goodman was unaware of Wilson's plan to resign in early 1976. In fact, it was a shock for everyone except Callaghan and a few others. Not even Foot knew. When Labour returned to power in March 1974, Wilson promised he would give himself no more than two years before retiring.[61] In Goodman's version of events, shortly before the surprising announcement, Healey learned the news standing in a toilet stall next to Wilson's stall. However, Healey did not get Wilson's support for the leadership. Days earlier, Healey blew up and shouted a profanity at Labour backbenchers, and this was, Goodman wrote, "a decisive factor in Wilson's mind" to back Callaghan.[62]

On March 25, 1976, the Labour MPs voted for the six leadership candidates: Foot, Callaghan, Benn, Healey, Roy Jenkins, and Anthony Crosland. The top three were Foot with ninety votes, Callaghan with eighty-four, and Jenkins with fifty-six. The second ballot was five days later between Foot, Callaghan, and Healey. This time Callaghan was ahead with 141 to Foot's 133 and Healey's 38. Dropping out after the first ballot and throwing his support to Foot, Benn wrote in his diary: "I must say the fact that Denis only got one more vote in the second ballot than I got in the first gave me great pleasure; he was utterly rejected really."[63] The final ballot was Callaghan 176 to Foot's 137. While the mixing of Keynesianism and socialism could be confusing, the moderates were victorious again. Goodman believed Wilson had "profound radical instincts," but, unfortunately, he "lacked the ideological courage to match them."[64] To his critics, Wilson made no apologies:

> To produce a policy on which the party could remain united, despite unhappiness on one or other wing—or both—inevitably evoked the phrase "devious." But in my view a constant effort to keep his party together, without sacrificing either principle or the essentials of basic strategy, is the very stuff of political leadership.[65]

According to Thatcher, Wilson had a "technically brilliant mind" and he was someone familiar with economic models. However, she could "say little in favour" of his record as prime minister, stating that his principles were "so obscured by artful dodging it was difficult for friends and opponents alike to decide what they might be."[66]

III

When Callaghan became leader on April 5, 1976, Benn wrote: "I would say that Jim will prolong this Parliament as long as he can because it may be his only period as Prime Minister. If he loses the next Election, in due time he too, will go."[67] Benn preferred Foot, but Callaghan had an impressive record of experience serving as chancellor, home secretary, and foreign secretary. His "avuncular" approach presented a challenge for Thatcher who wrote that his "patronizing" attitude in the House of Commons was difficult to counter without her appearing to be a "nag."[68] Labour political adviser and friend of Callaghan, Bernard Donoughue relished the way his boss handled Thatcher. In one episode in the House of Commons, Callaghan was at his best: "Totally relaxed and amusing, putting Thatcher down gently but with patronising contempt. Even the Tories were roaring with laughter." In one encounter between Donoughue and Thatcher at a cafeteria, Thatcher's response to a Donoughue comment revealed much: "I have had to learn to be hard."[69] Barbara Castle wrote of Callaghan's ability to run "rings round an uncertain Margaret Thatcher, metaphorically patting her on the head like a kindly uncle."[70] This was from someone who was no friend of Callaghan. When he became leader, he dropped Castle from her cabinet position of secretary of state for health and social services. Callaghan wrote of their political differences: Castle "thought that I lacked ideology, and I thought she sometimes allowed ideology to prevail even when her commonsense and instinct should have told her otherwise."[71] Moving Castle out of the cabinet was a bold move. In his memoirs, Healey wrote that Callaghan "had none of the middle-class socialist's illusions about how working people think."[72]

Despite Callaghan's confidence, he faced a troubling economy with few hopeful signs. The slide of the sterling pound a few weeks earlier was a major concern in the coming months of 1976. From the cabinet secretary, he received a "state of play" identifying a miserable economic forecast of high unemployment and inflation and a gloomy balance of payments. The Treasury advice was to avoid any radical changes to economic policy:

> We are sailing in a large unknown sea, and it could be damaging to take decisions based largely on the Treasury's computer prediction of where we shall end up if the economy behaves as it has done in the past.[73]

Despite his background as chancellor, or perhaps because of his background, Callaghan chose not to immerse himself into economic policy, preferring that Healey take care of the issue. Callaghan understood that the Exchequer was "the loneliest man in the Cabinet."[74] He asked Geoffrey Goodman to continue his CIPU work, but Goodman decided to return to journalism at the *Daily Mirror* and the job went to Hugh Cudlipp. The transition did not go well, and within a few months the inflation unit closed down; the government's claim that the work was complete was not believable.[75] One interesting component of the CIPU was that its existence and its mission to sell the Social Contract implied that labor union bargaining was the main cause of inflation. If wage bargainers were reasonable, wage restrictions were unnecessary.[76]

In June unemployment reached its highest number in decades, and throughout the summer the economy continued to falter and the declining value of the sterling pound on foreign exchange markets caused increasing alarm. The government attempted to boost the pound by drawing on the reserves and arranging stand-by-credit, but there appeared to be no escape from higher import prices and inflation. Another problem was choosing the correct path forward when much of the cabinet did not understand or consider the issue of "where the money had to come from to pay for their expenditure decisions." While everyone recognized the seriousness of the situation, there was much disagreement on economic policy. For some cabinet ministers, the government intervention and Keynesian-socialist spending of previous decades remained the best option. Callaghan and Healey pinned their hopes on an incomes policy. Others were less sure.[77] Anthony Benn wanted more government planning, specifically import controls and "compulsory planning agreements." In a mid-July cabinet meeting, Benn angered Healey when he said that the British Establishment "is now infected with same spirit which afflicted France in 1940, the Vichy spirit of complete capitulation and defeatism."[78]

A few days later, Benn watched Peter Jay's interview of Milton Friedman explaining his free-market ideas. Benn said nothing of Friedman's monetarism and only commented that it was easy to counter Friedman's point about coercion: "I felt as one was living in completely pre-socialist age; the contribution that Karl Marx has made to our thinking does enable one to see through that sort of argument very simply."[79] His lack of interest in learning more about monetarism continued years later. Asked by the BBC in early 1980 to join a discussion on monetarism with Jay, journalist Peter Jenkins, and Deputy Governor of the Bank of England Jasper Hollom, Benn found it annoying that the BBC gave so much attention to this "particular religion"; he rejected participation in the discussion, not wanting to be the only "token left-winger."[80]

In mid-July, 1976, William Rees-Mogg of *The Times* wrote how excess money led to inflation, a process that normally took two years. The title of his article was provocative: "HOW A 9.4% EXCESS MONEY SUPPLY GAVE BRITAIN 9.4% INFLATION." Focusing on the years 1964 to 1975, he compared "the increase in money supply each year in excess of the increase in output with the increase in prices two years later" and found they matched. Rees-Mogg himself admitted that the data changed his attitude on incomes policy: "If the Excess Money Supply determines the rate of inflation equally closely in years subject to incomes policy and in years without, there seems to be no evidence left that incomes policy has any significant influence on inflation." The agreement between the two numbers did not shock Milton Friedman, who noted the "storm of controversy" the article generated. He added to Rees-Mogg's analysis and wrote that Labour's social contract "will be another unsuccessful experiment."[81]

Callaghan's keynote speech at the Labour Party Conference on September 28 in Blackpool revealed how far he was willing to distance himself from socialist optimism.[82] It also demonstrated that he was no Friedman monetarist. He told the conference that the economy was in crisis, and there were limitations to what government alone could achieve as it pushed and pulled economic levers. He called for "a new spirit of co-operation" between employers and trade union leaders as they worked together with the government to honor the Social Contract and stimulate industrial growth.[83]

Callaghan's analysis was uncompromising, especially the section written by Peter Jay whose words "made the fur fly."[84] Britain's high unemployment was due to workers getting greater pay than the value of what they had produced, and British leaders were wrong to believe "that you could spend your way out of a recession, and increase employment by cutting taxes and boosting Government spending." The old option of spending and borrowing inevitably meant "injecting a bigger dose of inflation into the economy, followed by a higher level of unemployment as the next step." These were remarkable statements from a Labour prime minister. Callaghan admitted that both parties were guilty. It was time to "get back to fundamentals": first, labor costs could not be higher than Britain's major competitors; second, it was key to have improved investment and productivity; and third, it was time to reject the idea that "we can buy our way out by printing what Denis Healey calls 'confetti money' to pay ourselves more than we produce." The Labour government could no longer forge ahead on borrowed money from abroad while ignoring the fundamental problems of British industry. Callaghan explained that having a stronger economy was possible when a government stopped borrowing and printing money and, instead, focused on creating wealth "with the agreement and the support of the trade union movement."[85]

Given the pressure he received from Labour members demanding more socialism, equally astonishing was his message about industrial profits:

> Whether you call it a surplus or a profit, it is necessary for a healthy industrial system, whether it operates in a socialist economy, a mixed economy or a capitalist economy. If industry cannot retain and generate sufficient funds as

> a result of its operations, and replace old plant and machinery, then you will whistle in vain for the investment and we shall continue to slide downhill. These are elementary facts of life. They are known to every trade unionist. Who would they sooner go and negotiate with when they want an increase in pay: a firm that is bankrupt or a firm that is doing well and generating a good surplus?[86]

Callaghan still believed "in a high level of public expenditure," but wealth creation came first:

> I part company with those who believe we can rely indefinitely on foreign borrowing to provide for greater social expenditure, a better welfare service, better hospitals, better education, the renewal of our inner cities and so on. In the end these things, comrades, are only provided by our own efforts.

Once wealth creation occurred then there could be distribution. Callaghan concluded his speech with the promise of government being truthful to the people and working with the trade unions for a "new future."[87] Bernard Donoughue wrote in his diary that the speech had no humor, and there were few cheers. It was "Straight down the line. It also had some remarkably courageous words about the impossibility of simply reflating back to full employment—so the campaign by the monetarist economists had made an impact."[88]

As the Labour conference digested Callaghan's economic assessment, there was also drama with Healey in London. Earlier in the day before Callaghan gave his speech, Healey was set to fly to Hong Kong to meet with other Commonwealth finance ministers and then to the IMF meeting in the Philippines. Before he boarded his flight at Heathrow airport, he learned of the pound falling almost 5 cents to $1.63, prompting him to ask Callaghan if he should continue with his flight. He told the prime minister that bank experts forecasted a potential fall to $1.50.[89] Healey canceled his flight and deliberated with others about how the government should respond. Callaghan later regretted his failure to encourage Healey to continue his trip to Asia. The next day, September 29, Healey declared the government would apply to the IMF for stand-by-credit. The following day was no easier; Healey jumped on an RAF plane and went to Blackpool and addressed the Labour conference, now with even more journalists attending. His message was a hard sell, admitting the continuation of "very painful cuts in public expenditure" and sticking to the agreed-upon pay policy. Attacking inflation was paramount and he asked that the conference support him in his "trials." When Healey sat down, most of the room applauded.[90] One who did not applaud was Anthony Benn, calling the speech "vulgar and abusive."[91] Healey later described the autumn of 1976 as the worst period of his life as he negotiated with the IMF.[92]

Others viewed Labour's cutting government expenditures as a charade. As reported in the *Daily Mail*, Milton Friedman declared:

> Your government has gone to the IMF so that they can lay down rules for the management of your economy. . . . It's like the way big corporations use management consultants. The corporations know perfectly well what must be done, but they want to blame the unpleasant remedies on someone else.[93]

On the other end of the political spectrum, Bernard Donoughue had an interesting interpretation. He believed that the Treasury and the Bank of England did not want the IMF loan approved: "They think it will corrupt us. They want us to be forced to cut borrowing by £6 billion in one year, even if it kills off industry and produces five million unemployed."[94]

An IMF team of six arrived in London on November 1 and began the process of going through Britain's financial books to identify problems and suggest solutions. One month later the cabinet met to discuss proposals from various ministers, with those by Anthony Benn, Anthony Crosland, and Peter Shore receiving the most attention. Benn wanted no additional spending cuts and suggested an alternative strategy that favored nationalization and protectionism. Shore's proposal was a softer version of Benn's. Crosland looked to import deposits as the answer. The cabinet rejected all three. Healey's proposal got the nod, which included selling British Petroleum shares for £500 million, reducing the PSBR by £1 billion in 1977–1978 and £1.5 billion in 1978–1979.[95] The episode depressed Benn and other like-minded socialists, but "they did not want the Government to fall"; if there was a confidence vote, they planned to stick with Callaghan.[96]

On December 15, Healey presented in the House of Commons the details of the government's IMF plan, making it clear that a key objective was "to continue the attack on inflation."[97] Benn found the targets for the PSBR brutal, but Healey argued that £8.7 billion for 1977–1978 and £8.6 billion for 1978–1979 were necessary for creating the necessary monetary conditions for investment and growth and for controlling inflation.[98] There were many comments and questions, but one of the more probing questions came from Enoch Powell, former Conservative MP who became Ulster Unionist MP for South Down:

> Will the right hon. Gentleman confirm that these measures would have been equally necessary even if the IMF had not existed and that the decision to borrow from the IMF, whether right or wrong, is unconnected with the necessity of what he has put before the House?

The astute Healey answered in a manner that avoided Powell's point of failed Labour Party economic thinking.[99] Lamenting the inaccuracy of 1976 forecasts, Healey later claimed that the IMF loan was unnecessary. He also clarified his skepticism of Milton Friedman's monetarism and the ability to properly define and control money; no banker he talked to "believed the monetarist mumbo-jumbo." Healey even struggled to find a suitable economic adviser on the Left; he found the economic advice of Nicholas Kaldor, a foe of monetarism, inconsistent, and he seriously considered recruiting the American Arthur Okun, a Keynesian working at the Brookings Institute.[100]

Thatcher's assessment of Healey's plan is interesting. His significant cuts in spending and borrowing and his money targets, "though expressed in terms of domestic credit expansion," were similar to the "monetarist" approach favored by her. In her memoirs, she wrote that Healey's position gave her some political capital as she dealt with members of her shadow cabinet who were still "clinging to the outdated nostrums of Keynesian demand management." It was significant that the Tory Party abstained from voting on the measures.[101] Milton Friedman, however, was very critical of Labour's economics. In the *Financial Times* of January 6, he replied to Samuel Brittan's criticism of Friedman being inaccurate with his statement that British democracy had a 50–50 chance of falling apart within the next few years. In "Letter to the Editor: An Open Reply from Milton Friedman," the economist pointed to the unpleasant consequence of higher taxes to pay for government spending: "Government employment would simply replace private employment." Moreover, there was a significant flaw in Labour's redistribution of wealth. At the start, a government can provide welfare benefits for "a few by imposing light taxes on many," but with greater government expansion, politicians face the problem of extracting enough taxes from fewer and fewer. To pay for the benefits of a greater number of people, the government had the difficult political task of imposing higher taxes on the many. Friedman also presented a clear assessment on the issue of inflation: "the so-called, 'social contract,' Government price fixing, and the wide gyrations in the rate of inflation, not the level of inflation per se, are, I suspect, the chief culprits in Britain's current high unemployment."[102]

Weeks before his unexpected death in February 1977, Anthony Crosland wrote in a cabinet memorandum that "it is still sometimes said that the British people are not living within their means and need to be taught a sharp lesson about the reality of our condition. But on present policies we *shall* be living within our means by late 1977 or early 1978."[103] The Labour Party needed an economic boost of confidence in 1977, and the IMF loan of £3.9 billion was, some argued, a step in the right direction. Politically, the Labour government was in a precarious position when it only held a one-seat majority after losses in the January by-election. In March, Thatcher tabled a "No Confidence" motion and, to secure its position, Labour negotiated an alliance with the Liberal Party, a party of thirteen including leader David Steel. The "Lib-Lab

Pact," viewed by some as the "final abandonment" of radical reform by the Labour government, bought Callaghan more time.[104] Even before the official pact, Callaghan was in a fighting mood: "I had not lived through the previous autumn to surrender to the Conservatives at the moment when we were beginning to see the first glimmering of improvement in our economic and financial situation."[105] Healey could point to some positive economic signs and predict further drop in the inflation rate throughout the summer.[106] The Labour leaders were also confident knowing that Thatcher was often weak in the House of Commons. She could be "shrill," "humourless," and "boring." Her economic statistics did not appear to make an impression.[107]

Much of the Labour Party hope for a better future of lower inflation and higher unemployment did not come from economic theory. There were clear limitations to their understanding of inflation. It was common for Labour politicians to mostly blame international events for inflation whether it was President Lyndon Johnson's heavy spending on the Vietnam War, the Middle East oil crisis, the Iranian Revolution, or some other international reason. Locked into Keynesian and socialist thinking, Labour commentators failed to understand the combination of high inflation and high unemployment. They continued to dismiss new economic theories that some economists argued were more hopeful than the older economic models. Although the Labour Party was skillful in pointing out the grievances of workers, particularly wages unable to keep up with inflation, there was no deep analysis of how societies created wealth and improved productivity. Certainly, there was no consideration for Friedman's monetary solution that included rejection of government intervention in the economy. Thinking economically was an unpleasant task if it called into question the shortcomings of policies that were the lifeblood of Labour governments.[108] Actually, if a government could solve inflation by focusing solely on regulating money supply, it could stay clear of price and wage setting.[109] The Callaghan government went beyond old Keynesian thinking, but it did not pursue monetarism.

In the end, it was a battle for Denis Healey to push his economic policies ahead. To his credit, he had a better idea of the limitations of Keynesian and socialist thinking than many in his party. For example, he conceded that Labour's commitment to a "Wealth Tax" was not sensible; the administrative cost of the tax canceled any useful revenue yield. While he supported his party's commitment to public spending, he was critical of those reluctant to leave declining industries and consider "new techniques of production." He also understood the British resistance to radical change: "Our devotion to individual freedom limits our readiness to give central government the power to override our traditional power structures—except when our society as a whole is threatened by a foreign state."[110] The Labour instinct was to meet the needs of British workers, but inflation caused too much chaos for

Labour to continue its rate of borrowing and spending. Thatcher's clarity on monetarism was weak, but her constant messaging of Labour economic woes appeared to have an effect.

Harold Wilson lacked the energy to stay in the fight, and Callaghan let Healey do most of the heavy lifting. While Healey was not a monetarist in the strict sense of the word, his actions that upset people in the party and pleased others outside the party were enough to restore some confidence in the British economy. In fact, there were signs of an improved economy in 1977 and Callaghan looked stronger. Thatcher needed to find a way to keep pace with the popular Labour leader.

NOTES

1. Benn, *Conflict of Interest*, 42–43.
2. Nelson, "Milton Friedman and U.K. Economic Policy: 1938-1979," 488.
3. Bryan Magee, "Tony Crosland as I Knew Him," *Political Quarterly* 81, no. 2 (April 2020), 176.
4. Healey, *The Time of My Life*, 36.
5. James Callaghan, *Time and Chance* (London: Collins, 1987), 400.
6. Thatcher, *Margaret Thatcher*, 40.
7. Benn, *Conflict of Interest*, 34, 42.
8. Anthony Crosland, *The Future of Socialism* (London: Constable, 2006), vii.
9. Crosland, *The Future of Socialism*, 3–4.
10. Crosland, *The Future of Socialism*, 19, 21, 146–47, 326.
11. Benn, *Against the Tide*, 613. Thatcher, *Margaret Thatcher*, 83. John Saville, "Hugh Gaitskell (1906–1963): An Assessment," *Socialist Register* 17 (1980), 148–69.
12. Thatcher, *Margaret Thatcher*, 192.
13. Geoffrey Goodman, "Leading Labour Beyond Pipe Dreams," *The Guardian*, 25 May 1995.
14. Goodman, "Leading Labour Beyond Pipe Dreams."
15. Andrew Scott Crines and Kevin Hickson, eds., *Harold Wilson: The Unprincipled Prime Minister?* (London: Biteback Publishing, 2016). Goodman, "Leading Labour Beyond Pipe Dreams."
16. Benn, *Against the Tide*, 535.
17. Thatcher, *Margaret Thatcher*, 35.
18. Jenkins, *Mrs Thatcher's Revolution*, 123. Achin Vanaik, "Tony Benn (1925-2014): Committed Democratic Socialist," *Economic and Political Weekly* 49, no. 16 (2014), 26.
19. Benn, *Against the Tide*, 237.
20. Geoffrey Goodman, *From Bevan to Blair: Fifty Years Reporting From the Political Front Line*, (London: Pluto Press, 2003), 177.
21. Benn, *Against the Tide*, 443, 525.
22. Benn, *Against the Tide*, 609.

23. Wilson, *Final Term*, 144.
24. Healey, *The Time of My Life*, 28, 36.
25. Healey, *The Time of My Life*, 98.
26. Letwin, *The Anatomy of Thatcherism*, 58.
27. Healey, *The Time of My Life*, 105, 110, 144–45.
28. Healey, *The Time of My Life*, 377.
29. Benn, *Against the Tide*, 425.
30. Callaghan, *Time and Chance*, 149, 152.
31. Healey, *The Time of My Life*, 341.
32. Callaghan, *Time and Chance*, 281.
33. Benn, *Against the Tide*, 37.
34. Liz Davies, "Tony Benn: Liz Davies Pays Tribute to One of the Giants of the Labour Movement, Who Died in March 2014," *Socialist Lawyer*, no. 67 (2014), 13.
35. Moore, *Margaret Thatcher*, 345.
36. Jim Tomlinson, "British Government and Popular Understanding of Inflation in the Mid-1970s," *The Economic History Review* 67, no. 3 (2014), 755–56.
37. Healey, *The Time of My Life*, 388, 391–92.
38. Wilson, *Final Term*, 24–29.
39. Wilson, *Final Term*, 110.
40. Wilson, *Final Term*, 27–28.
41. Healey, *The Time of My Life*, 394.
42. Wilson, *Final Term*, 111.
43. Hansard, Ways and Means, column 282, 15 April 1975, https://hansard.parliament.uk/Commons/1975-04-15/debates/05a66797-c0a7-46f4-be2c-fe7885c2935c/WaysAndMeans.
44. Wilson, *Final Term*, 143–44.
45. Benn, *Against the Tide*, 397.
46. Hansard, Domestic Inflation, Vol 894 cc1189-200, 1 July 1975, https://api.parliament.uk/historic-hansard/commons/1975/jul/01/domestic-inflation#S5CV0894P0_19750701_HOC_172 .
47. Hansard, Domestic Inflation, 1 July 1975.
48. Wilson, *Final Term*, 116, 118, 266–68.
49. Benn, *Against the Tide*, 413.
50. Hansard, Attack on Inflation, 11 July 1975, https://api.parliament.uk/historic-hansard/commons/1975/jul/11/attack-on-inflation#S5CV0895P0_19750711_HOC_20.
51. Hansard, Attack on Inflation, 11 July 1975.
52. Wilson, *Final Term*, 119–21. Benn, *Against the Tide*, 414–17.
53. Goodman, *From Bevan to Blair*, 171. On Jones's character, see Healey, *The Time of My Life*, 396.
54. Benn, *Against the Tide*, 46.
55. "Geoffrey Goodman Obituary," *The Guardian*, 6 September 2013.
56. Tomlinson, "British Government and Popular Understanding of Inflation in the Mid-1970s," 762.
57. Goodman, *From Bevan to Blair*, 173, 175–78.

58. Goodman, *From Bevan to Blair*, 180.

59. Goodman, *From Bevan to Blair*, 181.

60. Callaghan, *Time and Chance*, 387. Callaghan wrote in his memoirs that he received the official news from Wilson on March 11, five days before the public announcement (390).

61. Wilson, *Final Term*, 227–28. Also, see Callaghan, *Time and Chance*, 386.

62. Goodman, *From Bevan to Blair*, 182. Others claim Healey found out in Wilson's office before the announcement. See Kathleen Burk and Alec Cairncross, *Goodbye, Great Britain: The 1976 IMF Crisis* (New Haven, CT: Yale University Press, 1992), 33. Also, Healey, *The Time of My Life*, 446.

63. Benn, *Against the Tide*, 549.

64. Goodman, *From Bevan to Blair*, 189.

65. Wilson, *Final Term*, 234.

66. Thatcher, *Margaret Thatcher*, 85, 192.

67. Benn, *Against the Tide*, 553.

68. Thatcher, *Margaret Thatcher*, 192.

69. Donoughue, *Downing Street Diary*, 59.

70. Campbell, *Margaret Thatcher*, 358.

71. Callaghan, *Time and Chance*, 402.

72. Healey, *The Time of My Life*, 448.

73. Quoted in Wyn Grant, "Economic Policy," in *James Callaghan: An Underrated Prime Minister*, eds. Kevin Hickson and Jasper Miles (London: Biteback Publishing, 2020).

74. Callaghan, *Time and Chance*, 415.

75. Goodman, *From Bevan to Blair*, 198–200.

76. Tomlinson, "British Government and Popular Understanding of Inflation in the Mid-1970s," 763, 766.

77. Burk and Cairncross, *Goodbye, Great Britain*, 20–21.

78. Benn, *Against the Tide*, 595.

79. Benn, *Against the Tide*, 597.

80. Benn, *Conflicts of Interest*, 577. He told the BBC producer that he would only agree to a discussion with Friedman.

81. Milton Friedman, "Money and Inflation," *Newsweek*, 20 September 1976.

82. Leader's speech, Blackpool 1976 http://www.britishpoliticalspeech.org/speech-archive.htm?speech=174.

83. Leader's speech, Blackpool 1976.

84. Callaghan, *Time and Chance*, 42.

85. Leader's speech, Blackpool 1976.

86. Leader's speech, Blackpool 1976.

87. Leader's speech, Blackpool 1976.

88. Donoughue, *Downing Street Diary*, 73.

89. Burk and Cairncross, *Goodbye, Great Britain*, 55. Also, Callaghan, *Time and Chance*, 427–28 and Healey, *The Time of My Life*, 429.

90. Callaghan writes that there was "hysterical panic" when Healey canceled his trip. See Callaghan, *Time and Chance*, 428. Healey's Finance Speech at Labour

Party Conference, 30 September 1976, http://www.aparchive.com/metadata/youtube/6b4343969f4513ed15a0ac1c393ad851. Healey, *The Time of My Life*, 429.

91. Benn, *Against the Tide*, 616.

92. Healey, *The Time of My Life*, 428–29.

93. Quoted in Nelson, "Milton Friedman and U.K. Economic Policy," 490.

94. Donoughue, *Downing Street Diary*, 80.

95. Burk and Cairncross, *Goodbye, Great Britain*, 97–98, 101.

96. Callaghan, *Time and Chance*, 37, 439.

97. Incomes Policy, 15 December 1976, https://api.parliament.uk/historic-hansard/commons/1976/dec/15/incomes-policy.

98. Domestic Monetary Effects, 15 December 1976, https://api.parliament.uk/historic-hansard/commons/1976/dec/15/domestic-monetary-effects.

99. Economic Prospects, 15 December 1976, https://api.parliament.uk/historic-hansard/commons/1976/dec/15/economic-prospects.

100. Healey, *The Time of My Life*, 381–82, 391, 434. He stated his distrust of "all systematic economic theories" (382).

101. Thatcher, *Margaret Thatcher*, 195–96.

102. Milton Friedman, "Letter to the Editor: An Open Reply from Milton Friedman," *Financial Times*, 6 January 1977.

103. Economic Strategy – IMF, 29 November 1976, http://filestore.nationalarchives.gov.uk/pdfs/small/cab-129-193-cp-76-118-8.pdf.

104. Matt Cole, *Richard Wainwright, the Liberals and Liberal Democrats: Unfinished Business* (Manchester; New York: Manchester University Press, 2011), 173–74. Also, see Thatcher, *Margaret Thatcher*, 199.

105. Callaghan, *Time and Chance*, 452.

106. Inflation, 24 March 1977, https://api.parliament.uk/historic-hansard/writtenanswers/1977/mar/24/inflation#S5CV0928P0_19770324_CWA_205. Also see David James Gill, "Rating the UK: The British Government's Sovereign Credit Ratings, 1976-8," *The Economic History Review* 68, no. 3 (2015), 1024–25.

107. For example, see Donoughue, *Downing Street Diary*, 186, 224.

108. A recent example of this approach is Tara Martin López, *The Winter of Discontent: Myth, Memory, and History* (Liverpool: Liverpool University Press, 2014).

109. Tomlinson, "British Government and Popular Understanding of Inflation in the Mid-1970s," 765–66. He suggests this was more problematic for Conservatives. Seeing monetary growth rather than trade union activity as the reason for inflation contradicted conservative "common sense."

110. Healey, *The Time of My Life*, 404–5, 407.

Chapter 5

Thatcher in Mid-Stream

Prime Minister James Callaghan told cabinet ministers in February 1978 that unlike any other Tory leader, Thatcher "was moving further and further to the right" whereas Conservative backbencher Norman Tebbit worried that Thatcher would be misled by the "Heathmen" with their entrenched policies of the past. She had "lackluster" speeches and there were signs of wavering confidence. According to Tebbit, she performed much better when upset. On one occasion he gave her infuriating news about the party, and she stormed into the House of Commons. Tebbit turned around and declared to nearby MPs, "I think she's at her best when she's angry—well I hope so or I'll be in terrible trouble." Her speech was a hit.[1] Yet, many of her other performances in the House of Commons were mediocre.

Thatcher faced the formidable Callaghan who "patronized" her constantly for her lack of experience in "high office."[2] He developed good relations with the British establishment when he was flexible with the demands of the International Monetary Fund.[3] Although unemployment remained high, inflation numbers were down by 1978. Callaghan declared that the British people recognized that working together for "social justice" and "fair play" was the path for a better society. It was a curious time in British politics as the Labour Party survived a sterling crisis by making spending and tax cuts while Thatcher struggled to gain momentum. At summer's end in 1978, the Labour Party looked strong enough to win another election despite friction between key cabinet ministers. The Tory Party also experienced division as some Tories remained wary of Thatcher's ideological opposition to popular economic policies of the past. Their concern was unnecessary. There were no clear declarations that Keynesianism was a failure and no well-defined statements of new economic thinking. Public discussion of incomes policy was infrequent. As others observed about Britain, the "money does not matter" brand of Keynesianism was more dominant and "extreme" than had been the case in the United States and its influence was not easily set aside.[4] Thatcher's progress as a leader in 1977 and 1978 was modest as she tread carefully on issues such as incomes policy and trade unions.

I

After the chaos of Labour economic policies in 1975 and 1976, monetarism, even though far from what Milton Friedman promoted, gained more attention with policymakers.[5] When Denis Healey revealed his mini-budget on December 15, 1976, Thatcher understood the implications for her party. Healey's cuts in public spending and added attention to domestic credit expansion represented a "turning point" that was a mixed blessing for the Tories. The fortunes of the Labour Party would improve as the economy became less dire, but the Tory Party, particularly the free marketers, could point out that even Labour leaders acknowledged the failure of socialist doctrine.[6] However, Thatcher was careful not to associate her economic approach directly with Friedman whose warnings of Britain's decline were controversial. According to the Daily Mirror, Friedman was the "smiling man of woe" with "doomsday solutions."[7] Still shoring up her place as leader, she needed to be acceptable to both Keynesians and non-Keynesians in her party.

Thatcher began 1977 believing that *The Right Approach*, published in late 1976, struck the proper balance for a "new Conservatism." There was a truce as moderates and conservatives agreed that prices and incomes policies, though unsuccessful in the long term, should remain an option to control inflation. At times, Thatcher did voice her unease with the process of finding a consensus on economic policy. She was less enthusiastic with *The Right Approach to the Economy*, published in October 1977.[8] It was the prime example of squaring the Thatcherites and progressives such as James Prior, described by one historian as the "custodian of the Heath inheritance."[9] Prior saw little hope for the Tories unless they remained open to an incomes policy and provided evidence of being able to work with trade union bosses.[10] He disagreed with Thatcher's desire to see no mention of a pay policy in the document, and he wrote "that it was nonsense to believe that a pay policy was not essential, at the very least in the public sector, where the Government had a direct responsibility."[11]

Written by David Howell, Geoffrey Howe, Keith Joseph, and Prior, *The Right Approach to the Economy* provided an outline of economic strategy for the next Conservative government. There was the typical Tory criticism of "Socialist policies" summarized as "massive public spending and borrowing, high taxation, controls and over-detailed planning." It was time to reject

Labour's "intolerant and narrow breed of State Socialism" that burdened Britain and reduce government spending, lower taxes, and insist on a freer society. The document reiterated the understanding that inflation was a "great destroyer" of employment, living standards, and a stable order. But there was no clear explanation of how the government would control the rate of the money supply "in line with firm monetary targets" nor clarification on the issue of an incomes policy. There was a vague suggestion of having a forum of "the major participants in the economy" to discuss "the Government's fiscal and monetary policies." Overall, the tone of *The Right Approach to the Economy* was far from inspiring. The document declared:

> There are no speedy solutions to be offered and no slick phrases to be paraded as the Conservative "answer." But if we work away with patience and understanding at the policies here outlined, then it is probable that our economic successes will grow and our economic problems be contained.[12]

Was the hope of containing economic problems enough? If Tory policymakers could not find encouraging language among themselves, would they be able to effectively defend and promote their policies?

On sensitive economic issues, Thatcher was often more forthcoming in private conversation than when she faced Callaghan. In a letter to trade unionist Jack Peel, she said that even voluntary incomes policies were counterproductive.[13] Perhaps it is not surprising that in the House of Commons the Tories often failed to score points against Labour leadership. Labour survived the sterling pound crisis the year before, and Callaghan's handling of the economy, including public spending cuts, resulted in declining inflation numbers throughout 1977. The economy was not good, but there had been some improvement. Thatcher admitted her party was "not a particularly successful Opposition." When the Labour government showed financial restraint to get the nation on a firmer economic standing, there was the expectation of some Tory support.[14] The British economic crisis was not just a Labour problem; the crisis was brought on by misguided economic policies of both Labour and the Tories.

Although the Tory Party was unable to offer a compelling argument against Labour economic policies, Thatcher saw promise in some recent Conservative recruits such as John Hoskyns who had assisted Keith Joseph with policy. Hoskyns was a former army captain and successful computer entrepreneur who viewed politicians as inept strategic planners. He worked closely with Norman Strauss, another policymaker, in planning how Conservatives needed to focus their attention on confronting labor union activism.[15] Their major achievement was the creation of a conservative strategic plan called "Stepping Stones." The two policymakers convinced Thatcher that fitting all policies into a single strategy would improve orderly and effective political action.[16] Even though the party did not publish it, the document was a good model for intelligent policymaking. It took time, but it was crucial to see "a complete change in the role of the trade unions movement." With this transformation, unions would go from Labour's weapon to its electoral liability. The tactics were not for the half-committed: "Drag every skeleton out of the union cupboard, linking it to Labour."[17]

By challenging Labour politicians to own or disown the radical components of the Labour program, Conservatives could show voters that British socialism was more radical than "Continental social democracy." The relationship between the Labour Party and unions was unique in that socialism "always has the real power, whatever people thought they had voted for." As stated in the Stepping Stones Report of November 1977, the Labour and union movement link explained why Britain was the "most socialist, as well as the poorest country in the Western world except for Italy which pursued similar policies of intervention, nationalisation and union appeasement."[18] Hoskyns wanted voters to get this conservative message loud and clear. He also countered the resistance by centrist Tories who saw Stepping Stones as too inflexible. Upset with Jim Prior's cautious approach with labor unionism, Hoskyns acted decisively and told Thatcher to get rid of him. With an election pending she continued to support Prior, but Hoskyns believed that she saw Prior as incapable of offering an effective and "resolute plan for recovery."[19]

With his working-class background, Norman Tebbit, MP for Chingford, was another conservative who was valuable. Except for the "Heath aberration of authoritarian centralist corporatism," he was confident that most Conservative values and policies had the support of many working-class voters.[20] Tebbit had no university education, but he was a brash and "maverick bank bencher" who had a natural talent for infuriating Labour politicians in the House of Commons. On one occasion Labour MP Tom Swain, a "tough old Derbyshire miner" with fists and biceps as hard as rocks suggested he and Tebbit go outside Parliament and settle a dispute one on one. Cooler heads prevailed and there was no fight, but strangely Tebbit and his wife encountered Swain a few days later in a bar where Swain, after a few drinks, explained to Tebbit's wife the finer points of pruning grapevines. Tebbit saw himself as a "gadfly" who provided strong support for thinkers such as Keith Joseph.[21]

Thatcher's closest supporters on economics typically had a connection with Joseph, the idea man. For Thatcher, "winning the battle of ideas" was more than having electoral success; there had to be "enduring popular support" for the rejection of expanding government management of the economy.[22] Joseph was passionate about his opposition to centralized economic decision-making and an incomes policy. In addition to Centre for Policy Studies (CPS) meetings, lectures at universities and elsewhere, he met and was in communication with many commentators and thinkers including F. A. Hayek who welcomed Joseph's assistance with his talk on the BBC in early 1977.[23]

Joseph's enthusiasm for learning and sharing free-market economics meant that he reached numerous people, but there were many who found his message misguided. He gave over 100 speeches at universities and colleges and there was much heckling and the occasional physical attack. At the London School of Economics, students attempted to ban him from speaking, and at other universities, opponents put up notices fraudulently claiming the cancellation of Joseph's meeting. At an Oxford speech, one student found the experience memorable:

> Going to a packed lecture hall to hear Sir Keith Joseph talk about free markets, about monetarism and the perils of corporatism . . . they were the sort of things that a rather respectable parent would warn his son against; the sort of thing that an ambitious tutor would be worried about if his students started flirting with.

At the universities, Joseph enjoyed the challenge of converting the "convinced statists if not socialists." He understood his words shocked listeners: "I'm sure they had never heard the moral case for capitalism."[24] Sir Edwin and Dame Bridget Plowden referred to him as a "silly man" who was "always wrong."[25]

Thatcher appreciated her idea man, but those favorable to the work of the CPS may have wondered if she underutilized him. Certainly, he was not as active in the House of Commons as outside of it. Journalist Frank Johnson wrote: "As he speaks, the veins are prominent on the forehead, the brows are coiled, the eyes are half-closed with concentration. The whole head comes to resemble an over-wound-up alarm clock about to go off or burst its springs." To "the glazed or baffled stares of Shadow Cabinet colleagues," he detailed "the efficacy of free enterprise."[26] Changing economic thinking was a mammoth task for anyone. Too many British politicians failed to acknowledge that the democratic socialism and Keynesianism of the past had no effective solutions for the nation's struggling economy.

II

In typical bombastic style, Alfred Sherman viewed the "Labour movement" as "an exploiting caste, giving political employment at high (disguised) living standards for tens of thousands of people 'on the backs of the workers.'" It did its business "against the national economic interest" and its expansion worsened the conditions of ordinary workers.[27] Whatever one thought of Sherman's blunt assessment, it was clear that labor unionism and inflation affected each other. Inflation and the poor economy drove many labor union leaders to take a more militant stand for their members. While incomes policy limited the union leaders' ability to push for higher wages, they continued the fight in other areas. Both Sherman and Joseph shared a contempt for the labor union activity they believed was unethical.

One major episode that engaged the attention of Joseph, who disagreed with those Tories preferring a diplomatic approach in dealing with labor unions, was the strike at the Grunwick Film Processing Laboratories in North London that began in August 1976. Run by Managing Director George Ward, an Anglo-Indian entrepreneur, the medium-sized Grunwick business employed about 500 workers, many of whom were females and immigrants. A labor dispute with a nineteen-year-old male worker, who demanded more pay, resulted in some workers walking off the job. When the company fired these workers, over 100 other workers went on strike, many of them joining the Association of Professional, Executive, Clerical and Computer Staff (APEX), the trade union for clerical employees. The workers demanded union recognition. In early September, the company fired the striking workers and, in response, post office workers refused to deliver the company's mail. In the courts, Grunwick argued that APEX sought to impose a closed shop even though most of the Grunwick workforce opposed joining APEX. The company sought the assistance of the National Association for Freedom (NAFF) to bolster the argument that a company had the freedom to hire and fire employees. The strike continued the following year and three Labour ministers appeared on the picket line in May 1977. In June the temperature rose even further when Arthur Scargill of the National Union of Mineworkers arrived on the picket line with hundreds of reinforcements. There were more than 1,500 policemen to keep order, but violence broke out.[28]

In a speech on June 20, Joseph discussed the "siege" at Grunwick and how neither the government nor the TUC was "guiltless of the violence, illegality, disgraceful behaviour of the rent-a-mob flying pickets mobilised by the revolutionary parties." He pointed out that Albert Booth, secretary of state of employment, inappropriately encouraged unions to use illegal means "to coerce workers, citizens of this country into joining organizations they do not wish to join."[29] This was troubling since a poll of the remaining employees showed less than 10 percent wanted union representation.[30]

Thatcher devoted significant attention to Grunwick in her memoirs. With socialist ideas playing a large role, the affair was "a clear case of the outrageous abuse of trade union power." She requested that Conservative MPs Adam Butler and Barney Hayhoe ride through the picket line with non-striking employees and they gave a report of employee fear and courage.

Demanding that the government clarify its position on the labor violence, Thatcher believed she had a winning issue. To one of the directors of NAFF, she wrote that the scenes of violence on television plus the "wild charges and allegations being thrown about in certain quarters, are enough in themselves to put most of the public on the side of right and are doing more than hours of argument." As bad as it was to give trade unions "virtually unlimited immunity in civil law," worse was the violence and breach of criminal law. The intimidation and militancy set a dangerous tone. Thatcher wrote how the rule of law appeared inconsequential to the "far Left." If labor leaders won the battle for the closed shop, they could advance their power with "further assault on liberty."[31] But some warned Thatcher to tread carefully with the Grunwick issue; there were large companies that preferred the closed shop system which allowed them to negotiate with only one group. Criticism of George Ward's business behavior was another reason for Thatcher to be cautious. Political adviser John Sparrow stated: "There would be quite a lot of unhappiness if it were felt that there was a close relationship between you and Mr. Ward."[32]

The stagnant economy and the effects of many months of inflation contributed to an uglier mood. In previous years, Labour and union leaders banned members of "far Left" organizations of Labour Party membership. The lifting of the ban signified to Thatcher "Labour's drift to extremism"; fewer Labour MPs hid their association with hard socialist or communist organizations. It appeared to her that no matter what the IMF or prime minister might think, it was "the extreme Left whose programme represented Labour's future, and that whether the tactics employed to achieve it were violent or peaceful was the question at issue."[33]

The disagreement among Tories on how best to tackle inflation mostly correlated with the divide concerning trade unionism. Compared to Joseph, Thatcher was circumspect with monetarism and trade union reform. The Grunwick affair was upsetting, but she sided with James Prior who warned against any major trade union reform that outlawed the closed shop. Effective reform was doubtful without the cooperation of trade union leaders. Joseph took an opposing position and argued against any tolerance of "collectivist bullying." The government set up an inquiry under Lord Scarman, but Joseph was highly critical of the Scarman Report of the Industrial Court which was more favorable to the "law-breakers" and recommended Grunwick accept union representation. Especially annoying for Joseph was the report's statement that a union "could, in the future help the company as well as its employees." What of the labour history, Joseph asked, of unions injecting "restrictive practices" which limit the productivity of a company? Repeating his question in another way: "Is not the Industrial Court aware that such a fairly common union attitude could jeopardize a firm's survival in a highly competitive market and hence the pay and even the job of its workers?"[34]

Joseph could not understand the "illegality" of the union. Yes, the employer was "less than perfect," but most of his staff preferred to stay with him while mass pickets attacked the police. Another "extraordinary" recommendation of the Industrial Court was that Grunwick reinstate the dismissed workers who, according to Joseph, had revealed their hatred of the company. In the end, the report was "not good for the country." Joseph, however, was happy that the Industrial Court had no legal force: "The phrase Industrial Court is itself something of a linguistic confidence trick—to try to give some of the legal sanctity of a Court of Law to a body that is, in fact, no party of the system of law courts."[35]

Norman Tebbit was in Joseph's corner, and he entered the controversy on September 12 declaring: "[T]oday the cloth-capped colonels of the TUC use their industrial power for political ends. They insist on the conscription of the closed shop as part of their price for allowing a government to stay in office." This was wrong and so was appeasement: "If an evil is so powerful that the faint hearts say it must be appeased, then that is all the more reason to deal with it before it becomes stronger still."[36] As a backbencher, he had more leeway to be frank. On the other hand, Thatcher thought Joseph's response was too harsh and she supported James Prior's favorable assessment of the Scarman Report.[37] She believed neither the Tory Party nor the electorate were ready for tough policy changes. A "long-term shift away from the policies which had let to Britain's decline" was necessary, but such "unpalatable medicine" would not work in 1977.[38]

III

As was the case in her first two years as Tory leader, Thatcher scored her most points as leader with important speeches outside of the House of Commons. For those preferring a more moderate Thatcher, on some occasions she did not disappoint. To the Institute of Bankers in early 1977, she declared: "I do not believe that the Trade Unions would deliberately stand in the way of wealth-creating economic policies, or the Party which advocates them." The labor unions represented millions of workers who had minds of their own; she expected workers to understand that a profitable industry was in their best interest. It was necessary for industry to adapt and change to stay competitive, but she advised against any abrupt action that could be "socially damaging."[39]

Thatcher avoided the topic of reforming the trade unions and she rarely discussed monetarism, still seen by some as extreme economic thinking. However, there was no lessening of her hard-hitting criticism of socialism.

She kept telling people that socialism was behind the compassionate and smiley faces of the Labour Party. In a February speech to Southampton Conservatives, she explained her efforts to get Callaghan to state whether the Labour Party "welcomed or condemned" Marxist supporters. According to Thatcher, Callaghan refused to answer since his answer would either offend most British voters or the Labour Party members who supported the "Labour's Programme 1976" policy document that called for "a new and powerful Socialist economic and industrial strategy." The document argued that the Labour government could only reach its goals by having more direct control of industry. Thatcher promised that the Conservative Party would get the country back on track: "Soon, now—perhaps very soon—we will rid the country of the evasiveness, the extravagances, and the dogmas of all kinds of Socialism."[40]

Other Thatcher speeches generated greater attention. Speaking to the Zurich Economic Society in March 1977, she quoted Callaghan's words from 1960:

> I have not the slightest doubt that the economic measures and the Socialist measures, which one will find in the countries of Eastern Europe, will become increasingly powerful against the uncoordinated planless society in which the West is living at present.

Thatcher asked how was it not obvious even to intellectual socialists that socialism had failed, either in compromised or extreme versions? Left policies sounded attractive, but there were more people experiencing the emptiness of "socialist illusions" and "class struggle." Higher taxes failed to finance the public sector and the government continued to borrow money internationally and print money which led to higher inflation. But there were clear signs of the end of a socialist trend, demonstrated by the revolt against excessive taxation, and the start of a "new renaissance." The future of Britain did not need to be dismal. Thatcher reassured: "I have reason to believe that the tide is beginning to turn against collectivism, socialism, statism, dirigisme, whatever you call it."[41] It is interesting that there was no mention of Keynesianism and its expansion of the role of government.

In Thatcher's June meeting with Westminster Conservatives, there was a souvenir booklet printed for the occasion that introduced the rumor of the Labour government planning for an October general election: the "Socialists and their Liberal accomplices" were on their way to presenting a "fresh face" to voters even as the nation experienced a 17.5 percent inflation rate. "Tricking" the people would not be easy. Thatcher explained in the booklet that three years of "Socialist rule" brought "reduced incentives, increased controls, and an ever-expanding interference by the state in their private lives." In her speech, she turned her attention to inflation and went deeper into the topic than had most of her speeches. Thatcher doubted the Labour government and the union movement could move beyond the Social Contract and reach the next stage of a counter-inflation policy. She applauded Denis Healey's July 1976 linking of the economy and money supply targets, but she wanted him to give money supply greater attention to fight inflation. The Bank of England, in the previous week, argued that money supply targets represented "a barrier to inflation, provided there is general understanding of their undoubted necessity." If the government's monetary expansion fell in the 9 to 13 percent range for the year, as planned, it was important to keep the rise in wage costs significantly below this range to realize economic growth. Even though Healey probably argued the case in private to slow wage hikes, Thatcher believed he did too little publicly and this left many people unaware of the relationship between monetary expansion and wage costs.[42]

In her July 22, 1977, speech in the House of Commons, Thatcher began with a Callaghan quote from the previous year:

> We used to think that you could just spend your way out of a recession and increase employment by cutting taxes and boosting Government spending. I tell you in all candour, that that option no longer exists and in so far as it ever did exist, it worked by injecting inflation into the economy.

Callaghan had admitted that unemployment rose. The pattern was "Higher inflation followed by higher unemployment." To stay consistent with this "sound" interpretation and win the inflation fight, Thatcher argued that the government had to further reduce the 9 to 13 percent money supply since it was "way above the productive potential of this country." Citing Treasury figures, she said that Labour's record on inflation was dismal: the average industrial worker experienced a loss of £5.32 a week in real terms and everyone experienced a declining living standard. Given the repeated failures of the Labour economic policies of the past three years, she had no confidence in Healey's July 15 forecast of single-digit inflation well before July 1978.[43] Thatcher lacked the ability to "command" the House of Commons and she failed to articulate that Keynesianism was a spent force, but her repetition of the damaging numbers of Labour's economic record kept the government on the defence.

In September 1977, Thatcher went on an eight-day visit to the United States where she gave important speeches with extensive content on the economy, unions, and freedom. Demonstrating her dedication to free enterprise, she chose the no-frills Laker Airways rather than state-owned British Airways.[44] To the British American Chamber of Commerce, she stated that Britain was soon to enter a "post-Socialist period," and to support her point she once again quoted Callaghan's you-cannot-spend-yourself-out-a-recessio n statement. She believed an increasing number of people saw the wisdom of abandoning four key fallacies of the past: government control brings prosperity; people accept higher taxation for government services; new taxes allow better redistribution of wealth; and state-owned businesses benefit workers and consumers.[45] In an interview by *Time* magazine's Herman Nickel, Thatcher explained that inflation, a lower living standard, and a heavy taxation system were the causes of much resentment, but it took the authority of the IMF to see any financial discipline. If someone desired to be a politician, "they'd better learn one of the lessons of the past. And that is: if you let your public expenditures rise too much, you'll not only have higher inflation, you'll have higher unemployment as well."[46] However, Thatcher provided no explicit discussion of monetarism. One month later at the annual Conservative Conference in October, Thatcher promised the day was coming when Conservatives threw "off the Socialist yoke" and began the task of setting Britain free and creating a lasting economic recovery, but she avoided discussion of money supply theory. She took the safe route and delivered a speech meant to have widespread Tory appeal:

> Britain will have a Conservative Government—a truly moderate government, moderate not by order of our foreign creditors, but by genuine conviction, in touch and in tune with the people, carrying out the sort of sensible, prudent, policies that work so well in other countries.

If there was any mistake about her approach, she responded to Labour's strategy of labelling her as an extremist: "So let me tell you a little about my 'extremism.' I am extremely careful never to be extreme."[47]

With many expecting an election in 1978, Thatcher was mindful of an economic message attractive to voters. The future looked promising for the Tories as the labor union movement became impatient with Labour leadership that restrained wages and reduced public spending. Before Jack Jones retired as general secretary of the TGWU months later, his union conference "howled" against his request for wage restraint. James Callaghan, confiding with Denis Healey, even contemplated legislation to control the behavior of the unions. Explaining how union leadership of the Trade Unions Congress had no control over constituent unions, Healey pointed to the power of local shop-stewards as the biggest obstacle for union cooperation; a government's incomes policy robbed the shop-stewards of their purpose.[48]

There was high unemployment, angry workers, and impatient trade union leaders. But most of Thatcher's speeches indicated no major changes. There was no heavy imprint of Keith Joseph's ideas. Rather than any clear monetary theme, her position was traditional Tory fare: responsible government spending, lower taxes, a free and open market, and a celebration of personal opportunity and enterprise. One exception was when she briefly discussed a monetary theme in a speech to a meeting of overseas bankers in London in February 1978. She lamented the "crippling burden of taxation" on the private sector and how the British economy cried "out for the restoration of incentives recklessly destroyed over the past four years." However, there was a hopeful development: there was some discrediting of the Keynesian approach of government spending to address recession. As Britain experienced declining inflation rates, mainly due to the intervention of the IMF, it was vital to stay vigilant and not return to excessive spending and regulation of wages. Thatcher declared:

> I regard monetary disciplines as of continuing overriding importance. When in the past, like some of our friends and neighbours overseas, we have set ourselves clear and specific monetary targets, they have proved effective here as they have abroad. We must not now abandon them just as they have begun to pull us round.[49]

There were Tories giving significant attention to monetary issues, but discussions remained mostly confidential. In a March paper on "Inflation, Pay Determination and the Labour Market," prepared by Adam Ridley, a non-monetarist, and the Conservative Research Department (CRD), there was agreement that solving inflation was "the most important single task which must be fulfilled if our society and economy are to be restored to health and economic growth resumed." The recent decrease in inflation rates was no reason to lessen the priority of fighting inflation; it was still too high by international standards, and it could "easily and quickly return" to peak levels. Ridley admitted that the old strategy of income policies was a failure: "The impossibility of lasting success with any centralised and detailed method of wage control outside a command economy should be self-evident." However, monetarism was risky. The significance of monetary targets "can only be learnt by a slow and painful process of conditioning (bursts of inflation followed by painful periods of unemployment and weakened output) until and unless that process can be pre-empted and short-circuited by education and explanation."[50]

Weeks later, Ridley argued that there was no certainty of a surge of monetary growth causing prices to rise in the next year. He repeated that there was at least a two-year lag before money supply affected prices. Other issues included imperfect monetary statistics, Britain's relatively open economy compared to the United States, and whether monetary growth is "reasonably sustained" or is a "transient surge." Over a shorter period of 6 to 18 months, wages, world prices, exchange rates, and tax structure were the main determinates of prices. Ridley's main point was that it was "extremely dangerous to make any precise forecasts about future price changes on the basis of monetary trends, particularly when they are not very well-established ones." He also believed that the Labour Party was close to eliminating price control which would make the counter-inflation policy of the Tory Party and the Labour Party similar.[51] In another CDR paper, Ridley wrote that most people favored income restraint and thus it was politically wise for the Tory Party to be sympathetic to "the idea that it is a duty of Governments to play some part, if only indirect, in ensuring moderation in wage settlements."[52] Ridley did his part to cool enthusiasm for monetarism. Given the division over economics, it is no wonder that the Tory Party sidestepped heavy public discussion of monetary policy.

IV

As many looked to an autumn election, the main objective of the Tory Party was to keep the pressure on Labour without getting lost in the intricacies of economic policy, notably the flaws of Keynesianism. Although they sounded like a broken record, the Tories pointed to Labour's poor economic results. There was also the warning that Labour's conversion to tax cuts was due to circumstances rather than conviction.[53] In the House of Commons on March 14, 1978, Thatcher voiced her confusion that Callaghan presented a White Paper that increased public expenditure while claiming to believe that people preferred cuts in taxation rather than an increase in spending. She asked, "Indeed, but how can the Prime Minister cut taxes and increase public expenditure when production is flat?" Callaghan wanted to get "the economy going again" and this meant both tax cuts and increased spending.[54] This appeared contradictory, but there was no guarantee of winning this argument with Callaghan.

The live radio broadcasts of Parliament that began in April 1978 gave Callaghan an advantage over Thatcher; his "easy mastery and her shrill nagging" resulted in an increase of popular support for the Labour Party.[55] With this disadvantage, Thatcher had to convince voters that the Labour Party was no closer to solving inflation and improving the economy than was the case in 1974 or anytime since. In the House of Commons on April 11, she congratulated Denis Healey for presenting a "much shorter" budget speech, but she noted his failure to keep his promise of clarity and using less jargon. Moreover, Healey made no comment on his previous thirteen budgets and the subsequent dismal productivity output and high unemployment. The 9.5 percent year-on-year rate of inflation was an improvement, but it was not the time for rejoicing:

> He omits to say that from the housewife's point of view this is 9.5 per cent. on top of 16.2 per cent. on top of 22.9 per cent. on top of 19.9 per cent. Therefore, it is not surprising that the housewife does not entirely see it in exactly the same way as the Chancellor.[56]

The improved inflation number was still three times higher than in Germany and two times higher than in Japan, and, of Britain's major competitors, only Italy had a higher rate of inflation. Thatcher declared that under Healey's stewardship there was a sharp rise in personal taxation and that Britain witnessed the greatest decline in the standard of living since World War II. A "prisoner" of Labour economic ideas, Healey "set out to create a Socialist paradise, and all that we have is Socialism." His economic strategy failed and rather than "tinkering with the system," such as his announcement of some tax cuts, "we ought to go in a totally different direction."[57] In a Tory Finance Committee meeting, Geoffrey Howe and John Biffen viewed Healey's budget as highly inflationary while some suggested it was rather dull and not an election budget of goodies for the "average man."[58]

In an April interview by the *Hornsey Journal*, Thatcher explained that her appeal went beyond the middle class: "I had a very ordinary background—probably a lot more ordinary than many of their own front bench." It was important to contrast her modest economic origins with the privilege and wealth of some Labour leaders. She valued the liberty of ordinary people and wanted them to "have the right to spend their own money in their own way" rather than have the government increase taxes. Her calculation had the government taking about 55 percent of the national product which resulted in the average worker earning "about £6 a week less." In addition to the issue of government overreach, she briefly discussed her opposition, in simple terms, to government controlling wages: "There's only one way, in the end, to get control and that's to get people to realise that they cannot have more unless they produce more." Expansion was the answer, but was difficult to achieve when restrictive practices caused restrictive wages. Too many businesses who obtained success eventually succumbed to high taxes and burdensome regulations.[59] Shortly after the interview, Callaghan in the House of Commons explained the reason for higher taxes: "Taxes have gone up in an effort to secure national recovery, and they have had an impact. Obviously Conservative policy is to relieve the richer taxpayers and to see that poorer people spend more."[60]

While Callaghan and Thatcher traded blows in the political forum, there were healthy debates on collectivism and newer economic approaches for those interested. Some gathered to hear Milton Friedman lecture at Strathclyde University Business School in Glasgow, Scotland on April 21, 1978. Broadcasted on the BBC-2 for *The Money Programme*, the lecture introduced many listeners to his assessment of Keynes, socialism, British economic life, and monetarism. Although Friedman felt at home intellectually, given that Adam Smith taught there 200 years ago, and welcomed that fewer people had "a good word to say about nationalization," he worried about Britain's economic performance hampered by government control. In his opinion, British policy makers erred in not doing enough with monetarism and monetary targets. Labour gave hopeful statements, but as it continued to fine-tune budgets there was a lack of "steadiness and predictability" with monetary targets. Old ways died hard. Too many on the Left believed in the system of governmental control and judged past failures to improper application rather than problems with the system itself. Friedman sought to change people's thinking. He believed thinkers had a role to play, but he expected "the brute force of events" would have greater influence: "The tide is turning, if it is, not because people like myself have preached the fallacy of the erroneous elements in Keynesian thinking, but because demand management has been a clear failure." Far from achieving a strong economy of good jobs and stable prices, "it has managed to achieve the worst of both worlds: high inflation and high unemployment." He looked to Britain to break from collectivism and embark on the path of greater freedom, opportunity, and prosperity.[61] While impossible to measure, Friedman's efforts helped prepare the way for economic ideas that many in the past viewed as extreme. By 1976, he had his Nobel Prize in economics and his critics weakened their position if they dismissed him without addressing his evidence-based research.

As the summer months approached, both the Labour and Tory parties jockeyed for the support of the British public. The last general election was almost four years ago and there were significant strategic sessions on what lay ahead. One interesting development in early 1978 was the selection of the Saatchi and Saatchi advertising agency to get the Tory message to voters. From a family of Baghdad Jews, the Saatchi brothers Maurice and Charles began their company in 1970. For the Tory Party, the agency created the clever slogan "Labour isn't working" that focused on people's frustration with the Labour government and high unemployment. Denis Healey raged against the Saatchi poster that showed a long line of unemployed people waiting to enter the unemployment office. Thatcher initially failed to see the effectiveness of the poster, complaining that "Labour" was the largest word. Quickly, she changed her mind and the poster had an effect on countless people, including James Callaghan who in the summer nervously pondered when to call an election.[62]

Certainly, an election was on the minds of many. In early June, Alfred Sherman sent Thatcher a confidential memorandum stating the vulnerability of the sterling pound if Healey adopted "electioneering economics." Sherman raised the possibility of Callaghan taking advantage of an economic crisis and dragooning the Tories into a coalition, thus creating "a counterweight to the Labour left" and perhaps splitting the Tory Party. The Tories needed a contingency plan that included "proleptic counter-proposals for a common programme of national recovery" attractive to the public, but unacceptable to socialists.[63]

In his speech to Conservatives in Kirtlington, Geoffrey Howe explained how the strict supervision of the IMF and Labour's lack of a parliamentary majority had kept the government more economically accountable the previous year. But the party showed signs of its old ways. The National Institute of Economic and Social Research predicted a return to "near-stagnation" and Howe argued that there was nothing in the Labour Party's record to suggest it understood "what needs to be done." A vote for Callaghan was a vote for Anthony Benn socialism: "for more nationalisation and for less enterprise, for more equality and for less opportunity, for falling living standards and for fewer jobs." In one case, a builder searched seven job centers before finding a skilled craftsman for his project. People went to Canada or elsewhere for new opportunities. The finance director of Rolls Royce reluctantly left Britain to work in "North America." There was proof of some trade union leaders openly "playing their part in institutionalising Socialism as the British way of life." Howe claimed one could not exaggerate the "urgency and the importance of the task" required to halt and reverse the trend of "an increasingly sick economy."[64] Days later, when the bank rate increased to 10 percent, Howe believed the prediction of a worsening economy was "now coming true."[65] This was bad news for the nation, and the Tories saw no hope in Labour economic policies. As conservatives within the party prepared for the eventual election, they began working closely with academics such as Peter Bauer, economic professor at the London School of Economics, and former *New Statesman* editor Paul Johnson, who had recently recanted his socialism.[66] Later Johnson argued in *Modern Times*, his *New York Times* book of the year, that trade unions destroyed the governments of Harold Wilson, Edward Heath, and James Callaghan.[67] Some viewed Bauer as the "world's foremost authority on economic development" in the Third World. He was critical of scholars who applauded government intervention but failed to examine the economic costs of such action.[68]

At the end of July, Thatcher presented a major economic speech in the House of Commons that explained where the Tories stood on the government's performance and what policies Britain needed to move beyond socialism. In her first sentence, she noted the Labour record of unemployment, stagnant living conditions, and blacklisting tactics to enforce pay limits. She taunted Callaghan for sitting down when he did: "I was waiting for him to develop an intellectual argument. Perhaps that was a little optimistic. He is long on words; what a pity it is that he has been so short on achievement."

She noted that his speeches usually began with a reference to the "unsavoury inheritance," but his government was in power for almost 4.5 years.[69] Was it not time to take ownership of Labour policies?

One troublesome issue for Thatcher was the heavy-handedness of Labour's White Paper on Industrial Democracy presented in Parliament two months earlier. There were laws properly passed in Parliament and "[t]hen we have White Paper law or diktat which is arbitrary, secret and Socialist. It is passed by those who wish to control other people's lives but who have envisaged themselves only as controllers, not as the controlled." As she saw it, the White Paper upheld "black lists and arbitrary sanctions" that, "at the whim of the Government," hurt companies. Thatcher applauded the White Paper objectives on jobs, prices, and growth, "but the truth is that the policies to put them into effect are just not forthcoming, and they never have been." Excessive public spending killed growth, high taxation killed incentive, and burdensome regulation killed jobs." The facts were there for anyone to see:

> We contrast Labour's record of economic failure. It is its own condemnation. It is a record born of envy and hostility to wealth creation. The unemployment queues spell the despair of Socialism. The record of inflation tells its own story of Labour incompetence. The present level of interest rates condemns the fiscal and monetary judgments of the Chancellor of the Exchequer.

Although she ducked the topic of monetary policy, she did go on record rejecting statutory incomes policy for the future.[70]

By the end of the summer, the Conservative Party was ready for the election. For the most part, Thatcher had played it safe. There was no articulation of the flaws of Keynesianism and no strong anti-union language or clarification of economic ideas directly linked to Milton Friedman's monetarism. Even Keith Joseph kept his economic message straightforward, focusing on the argument that the Labour Party was a job killer. In late August, he had three speeches set to go: "Wasteful Spending Kills Jobs—Cuts Save Them," "Do Job Rescues Rescue Jobs?," and "Jim Callaghan the Job-Killer." Joseph was hopeful these "pre-election" speeches would be useful to other Tories. The tone was aggressive rather than defensive: "I am saying that the policies he [Callaghan] follows, the policies that the Labour Party is bound to follow until it accepts free enterprise whole-heartedly and drops it class war, Marxist trends, are bound to create unemployment."[71]

V

The Labour Party was in a tenuous position in August. In 1976 and 1977, its majority eroded mainly due to by-election losses and defections to the

Scottish Labour Party. If challenged, Callaghan did not have enough votes to keep the government in power. On March 18, 1977, the party faced a Commons motion of "No confidence" and shortly after Callaghan saved his government by signing a formal agreement with the Liberal Party and its thirteen MPs led by David Steel. By a majority of twenty-four, the government won the vote of confidence. Norman Tebbit wrote that he never forgave Steel "for sustaining Labour at a moment when we could have won a sweeping victory."[72] Benn saw the pact as an obstacle for carrying out a socialist manifesto whereas Thatcher took the opposite position: "It did not halt, let alone reverse, the advance of socialism; indeed, it kept the Labour Government in office and enabled it to complete the nationalization of the aircraft and shipbuilding industries."[73] The pact bought the Labour Party time before it formally ended in August 1978.

Callaghan spent most of August at his Upper Clayhill Farm at Ringmer in the Sussex Weald. Enjoying country life, he contemplated when the British should go to the polls. Much of his reading was dry: Parliamentary processes, election surveys, and voting opinion data. He made his decision in mid-August, but he kept it to himself. Confident in Callaghan's record and political knowledge, "most Labour politicians and party voters" expected him to make the right decision.[74] When six senior TUC leaders met with Callaghan at his farm, only one advised him to delay the election. The message from the five others was: "Go now. Don't wait until next year. We cannot guarantee industrial peace in the coming winter."[75] Callaghan was willing to gamble and when he returned from his holiday, he confided to Ken Stowe, his principal private secretary, that "the great issue was economic recovery and the conquest of inflation in which the wages policy was essential." The best option was "to fight the battle during the winter, hope to win it and then go to the country."[76] His own "amateur calculations" had Labour with 303 seats and the Tories with 304: "I made up my mind. The Government should aim to consolidate the progress we made and then ask the country to confirm us in office on a progressive manifesto in the spring."[77]

Callaghan believed victory in October was a long shot and he had the support of Michael Foot who favored more time before going to the polls.[78] When Anthony Benn made his way to the September 7 cabinet meeting, he expected a fall election. The announcement of no election angered him because he believed the cabinet had no say in the final decision: "The letter to the Queen had been sent, and that was it." According to Benn, Callaghan explained that the party could win in the fall, but he expected the economy to improve in the coming months.[79] The British people who watched Callaghan's September 7 television broadcast heard Callaghan admit the vulnerability of his minority government due to the ending of the Liberal-Labour pact and his request that the British people "carry on with the task of consolidating the improvement now taking place in our country's position."[80] The announcement caught many off guard; the British public, journalists, union leaders, and politicians from all parties expected an early election. The *Daily Mirror*, a friend of the Labour Party, printed that October 5 would be election day. After he heard Callaghan's broadcast, *Daily Express Leader* writer Edward Pearce hastily re-wrote his story of the coming election before it went to print.[81] No less surprised were Callaghan's political advisers, as Bernard Donoughue admitted: "Most of the watchers were astonished by the news of no election. [Roger] Carroll and [David] Lipsey were totally speechless." Labour's Tom McNally concluded: "Either he is a great political genius or he has just missed the boat."[82]

Norman Tebbit's analysis was that the Labour Party was in good shape to secure a majority if there had been a June election: "Although inflation and unemployment were unpopular the policies which lead to them were not." In essence, most British voters were fine with Keynesian intervention to restore a poor economy. Tebbit's advice was for the Conservatives to distract Callaghan throughout the summer with issues since he was "very bad at taking considered decisions." When Callaghan failed to call an election, Tebbit knew the Conservative Party "had got him."[83] Thatcher responded to Callaghan's decision with a "general sense of anti-climax," knowing that an autumn election would have given the Conservative Party "a small overall majority." There was no sense of a guaranteed landslide.[84]

When Thatcher delivered her speech at the Conservative Party Conference in October 1978, opinion polls had the party trailing Labour. There was some confusion on what the Tories stood for. Before the conference, James Prior gave a radio interview suggesting that the Tory Party supported a statutory incomes policy. At the conference, Edward Heath warned against dogmatism and any outright rejection of an incomes policy. When asked on television whether the Conservative Party should accept the Labour's pay policy, he declared his support for it if the alternative was "roaring inflation."[85] Thatcher was not happy that Heath continued to oppose her, but she played it safe. In her conference speech, the only mention of incomes policy and money supply was one sentence stating that Germany opposed them. She declared that the Conservative Party offered Britain "nothing less than national revival" and she hoped for the people to accept the "basic Conservative belief that the State is the servant not the master of this nation." Labour politicians had good intentions, but they upheld misguided illusions including

> the illusion that real jobs can be conjured into existence by Government decree like rabbits out of a hat [and] the illusion that there is some other way of creating work and wealth than by hard work and satisfying your customers.

Conservatives were "as fallible, as human and therefore as given to making mistakes as the next man. But we don't preach hatred and we are not a party of envy." In short, "Class warfare is immoral."[86]

Although Thatcher's criticism of Labour and its theme of class warfare was clear, it was not her best speech and there was little enthusiasm among the Tory rank and file. Heath continued to cause confusion with his public support for an incomes policy. Thatcher supporters viewed him as disloyal and George Gardiner, remaining faithful to Thatcher, declared in late October that getting "support from Ted Heath is like being measured for the undertaker."[87] Troubling for Thatcher was a November poll showing a 14 percent advantage over the Labour Party if Heath was the leader. With Thatcher as leader, the Tory Party and Labour Party were close in the polls. British opinion appeared to favor an incomes policy plan rather than Thatcher's "free-for-all" that might result in an explosion of wage increases and out-of-control inflation.[88] Labour Party insiders were hopeful of winning the next election.

Events in the subsequent months transformed the political landscape. In the autumn of 1978, there was ample uncertainty and disappointment as the British people witnessed economic stagnation. Even popular culture captured the rise of tension over the lower standard of living and concern for the future. One example was Peter Flannery's play *Savage Amusement* premiered by the Royal Shakespeare Company in July 1978. The story follows young squatters in the decaying and chaotic setting of a future Manchester. The government relocated the family of Teenager Fitz to a new high-rise in Hulme which is unsanitary. In these conditions, Fritz's father resorts to drinking and then abandons the family.[89]

Real people experienced the social cost of low wages or joblessness. The Labour Party's pay policy was in jeopardy and there were signs of union leaders taking a more aggressive stand against the government. But many were not ready to turn to Thatcher, who was less popular than Callaghan. People going back to his speech of 1976 could see a leader willing to take a tough stand, even if it upset dissenters in the Labour Party. When Callaghan declared the impossibility of spending "your way out of a recession," foes and friends took notice. None of Thatcher's declarations captured the same degree of attention; she held back on the issues of incomes policy and trade unions. It had been a formidable task to combat a prime minister who had the confidence of most voters and, thus, her progress as leader was modest at best. There was uncertainty for both the Labour and the Conservatives, but each knew the 1979 election would answer many questions. However, neither side imagined the level of anger and protest that the year would bring.

NOTES

1. Benn, *Conflicts of Interest*, 282. Tebbit, *Upwardly Mobile*, 180, 184.
2. David Cannadine, *Margaret Thatcher: A Life and Legacy* (Oxford University Press, 2017), 24.
3. Young, *One of Us*, 121–23.
4. Nelson, "Milton Friedman and U.K. Economic Policy," 466.
5. Keegan, *Mrs Thatcher's Economic Experiment*, 61.
6. Thatcher, *Margaret Thatcher*, 196, 221.
7. Nelson, "Milton Friedman and U.K. Economic Policy," 493.
8. Thatcher, *Margaret Thatcher*, 196, 221.
9. Young, *One of Us*, 107.
10. Moore, *Margaret Thatcher*, 355.
11. Prior, *A Balance of Power*, 109.
12. MTF, *The Right Approach to the Economy*, 8 October 1977, https://www.margaretthatcher.org/document/112551. Also, see Moore, *Margaret Thatcher*, 357.
13. Moore, *Margaret Thatcher*, 358.
14. Thatcher, *Margaret Thatcher*, 193.
15. Denham and Garnett, *Keith Joseph*, 306–7.
16. Thatcher, *Margaret Thatcher*, 231.
17. Young, *One of Us*, 115–16.
18. MTF, Economy: "Stepping Stones," 14 November 1977, https://www.margaretthatcher.org/document/111771.
19. Moore, *Margaret Thatcher*, 362–63.
20. Tebbit, *Upwardly Mobile*, 172.
21. Tebbit, *Upwardly Mobile*, 181, 190–91.
22. Thatcher, *Margaret Thatcher*, 193.
23. MTF, Sir Keith Joseph to Hayek (talks for BBC), 1 February 1977, https://www.margaretthatcher.org/document/114623; Hayek to Sir Keith Joseph (talks for BBC), 23 March 1977, https://www.margaretthatcher.org/document/114625.
24. Yergin and Stanislaw, *The Commanding Heights*, 102–3.
25. MTF, Hailsham diary, 9 March 1977, https://www.margaretthatcher.org/document/111176.
26. Quoted in Halcrow, *Keith Joseph*, 124.
27. MTF, Sherman memorandum to CPS Management Board, 20 July 1978, https://www.margaretthatcher.org/document/111999.
28. Denham and Garnett, *Keith Joseph*, 308–9.
29. MTF, Speech in Chelmsford, 20 June 1977, https://www.margaretthatcher.org/document/111257.
30. MTF, Scarman Report, 26 August 1977, https://www.margaretthatcher.org/document/111943.
31. Thatcher, *Margaret Thatcher*, 217–18.
32. Moore, *Margaret Thatcher*, 359.
33. Thatcher, *Margaret Thatcher*, 218.

34. MTF, Speech at Hove Town Hall, 1 September 1977, https://www.margaretthatcher.org/document/111945.

35. Speech at Hove Town Hall, 1 September 1977.

36. Tebbit, *Upwardly Mobile*, 195.

37. Thatcher, *Margaret Thatcher*, 219. Thatcher admitted Joseph was right and she was wrong.

38. Thatcher, *Margaret Thatcher*, 215.

39. MTF, Speech to Institute of Bankers, 19 January 1977, https://www.margaretthatcher.org/document/103303.

40. MTF, Speech to Southampton Conservatives, 11 February 1977, https://www.margaretthatcher.org/document/103315.

41. MTF, Speech to Zurich Economic Society, 14 March 1977, https://www.margaretthatcher.org/document/103336.

42. MTF, Speech to Westminster Conservatives, 22 June 1977, https://www.margaretthatcher.org/document/103400.

43. MTF, Counter-Inflation Policy, 20 July 1977, https://www.margaretthatcher.org/document/103421.

44. Moore, *Margaret Thatcher*, 367.

45. MTF, Speech to British American Chamber of Commerce, 8 September 1977, https://www.margaretthatcher.org/document/103436.

46. "The World: Thatcher: 'We Shall Win,'" *Time*, 19 September 1977.

47. MTF, Speech to Conservative Party Conference, 14 October 1977, https://www.margaretthatcher.org/document/103443.

48. Healey, *The Time of My Life*, 398–99.

49. MTF, Speech to Overseas Bankers, 7 February 1978, https://www.margaretthatcher.org/document/103609.

50. MTF, Adam Ridley paper for pay meeting, 16 March 1978, https://www.margaretthatcher.org/document/109759.

51. MTF, Adam Ridley note for Keith Joseph, 26 June 1978, https://www.margaretthatcher.org/document/109763.

52. MTF, Adam Ridley paper, 30 June 1978, https://www.margaretthatcher.org/document/109764.

53. Also see, Gamble, *The Free Economy and the Strong State*, 99.

54. MTF, Hansard, House of Commons PQs, 14 March 1978, https://www.margaretthatcher.org/document/103642.

55. Campbell, *Margaret Thatcher*, 359–60.

56. MTF, Budget Resolutions and Economic Situation, 11 April 1978, https://www.margaretthatcher.org/document/103653.

57. Budget Resolutions and Economic Situation, 11 April 1978.

58. MTF, Report of Conservative backbench Finance Committee meeting, 11 April 1978, https://www.margaretthatcher.org/document/109762.

59. MTF, Interview for *Hornsey Journal*, 21 April 1978, https://www.margaretthatcher.org/document/103662.

60. MTF, House of Commons PQs, 27 April 1978, https://www.margaretthatcher.org/document/103665.

61. Milton Friedman, "Has the Economic Tide Turned?," Glasgow: Strathclyde Business School, University of Strathclyde, 1978, https://miltonfriedman.hoover.org/objects/57654/has-the-economic-tide-turned.

62. Moore, *Margaret Thatcher*, 384–86.

63. MTF, "Stand by to Repel Coalition - Press-gangs," 1 June 1978, https://www.margaretthatcher.org/document/111993.

64. MTF, Sir Geoffrey Howe speech in Kirtlington, 2 June 1978, https://www.margaretthatcher.org/document/109798.

65. MTF, Sir Geoffrey Howe statement, 8 June 1978, https://www.margaretthatcher.org/document/109799.

66. MTF, Centre for Policy Studies Management Committee minutes, 20 June 1978, https://www.margaretthatcher.org/document/111956.

67. Paul Johnson, *Modern Times: The World from the Twenties to the Nineties* (New York: HarperPerennial, 2001), 740.

68. See P.T. Bauer, *Reality and Rhetoric: Studies in the Economics of Development* (Cambridge: Harvard University Press, 1984).

69. MTF, The Economy, 25 July 1978, https://www.margaretthatcher.org/document/103736.

70. The Economy, 25 July 1978.

71. MTF, Sir Keith Joseph to Thorneycroft, 29 August 1978, https://www.margaretthatcher.org/document/111865.

72. Tebbit, *Upwardly Mobile*, 198.

73. Benn, *Conflicts of Interest*, 91. Thatcher, *Margaret Thatcher*, 215.

74. John Shepherd, *Crisis? What Crisis?:* The *Callaghan Government and the British 'Winter of Discontent'* (Manchester: Manchester University Press, 2013), 21. Kenneth O. Morgan, *Callaghan: A Life* (Oxford: Oxford University Press, 1997), 626, 636–37.

75. Shepherd, *Crisis? What Crisis?,* 29.

76. Shepherd, *Crisis? What Crisis?,* 24.

77. Callaghan, *Time and Chance*, 516.

78. Shepherd, *Crisis? What Crisis?,* 21.

79. Benn, *Conflicts of Interest*, 334.

80. For his full broadcast, see Callaghan, *Time and Chance*, 517–18.

81. Shepherd, *Crisis? What Crisis?,* 18–19.

82. Donoughue, *Downing Street Diary, Volume Two*, 359.

83. Tebbit, *Upwardly Mobile*, 198–200.

84. Thatcher, *Margaret Thatcher*, 227.

85. Thatcher, *Margaret Thatcher*, 228–29.

86. MTF, Speech to Conservative Party Conference, 13 October 1978, https://www.margaretthatcher.org/document/103764.

87. Moore, *Margaret Thatcher*, 396.

88. Moore, *Margaret Thatcher*, 395–96.

89. Phil Tinline, "Back to the Future: What the Turmoil of the 1970s Can Teach Us Today," *The New Statesman*, 8 May 2019.

Chapter 6

The Winter of Discontent

In a documentary film about the infamous band the Sex Pistols, band members Steve Jones and John Lydon narrated their impression of England in the 1970s:

> It was cold and miserable, no-one had any jobs, you couldn't get a job. Total social chaos. There was rioting all over the place, strikes on every kind of amenity you could think of. The TV channels would go on and off randomly.[1]

It may be an exaggerated assessment of the decade, but it probably was a dominating perception during the "Winter of Discontent." When the Labour government imposed a 5 percent limit on wage increases in late 1978, British workers ranging from nurses to gravediggers participated in over 2,000 strikes in the subsequent months. The trade unions appeared to hold the balance of power since over half of the total British workforce belonged to a union, the greatest total in British history. Three years earlier on American television, Milton Friedman had generated a storm of protest in Britain when he suggested that there was a 50–50 chance that British freedom and democracy would be destroyed in the near future.[2]

The winter months of early 1979 were tragic: gravediggers refused to bury their dead, refuse accumulated in the streets, and hospitals postponed operations for cancer patients. These and other horrible incidents pointed to, in Conservative Lord Hailsham's words, "the law of the jungle." In his letter to the *Manchester Evening News*, W. Ashcroft declared:

> Trade unions have declared war on society. Some of us believe that work must be for the well-being of society. We are all now being bullied. Pickets don't

> bother me, woe betide any who try to stop me from earning a living. If the government can't look after us, it is up to us to look after ourselves.[3]

The outcome was dire with businesses and schools closed and transportation marred with national rail strikes, all while Britain experienced appalling cold weather. At the height of chaos from January to March when 5 million working days were lost, the British people watched television scenes of dramatic strike action. In mid-January, one person declared in the *Manchester Evening News* that after voting "Socialist" for forty-two years he planned to vote Tory. He wanted to send a message to the "wildcat dictators" and give Thatcher a chance to restore "some sense of sanity."[4] It became clear that Callaghan's decision not to go to the polls in 1978 was a fatal mistake for the Labour Party.[5] The no-confidence motion of March 30 went 311 votes to 310 against Labour; Callaghan called an election for May 3. The Tory election manifesto offered few innovative economic policy statements. With or without them, it did not matter. The voters had enough, and they carried out a "sea of change" that saw the Conservative Party gaining an overall majority of forty-three. On May 4, the grocer's daughter became the first female prime minister in British history.

I

Throughout the 1970s an increasing number of British families faced difficulties in getting ahead financially. Days after the Labour Party won the general election in October 1974, a Mrs. M. P. Blackey explained in a letter to the *Manchester Evening News* that she and many of her friends worked to supplement their husband's wages:

> I work a full day, from 8:30 am to 5 pm, and I work! Our family does not have a colour TV set or a car. I don't play bingo or visit the pub except on the very rare occasion when my husband and I go out for a quiet drink. We haven't even a washing machine.[6]

Four years later, many ordinary British families continued to experience difficult economic conditions. Pam Clemens, a laundry worker at Northhampton General Hospital, lamented the poor pay of her job: "Most of us here helped to pay mortgages and buy food, but it's got so it's not worthwhile. And if you use the creche (nursery), it is £9 a week for a child."[7]

The British economy captured the interest of economists seeking to understand why Keynesian and socialist policies had failed. For many years, Milton Friedman devoted significant attention to the state of the British economy in lectures, articles, and media presentations. In November 1976, the weekly magazine *The Listener* published a Richard Kershaw interview of Friedman that discussed his "apocalyptic conclusion" of Britain's future. Friedman argued that for the previous seventy years Britain embarked on "bigger and bigger government" that lessened individual responsibility. Britain's spending was more than 50 percent of its income and the government "has been forced" to impose "the tax of inflation" and to borrow. There was less incentive for anyone to save, invest, and use their resources within Great Britain. This could not continue. The only hope was for the Labour government to revise its policy direction by eliminating the social contract and its price and wage controls, policies that represented a misdiagnosis of Britain's economic problems. Wages did not cause inflation; wages were a consequence of inflation. Friedman found Callaghan's 1976 warning about overspending encouraging, but action was necessary: "If that is more than words, if it means a fundamental change in the direction of policy, then I will have to revise my probabilities [on Britain's decline]."[8]

Kershaw asked Friedman: "Would not your solution of a monetary squeeze make unemployment worse?" Friedman responded: "Is there a solution that won't? You have got a patient who is very sick. What makes anybody believe that there is an instant cure that will enable him to rise from his sickbed, tomorrow, a healthy man?" He conceded this was not politically appealing, but conditions demanded courageous action without the assistance of the IMF: "If, indeed, Britain were to demonstrate internally a radical change in its policy, I think there would be no problem whatsoever in international finance arising from private sources that would be more than ample to handle these transitional problems."[9] Why give up democratic freedoms to a committee of the IMF? There were both blunt words by ordinary British people burdened by difficult living conditions and by economists such as Friedman; however, the Labour Party could not possibly take the road that Friedman suggested. Labour held on with some minor tinkering, hoping for better economic results.

It became obvious that the Labour government fell short of its promises of a stronger economy. Too many politicians believed Keynesianism could solve inflation. Part of the problem was the persistent belief among commentators and academics that poor economic conditions were mostly due to a global financial crisis rather than bad economic policies by both Tory and Labour governments. On September 18, 1978, National Union of Public Employees (NUPE) general secretary Alan Fisher presented a strong message to the Labour party. The *Daily Express* recorded, "If the Government fails to understand the problems of the low-paid and to act to overcome them, they are in for a serious winter of discontent," and the *Daily Telegraph* provided additional details:

> We are prepared to fight for the policy of the TUC in seeking our objective of a £60 per week minimum rate of pay. The government's pay policy comes nowhere near that objective . . . it may lead to a major confrontation in the public sector.[10]

The Labour government insisted on a 5 percent pay limit, but this policy began to unravel soon after Callaghan's announcement of no election in the fall of 1978.

From September 29 to October 6, the Labour Party conference took place in Blackpool where Callaghan unsuccessfully attempted to win support for the government's incomes policy. His speech received a standing ovation, but there was a resolution passed that the government "immediately cease intervening in wage negotiations and recognise the right of trade unions to negotiate freely on behalf of their members." There would be no "planning of wages" unless "prices, profits and investment were also planned." In essence, this was a call for a more socialist economy. In his diary, Anthony Benn saw the conference as a triumph for the Left. No amount of arm twisting by Labour leaders altered trade union opposition.[11] Although this development suggested difficult times for the government in the future, at least in the short term, Callaghan's strong speech helped change opinion polls to favor Labour over the Tory Party by 5 percent.[12] On November 20, Bernard Donoughue wrote in his diary that "Thatcher is a long way behind the PM, and even running behind Heath."[13]

II

Since the 1941 arrival of unions in the British Ford Motor Company plants, there was evidence of increasing shop-floor militancy. The 1950s and 1960s witnessed the rise of unofficial strikes as rank-and-file members bypassed trade unions and confronted management. The 1970s saw greater labor unrest with the emergence of young workers from families immersed in trade unionism and Labour party politics. Born into an Irish immigrant family, Ford worker John Bohanna recounted when as a child, his father got him to go around the neighborhood with "Vote Labour" signs.[14] By the end of the decade, radicalism became more obvious and at the Ford Dagenham plant in London the Communist Party wielded influence on the shop floor. One Ford worker identified several radical groups at Dagenham including pro-Serbia Communists, pro-Albanian Communists, Chinese Communists, and a variety of Trotskyite groups. The shop floor militancy at Ford plants also had links to the International Socialist Group and the International Marxist Group.[15]

In early September 1978, H. A. Polling, chairman of the board of Ford Europe Incorporated, wrote to Callaghan expressing his concern with union demands for wages much higher than the government's 5 percent limit. With the assistance of the Industrial Relations Unit at Ruskin College, the TGWU calculated that Ford, with its profits, could afford to pay its workers a higher wage. A common message of the auto workers was: "We helped make the profits, now we want our fair share!" When Ford announced a wage increase of 5 percent in September 22, employees at the Halewood plant stopped working and the night shift did likewise. The strike action spread and in the next few days over 50,000 workers at Ford plants at Dagenham, Daventry, Swansea, Basildon, Dunton, Southampton, and Langley walked off their jobs. Ron Todd, chairman of negotiations for the TGWU, expected a period of negotiations, but instead the workers' actions were abrupt with thousands walking out, frustrated with the years of incomes policy.[16] Due to the large number of Ford workers, the organization depended on close coordination. At the Dagenham plant there were twenty-five entrances that required picketing twenty-four hours a day. The nights were cold, and some workers were creative and kept warm by burning coke and broken wooden pallets inside iron oil drums.[17]

The British people were split over the strike. The workers found support from other labor groups. The International Metal Workers' Federation promised financial assistance and approximately 100 nurses arrived at the Dagenham to help guard the picket line. Those opposing the strike included wives of Ford workers. Susan Charlton, a member of a Southampton group, organized a petition for a secret ballot for the workers to decide whether to keep striking or return to work. One woman of the group whose husband and son worked for Ford claimed that many workers wanted to return to their jobs. The "silent majority" opposed the strike. Other women formed the "Ford Women's Action Group" and held counter demonstrations to those who wanted to end the strike.[18] After nine weeks of strike action, Ford offered workers a 16 percent increase and the final agreed settlement was 17 percent. Callaghan saw this capitulation of the private sector as a heavy blow:

> The Ford pay claim was the bellwether of the flock, watched by other unions and highlighted by the press. Where Ford would go the others would follow, and such a flagrant breach of the guidelines could not be ignored if the policy was to be left with any content.[19]

Thatcher made headway when she fought the government's attempt to punish Ford by withdrawing government contracts and not purchasing Ford vehicles. In the House of Commons on November 28, she asked Callaghan:

> Does not the Prime Minister recognise the blatant injustice of imposing sanctions on Ford, when that company has already suffered the worst strike in its history because it has tried to support the Prime Minister's rigid 5 per cent pay policy?

As she saw it, Ford had an excellent record on providing jobs and exports for the nation and Callaghan's threat jeopardized this beneficial arrangement. When pressed by Callaghan, she stated her opposition to a "wages explosion," but without saying so, she also appeared to take a Milton Friedman position—that higher wages did not cause inflation—when she supported Ford's right to negotiate a higher wage for workers.[20]

On December 14 in Parliament, she repeated Michael Foot's March 1974 statement on government sanctions:

> I have always thought that one of the reasons why the discussion of incomes policy, so called, has been so difficult has been that, very often, the well-to-do or—even more offensively perhaps—the truly wealthy have been inclined to threaten sanctions or preach sermons to people who have to fight every day of their lives to keep their heads above the inflationary flood. But the threat of sanctions in such cases does not work.[21]

Thatcher was in a good position; the day before, the Labour government lost a vote to have sanctions against employers. She began to be more forceful on the issue of wage controls, pointing out that strict control on prices resulted in a larger rise "than at any previous time in our history." Supporting competition and reducing government spending was the best approach to keep prices reasonable. However, this went against Labour ideology: Labour knows "better how to spend people's money than people do themselves. . . . Socialism prefers to take away that money and to spend it through the collective genius, if I might put it that way, although I doubt it, of the Government."[22] According to Bernard Donoughue, her performance lacked "a touch of show-biz" necessary to effectively engage the House. She rambled on with statistics "and very soon people were chatting on the back benches or leaving for tea—because she does not *involve* them."[23] If this was the case, others were thankful for her stand against sanctions. The next day, Sir Terence Beckett, chairman and managing director of the Ford Motor Company, sent Thatcher a copy of one his speeches and thanked her for addressing the issue of sanctions in Parliament.[24] With the defeat of sanctions, trade union leaders increased action to win higher wages. For example, before Christmas the BBC staff gained a 12 percent wage agreement.

Callaghan's New Year's address warned against a militant response by labor leaders: "Let those who possess industrial muscle and monopoly power resolve not to abuse their great strength. Individual greed and disregard for the well-being of others can undermine and divide our society."[25] This statement demonstrated the weakness of Labour's claim of being the only party to be able to negotiate and work successfully with union leaders. Complicating the issue was the persistent belief among commentators and academics that poor economic conditions were mostly due to a global financial crisis rather than bad economic policies by both Conservative and Labour governments. The focus of trade unionists was on the difficulty of workers to get by on modest wage hikes rather than an analysis of why there was too little wealth creation. In the *Daily Telegraph*, one high-ranking union leader explained it was not his responsibility to manage the economy. His job was to get higher wages for workers.[26] There was hardly any discussion on why the economy was stagnant; it seemed that all that mattered was to force employers to increase wages, whatever the pressure tactic. As the *Socialist Worker* saw it, "ALL-OUT STRIKE!" was the answer.[27] As for voters, many lost patience with militant acts by industry and public sector strikers. When Callaghan canvassed an old couple from his Cardiff constituency, the wife jabbed him in the chest and asked, "Now, when are you going to something about these vandals, then?"[28] He lost credibility with some voters and Thatcher gained strength to the point of silencing the main objections of her Tory critics.[29]

It looked like a rough start for 1979. On January 3, the road hauliers' strike began with drivers refusing to work in Scotland and Britain. As it did with other trades, the three years of pay restraint hit the truckers hard. From the perspective of TGWU shop steward Fred Beach, the working conditions and wages of truckers were dismal. "Drivers were ten-a-penny," on the road for long hours, working for low wages. According to Beach,

> The lorry driver was a mobile tramp, a nonentity. The lorry driver didn't have any respect; their employers didn't have respect for them. If you don't like it, lump it. A heater in your cab? Never heard of it. Good training for a cold picket line.

With the trucks off the road there were no deliveries to hospitals, industry, power stations, and schools. As for hospitals, union activists attempted to balance the need for effective strike action without causing too much tension for the British public concerned about receiving health care. Organizing lookouts on the roads, strikers were successful in turning away deliveries to local hospitals while allowing access for ambulances. For inland Britain, trucking, not railway, was the main form of moving supplies, and thus the truckers' strike had a much greater impact on society than the Ford strike. Labour politician Roy Hattersley explained that the drastic reduction of transporting of goods "was spreading the bad news throughout the country. Every town and village felt like they were affected by the Winter of Discontent."[30] There were cities especially vulnerable. Hull had only two major roads connecting the city with other centers, and it was easy for truckers to set up blockades so that nothing came in or out. Fred Beach and other labor activists found their power emboldening:

> They [employers] were coming to beg. I use the word without any pleasure because it gives me no satisfaction to recall some of our arrogance or impudence of that day or that time. I don't think we were consciously arrogant or impudent. It just went along with the job.[31]

Unions leaders adopted secondary picketing and flying pickets as their main strategies to get their demands met. Secondary picketing consisted of picketing industries not directly involved in a dispute. One letter to the editor in the *Guardian* lamented the lawlessness of such action: "Sooner or later society will have to grasp the nettle and support the full enforcement of laws which ban secondary picketing—entirely, and make holding the nation to ransom less of a paying proposition." An example of flying pickets was when picketers in vehicles, "like a game of 'cowboys and Indians,'" met tankers on the roads, forcing them to return to the refinery. Some truckers returned without complaint, waving at the pickets and giving them a thumbs up. The flying pickets were successful and, consequently, frustrating for many. In the *Manchester Evening News*, A. B. Volk wrote:

> We are, I suggest, fed-up with the bully-boys, flying pickets and general intimidation of the silent public. Recognizing that the unions did so much good in the past, I now fear that they may do equally as much harm in the future, in the opposite direction.[32]

The slow delivery of food became a serious concern for many. Union leaders such as Bill Astbury, chairman of the Greater Manchester strike committee, hurt the cause of the labor unions with rash statements: "If we can't afford the food why should anyone else have it?"[33] Food for animals was also not getting through the Hull blockades and farmers in the region staged a dramatic event in full view of television cameras. A farmer exited his vehicle on a Hull street to begin a speech, but he dropped the door down of his Land Rover to reveal dead piglets. Calling it a publicity stunt, the union activists argued that starvation did not kill them. Rather, "the mother had laid on them all." The true cause of death did not matter; farmers worried about the shipment of animal feed made a dramatic point.[34]

Another issue with the transporting of goods was how the industrial stoppage prevented the maintenance of roads, many of them frozen and needing an application of grit. People asked unions leaders, "Don't you care about the children not being able to get around?"[35] One letter to the *Manchester Evening News* cautioned people not to get sick since there was no guarantee of safe roads to hospitals. To reach their goals, trade unionists made hard decisions. In Middlesborough, located in northeast England, shop steward Betty Hughes was a member of the Cleveland County Strike Committee that decided which NUPE workers were or were not on strike. Seeking to have the roads worked on one snowy and cold day, the chief executive of Cleveland County attempted to enter the town hall, but Hughes barred his entrance asserting that only the strike committee had the power to grit the roads.[36] Reports indicate that some women found trade union activity especially exciting. A member of the Strike Committee in the town of Darlington (also northeast England), shop steward Anne Gardiner witnessed how the decisions of the committee crippled the business of Darlington. She found her committee involvement enjoyable: "I got really into that. I enjoyed the hassles and the fighting. Then, of course, I think I proved myself, with the men." One older NUPE official said Gardiner went too far with the publicity stunt of threatening to have all the care staff go on strike and leaving older patients to fend for themselves.[37]

III

The media critical of the Labour government received a gift when James Callaghan, normally skilled in handling the press, made a serious error on January 10, 1979, when he returned to England from an international summit on the Caribbean island of Guadeloupe attended by President Jimmy Carter and other world leaders. At Heathrow airport with the temperature at minus 7 Celsius, the sun-tanned Callaghan gave a press conference on Britain's domestic problems, hoping to show his leadership qualities and explain the economic problems in the context of world events. When an *Evening Standard* journalist asked about his response to the ongoing industrial chaos, Callaghan gave the impression that there was no "mounting chaos" in Britain. The next day on the front page, the *Sun* published its report with the title: "Crisis? What crisis?" Other newspapers went with this narrative of an uncaring leader. On its front page, the *Daily Mail* wrote: "THE OSTRICH PRIME MINISTER: He's back from the beaches but his head is still in the sand."[38]

Damage control was difficult since the media was full of stories and photographs of Callaghan enjoying himself in the surf in Barbados. The prime minister fumed over how someone on a boat thousands of yards away was able to photograph him. He expected to let people know that he had done serious work in the Caribbean, keeping abreast of daily events, and planning how best to address Britain's problems. Not heeded was the advice of Bernard Donoughue for Callaghan to return earlier. On January 9, he wrote:

> I think they are mistaken to sit out there in the sun, with photographs of them lazing on beaches surrounded by topless women, while this country is increasingly paralysed. There will be a backlash and it won't help the PM's authority when he comes to tell the unions that they must take a more puritanical line.

The week after Callaghan's return was brutal and Donoughue wrote: "The end of the worst week—worst, politically, that is—since I came to No. 10."[39]

The conservative press watched carefully for any capitulation to the labor unions, but even some within the Labour Party were on guard against Labour surrender. In a January 18 letter to Callaghan, William Rodgers wrote:

> I assume that the Government must stand and fight somewhere and at some time. But in this case the Government is not even in the front line. To suggest to others that they should now give in would be defeatism of a most reprehensible kind. I could not be party to it.[40]

Educated at Oxford and a leader of the Fabian Society, Rodgers entered Parliament in 1962. He moved up the ranks and became the secretary of state for transport in Callaghan's government. He was no radical; his moderate approach was to restrain the worst excesses of capitalism.[41]

The National Day of Action of January 22, 1979, mainly pushed by the NUPE, saw health service workers take strike action. At a Hyde Park rally, Albert Spanswick, general secretary of the Confederation of Health Service Employees, declared: "This is the first time ever that the public service manual unions with the nurses have come together to fight the shame and indignity of low pay." Large demonstrations of public sector workers spread to Glasgow, Manchester, Liverpool, Belfast, and other urban centers.[42] It was frightening for many British citizens and the statement by union leader Bill Dunn made matters worse: "If it means lives are lost, that is how it must be."[43]

January 22 was very cold as 70,000 demonstrators gathered outside the House of Commons to protest low wages. Socialist commentators claimed that the lack of widespread sympathy from the British people for these demonstrations was due to unfavorable media. One study argues that approximately 40 percent of the national press was supportive of the Conservative Party in 1974, but five years later there was a conservative transformation and almost 70 percent of British national daily newspapers were pro-Conservative. An important example was the growing conservative bias of the tabloid *Sun*, with a circulation near 4,000,000, under the ownership of Rupert Murdoch, the forty-seven-year-old Australian-born American tycoon. The Trades Union

Congress (TUC) was critical of the media's portrayal of the trade union movement, notably the dramatic headlines such as one from the *Sun*: "Angry mums rolled up their sleeves and went into action yesterday against hospital strikers threatening the safety of their sick children."[44] Equally powerful was the *Daily Mail* headline: "They won't let us bury our dead." The story referred to the Liverpool strike by gravediggers and crematorium workers, with the former demanding a 46 percent pay raise. Bodies piled up in the city's mortuaries and the *Daily Mail* article explained that family had "to ask the strike committee first" for the possibility of a burial.[45] To the *Liverpool Echo*, Brenda Pratt shared her sad story of losing her mother and being unable to bury her: "All I want is to give my mother a decent funeral she would have wanted. It is heartbreaking to think of her body lying in a coffin with hundreds of others in an old factory."[46]

On February 2, the *Express* published the headline: "SICK, SICK, SICK: After the ill, the bereaved, the elderly—it's the children's turn to suffer hospital chaos." In London, porters and kitchen staff at the Great Ormond Street Hospital for Children were on a temporary strike and there was a one-day strike at the Queen Elizabeth Hospital for Sick Children. While making the case for higher wages, the shop steward at the Great Ormond Street hospital reassured the public that the union kept the striking action brief so as not to cause much disruption: "I must stress we do not want the children to suffer."[47] In his diary, Anthony Benn gave his assessment of the media: "The press is just full of crises, anarchy, chaos, disruption—bitterly hostile to the trade union movement. I have never seen anything like it in my life."[48] Reporting on an inaccurate story of the incident where a lorry driver was the victim of a beating by four picketers, Chris Hitchens wrote: "The *Daily Mail* has long been famous for two things: its bitter and hysterical hatred of the Labour movement and its abysmal failure as a newspaper to get at the truth."[49]

Certainly, the Tories looked stronger and Thatcher's critical assessment of the Labour government garnered significant support. In the House of Commons on January 16, she declared it was imperative for the government to reorient its policies and focus on limiting the money supply and spending and borrowing less to encourage productivity and improve the economy. In the short term, however, more pressing for Thatcher was the Labour support for closed-shop agreements and the crisis of industrial unrest worsened by criminal picketing and control by strikers' committees: "Intimidation and violence are unlawful. I believe that intimidation and violence are happening and are a daily occurrence. If the present law is unenforceable, we must change it so that it becomes enforceable." She found it remarkable that the simple report from British Rail was "There are no trains today," that the Freight Transportation Association confirmed the stoppage of basic food supplies and shortage of diesel fuel, and that the Confederation of British Industry reported the strangling of many industries. Callaghan's response was to stand firm. Despite all the problems, he concluded that Labour's approach on incomes, industrial strategy, and labor unionism were correct: "Is the present setback a reason for going into reverse on all our policies? The answer is 'No.'"[50] Labour was on the defensive and Bernard Donoughue wrote that if Thatcher came to power, it would be "wholly because of the trade unions."[51]

On the following day, with good composure before the television camera, Thatcher gave a broadcast that presented the theme of law and order. Eight minutes long, her speech began outlining the unfortunate state of the nation and how industrial action hurt countless people, notably the sick and disabled. She believed most trade unionists opposed the type of picketing that threatened "to bring the country to its knees—emptying our shops, endangering our farms, closing our factories, taking our jobs." Recognizing the Labour Party's close connection with the unions, she hoped Labour would accept the challenge of trade union reform to "avoid not just disruption but anarchy." She desired that both the Labour Party and the opposition work together for "the national interest." Three areas required immediate attention: amend the law on picketing to eliminate secondary picketing; have secret ballots to make the trade unions more democratic and representative of their members; and prohibit the public services of fire, hospitals, gas, water, and electricity from taking strike action. Thatcher concluded on a diplomatic note:

> If the present crisis has taught us anything it has surely taught us that we have to think of others as well as ourselves; that no-one, however strong his case, is entitled to pursue it by hurting others. There are wreckers among us who don't believe this. But the vast majority of us, and that includes the vast majority of trade unionists, do believe it, whether we call ourselves Labour, Conservative, Liberal—or simply British.[52]

Thatcher presented herself as both tough and non-partisan, an appealing combination.[53] She received over 200 letters from ordinary people commenting on her broadcast. The playwright Ronald Millar, one of her speechwriters, stated that her performance "did more to swing the country behind her than any subsequent speech." According to historian John Shepherd, Thatcher emerged "for the first time like a Prime Minister in waiting."[54]

IV

According to a *Daily Press* opinion poll, the Tories had a 19 percent advantage over Labour in February. However, there were no attempts to defeat the government before the devolution referendum of March 1. When the Scottish votes failed to reach the required 40 percent threshold and the Welsh vote was a clear "no," the government was in a precarious position. It could not count on key non-Labour politicians to keep it in power. In the last week of March, the Tory Party tabled a vote of confidence expecting enough Liberal, Nationalist, and Unionist support to force an election. During the March 28 debate, the House of Commons catering employees were on strike and two Tory whips brought food and alcohol for the vote.[55]

Thatcher's speech avoided any controversial material and presented no new arguments; she claimed that the Labour government failed miserably on its three objectives of overcoming inflation, reducing unemployment, and achieving a high-wage economy. She listed four reasons for Britain's decline: a focus on wealth distribution without an appreciation for wealth creation; a powerful centralized state; irresponsible trade union actions; and Labour abuse of the rule of law. Her analysis was routine conservatism: "There has been a failure not only of policies but of the whole philosophy on which they are based—the philosophy which elevates the State, dwarfs the individual and enlarges the bureaucracy."[56] Callaghan performed better for this crucial debate, yet neither party were confident and it came down to a one-vote defeat for Labour—310 to 311.[57] Not since 1924 had a government lost a confidence motion on the floor of the House. The last possible date for an election was May 3 and Callaghan went with this date hoping there was enough time to bounce back. He saw Thatcher as extreme, and the strategy was to highlight his moderation. He stated that the campaign hinged on how voters perceived her: "If we win, it will be because people cannot take her."[58] Political journalist Hugo Young argues she "was not born to rule," lacking the type of leadership that was natural for Balliol College men Macmillan and Heath; she was an outsider unknowledgeable of the social and political establishment.[59]

The election campaign of 1979 was notable in many ways. First, the last British general election campaign in April was in the nineteenth century. Second, the Easter break occurred in the middle of the campaign, thus a longer than typical period of campaigning. Third, security was higher than in previous campaigns because of the tragic murder of Conservative Airey Neave by Irish terrorists on March 30.[60] Finally, the election's most unique feature was the first woman vying for prime minister of the United Kingdom of Great Britain and Northern Ireland. Thatcher was popular with most women, but did voters believe she was up for the task of dealing with the British economy?[61] Did she make a convincing case against socialism?

Polling favored the Conservative Party when Callaghan announced the election, but in personal ratings Callaghan polled higher than Thatcher who made no effort to woo the BBC that she believed was a leftist organization partly responsible for British decline.[62] Some of her advisers had concerns about her debate performance on television; there was too much risk. Callaghan agreed to participate in a televised leaders' debate, and while Thatcher was keen, her inner circle discouraged her to refuse. Political strategist Gordan Reece even hid the first invitation sent, a move that angered Thatcher. He wanted the election to focus on the winter of discontent rather than "the election to be about the election."[63] On April 3, to Reece's relief, she sent a letter to David Cox of London Weekend Television rejecting a televised debate with Callaghan.[64] As for campaigning, Thatcher decided against it until after Easter (April 13–16) and in the meantime she attended three theatrical plays including the American musical Annie which she enjoyed. After the play, Thatcher went backstage to meet Sheila Hancock, but the socialist actress avoided meeting her by withdrawing to her dressing room.[65]

The Tory Party published the final text of its election manifesto on April 11, an 8,900-word document that went through many drafts. In early February, Thatcher argued for a radical change to the document with a "much more robust union policy." The following month, she told Chris Patten, who oversaw the drafting, to eliminate vague, feeble, or incorrect statements. For example, she disagreed with and crossed out the following sentence: "Our economic weakness has been partly caused by failure to accept that the interests of all classes within the nation are ultimately the same." Especially irritable for her was the consensual tone. How could one be "moderate" on important issues such as liberty and the rule of law? Despite her criticisms, the final version "was not at all rabid in tone."[66] In the wake of crippling union activity the section on trade union reform was conciliatory, pointing to the desirability of management and unions working together peacefully to improve living standards. Voicing traditional Tory points, it was a document that centrist Tories could embrace. In his assessment of the manifesto, James Prior wrote that it was "reassuringly moderate in content and tone."[67]

Of the party's five major tasks, "Restoring the Balance" and "A More Prosperous Country" focused on economics. Here one can see the influence of Keith Joseph. Price controls were a failure and the best approach to master inflation was reducing government borrowing, exercising "proper monetary discipline," and following "publicly stated targets for the rate of growth of the money supply." History demonstrated that when the government spent and borrowed too much, the nation experienced rising taxes, interest rates, prices, and unemployment. Scrapping costly "Socialist programmes," including the nationalization of land, aerospace, and shipbuilding concerns, was an important step in savings. As for taxation, the Tories wanted to cut income taxes more in line with European averages, reformulate capital transfer and capital gains taxes, and reject Labour's plan of a wealth tax, believing instead that "Profits are the foundation of a free enterprise economy."[68]

On a hot day in a conference room without air conditioning, Thatcher was on the platform with six members of her shadow cabinet including conservatives Keith Joseph and Geoffrey Howe and moderate Prior. Much of the press coverage of the manifesto launch was positive, including the BBC summary by David Holmes. Due to a clash with labour unionism, *The Times* was not operating throughout the campaign. Of the other major newspapers, those favoring the Tories were the *Financial Times*, *Daily Express*, the *Sun*, the *Daily Mail*, and the *Daily Telegraph* and the main pro-Labour newspapers were the *Daily Mirror* and *The Guardian*. The weekly magazines had the *New Statesman* supporting Labour and the *Spectator* and the *Economist* siding with the Tories. In its coverage of the manifesto launch, the *Financial Times* wrote of a "confident and relaxed" Thatcher answering questions and predicting "a new era of economic expansion in Britain marked by steady change." The *Sun* noted Thatcher, "brimful of confidence," was ready to lead the Tories to ten years of rule. In his lively account, the *Guardian*'s Michael White offered an interesting description of Thatcher's shadow cabinet: "Sir Keith retained his stiff upper lip, Mr. Whitelaw his limp lower one. Jim Prior's face turned from its usual light Burgundy to the darker hues of claret." Another *Guardian* article pointed to the Tory proposal of "a reduction in state benefits to strikers' families" and it repeated Denis Healey's warning from the Labour press conference: The Tory "manifesto was, in its way, more revolutionary than the Communist manifesto, because it was 'trying to abolish the laws of mathematics.'" They said the Tory numbers and proposals did not add up.[69]

The Labour manifesto titled *The Labour Way is the Better Way* argued that there was too much at stake to allow the Tories to take power and "return to the nineteenth century free market." The last Tory government, with its program of confrontation and social injustice, "brought the country almost to its knees." Once again, the Tory Party with its free-market approach "would mean soaring inflation, rising prices and growing unemployment." The way forward was a partnership of government, unions, and business; the government's role was to create jobs, control prices, and help modernize industry. As a contrast to the Conservatives, Labour would continue an incomes policy. Only the Labour Party could "overcome the evils of inequality" and assist "men and women struggling with low pay, mothers stretching the household budget to make ends meet, youngsters in search of a job, children learning in out-of-date classrooms, patients queuing for a hospital bed or families without a decent home." On policy goals, Labour would work with the TUC and lower inflation to 5 percent by 1982 and set up planning agreements with business to create employment and reach a 3 percent rate of growth. In addition, there would be restrictions on imports, a move to a thirty-five-hour working week, and a wealth tax for "people whose total net personal wealth exceeds £150,000." The Labour Party's economic policies represented prosperity and compassion.[70]

The Labour manifesto did not receive serious attention in the *Sun* newspaper; it was on an inside page and the analysis was trivial. The *Daily Mirror* praised Callaghan for outmaneuvering Labour radicals; the manifesto rejected the nationalization of banking, insurance, and the drug industry. The *Daily Express* viewed the "unhappy compromise" as a formula to hold the Labour Party together rather than providing "a constructive theme for the nation." According to the *Daily Mail*, Labour's "Steady as she goes" message was unappealing. Where did Callaghan take Britain in the past five years? "Nowhere."[71] The only newspaper that reprinted both the Labour and Tory manifestos in full was the *Financial Times*.[72] The *Daily Star* gave less attention to the election than the other papers and it took a neutral position. Its April 25 editorial simplified the dilemma for voters:

> The Tories are good at making money. Labour is good at spending it for the good of the largest number of people. So, if you favour means first you should vote Tory, if you favour ends then vote Labour. There's no alternative.[73]

As Thatcher saw it, the Labour government mostly ignored its manifesto and focused on the dire consequences of Tory policies. It made no sense for Labour to explain the state of the economy of the previous five years. Gone was Callaghan's "image of avuncular *bonhomie*." Labour resorted to negative campaigning, including many scare stories fed to the media and portrayal of Thatcher as a "dangerous right-wing ideologue."[74] One coup for Labour was the *Daily Mirror* publication, on March 30, of an insensitive letter sent by a youthful member of the Conservative Research Department to a British lady concerning her council home. The letter informed the lady she was "lucky to have been given something, which the rest of us are paying for out of our taxes." Thatcher apologized for the "offensive" message, but the Labour Party delivered 3,000,000 copies of the letter to council households across the nation.[75]

V

Thatcher's first day of "serious campaigning" was April 16 in Wales. At her Cardiff rally, she referred to "socialist" or "socialism" eleven times. It was a supposedly "inevitable" system so claimed the experts, but the new order of state control "somehow turns out to be the old order gone sour, in which people come second and the political boss and the party officials come first." The socialist preaching that communal benevolence must replace individual ambition failed to see that industrious job creators benefited society just as much as themselves. She asked: "And aren't the urge to save and to invest powerful engines of wealth creation which work efficiently and silently for every one of us if only we'll let them?" Although she provided no specifics on economic policies, she maintained Britain was long overdue for change:

> In politics, I've learned something you in Wales are born knowing: if you've got a message, preach it. I am a conviction politician. The Old Testament prophets didn't merely say: "Brothers, I want consensus." They said: "This is my faith and vision. This is what I passionately believe. If you believe it too, then come with me."[76]

However, some of her statements lacked conviction. When asked specifically about economic policy, Thatcher was careful not to sound extreme as was the case when BBC's Brian Curtois raised the issue of price controls at a London press conference on April 18. The Price Commission favored by Labour had useful sections, Thatcher claimed, but business competition was more effective in keeping prices down, something most housewives could confirm.[77] Behind some of her concessions to moderation was the increasing pressure from Party Chairman Peter Thorneycroft and others to tone down any Tory branding of conviction politics. When she gave her second major campaign rally, in Birmingham, absent was a strong passage on unions written by former socialist Paul Johnson who she respected. Thorneycroft's intervention was infuriating: "So I angrily tore out the relevant pages of my draft speech and inserted some more innocuous passages." Given the experience of the winter of discontent, she believed a cautious approach was "bad tactics." At an April 22 strategy meeting, she opposed complacency and took the position that energizing voters with non-compromising statements, providing it was a policy direction favored by voters, was crucial for winning elections.[78] However, when pressed two days later in a television interview by Denis Tuohy, Thatcher stated it was irresponsible for a politician to rule out a price freeze: "It is something that any government may have to introduce for a limited time."[79]

Although in the final days of the campaign the gap between the two parties narrowed, Thatcher remained confident. Nonetheless, Thorneycroft wanted her to share a platform with Edward Heath to protect centrist votes, a plan that infuriated her: "If Peter Thorneycroft and Central Office had not yet understood that what we were fighting for was a reversal not just of the Wilson-Callaghan approach but of the Heath Government's approach they had understood nothing." Heath represented the failed path and an invitation for him to deliver a "Party Political" represented a rejection of her policies.[80] In a BBC interview on April 27, Michael Cockerell made the point of Thatcher knowing "that her aggressive brand of Conservatism frightens many of her colleagues."[81]

However, there was nothing radical about her final speeches. Speaking to the Conservative Trade Unionists, she said it was time to bury the myth that all trade unionists were "dogmatic Socialists." There were trade unionists who were Marxists causing much damage, but most rejected socialist doctrine and were "first and foremost members of families, mothers, fathers, sons and daughters who share our values and who want to see once more a healthy Britain." She maintained that many were receptive to a Conservative rebuilding of the economy that encouraged a partnership of unions and management working together to lower inflation, bring greater productivity, and uphold the economic freedom of free enterprise.[82] For decades, Milton Friedman was direct on linking a compromised democracy to the damaging effects of inflation, but Thatcher was subtle when making that connection.[83] In her final press conference on May 2 with Geoffrey Howe, Peter Carrington, and Thorneycroft, she highlighted the theme of change that Britain needed to realize a higher standard of living. Key were economic and individual freedoms:

> We have passionate beliefs in the individual, the family, and the right of individuals to lead more of their own lives and to become a nation of independent individuals rather than the alternative, which is a nation of people constantly more and more dependent on the state for their jobs, for their houses, for the solutions to some of the problems which have been created by the state themselves.[84]

This dependency came at a cost. Greater state control meant higher taxation, and one thing people desired, Geoffrey Howe discovered on the campaign trail, was lower taxes. But as was the case with the whole campaign, discussion on taxation was brief and lacked specifics.[85]

Tory centrists were typically not bullish on Thatcher, but more worrisome was the less-compromising rhetoric of Keith Joseph. The *Guardian* reported that Joseph was keeping out of sight, something Joseph denied.[86] Several weeks earlier at the Bow Group, a conservative think tank, he discussed monetarism that Thatcher said little about. The focus of his talk was on the "union problem" and he clarified the important role of inflation in provoking union militancy. Inflation upset rational economic behavior and, in a climate of anger and mistrust, workers turned to trade union action to gain "the largest possible share of next year's banknotes." Echoing Friedman, Joseph declared that trade unions did not directly cause inflation, but they made it worse. He explained that the roots of inflation were from earlier decades when political parties failed to recognize the value of monetary discipline for economic growth and stability. As for the Labour government, Callaghan and Healey "denounced monetarism while practising it" poorly. It was Joseph's view that their public explanations of monetary targets and their effects were vague. If Labour was serious about squeezing inflation out of the system, it would need to both take ownership of its monetary policy and reduce state spending. This was highly unlikely given the party's acceptance of the belief there was "a war between 'good' socialism and 'bad' capitalism." Joseph was unequivocal; Labour was incapable of curing inflation. Taking a shot at both Labour and Tory economic thinking, he also clarified that twenty years of income policies were a disaster for Britain: "When we look at the evidence, do we really believe that without all these attempts at government controls, we would have done worse?" Furthermore, when socialists ignored the link between productivity and real pay, the expectation of the labor movement improving the standard of living was fanciful.[87] Anyone paying attention could see that socialists skirted the issue of wealth creation.[88] Joseph's deeper presentation of free-market economic ideas offered a clear contrast to the safer political strategy endorsed by centrist Tories. The moderates did not want to discuss monetarism or any hint of the role the Tory Party played with the inflation that burdened the nation.

Intellectually, Thatcher was sympathetic of monetarism, but she understood the political risks. Free-market journalist Patrick Cosgrave wrote in 1978: "She realises that a remarkable and perhaps unprecedented degree of consistent and powerful public support would be necessary to give it a trial in policy."[89] In his December 1978 letter to Ralph Harris, Friedman said that he and his wife enjoyed having dinner with Thatcher and the Harris couple, but he reserved judgement on whether she had "the capacities that Britain so badly" needed.[90] The tension between Thatcher and more moderate Tories was something she had lived with from the first day of her leadership. Biographer John Campbell views her campaign approach as "simultaneously radical and vague." Since 1975 there were two Thatcher voices: "one clear, didactic and evangelical, the other cautious, moderate and conventional." It was a confusing combination of confidence and caution, but the goal was not "getting too far ahead of her party."[91]

Did Thatcher play it correctly? On April 30, the *Daily Mail* published a NOP poll showing Labour with a 0.7 percent lead. This added to the nervousness of Tory insiders, but Thatcher remained confident, and even Callaghan recognized a Labour victory was a long shot. During the campaign he told Bernard Donoughue: "It does not matter what you say or do. There is a shift in what the public wants and what it approves. I suspect there is now a sea-change—and it is for Mrs. Thatcher."[92] Three days before the vote, *The Granada 500* television show presented a forum where all three party leaders, each separately, took questions from an audience in Bolton, a representative town that always voted for the winning party. Although Liberal leader David Steel performed well and answered the questions directly, the expectations for the Liberal Party were modest. During the campaign, Steel adopted the strategy of being photographed in narrow streets to give the impression of large crowds listening to him.[93] Television broadcaster Gordon Burns recalled that Callaghan arrived nervous, muttering "I wish I'd never agreed to do this." It did not go well when he told a nurse questioner that nurses were irresponsible for their complaints about work. Burns wrote: "You don't attack nurses—they are the darlings of the community! And yet he went into them—and it was a big mistake." Thatcher, on the other hand, received much applause for her answers on a variety of topics.[94]

Thatcher was not the right-winger that Labour portrayed. If she did not win the campaign as some claimed, she performed well enough to give her party electoral victory—the results that counted. Conservatives won 339 seats, Labour 269, Liberal Party 11, and 16 for the remaining parties. Tom McNally, a Callaghan adviser who later left the Labour party, blamed the trade union movement for mishandling the events that led to the demise of the Callaghan government. Up to the end of 1978, trade union leaders "had more direct power and influence over government policy than any time in their history, and they blew it in the Winter of Discontent."[95] The episode demonstrated the weakness of Labour's claim of being the only party to be able to negotiate and work successfully with union leaders.

Certainly, the Labour defeat stung. Although Anthony Benn wrote the day before the election that Tory victory was a sure thing, he found it difficult to process the final results: "A dramatic day in British politics. The most right-wing Conservative Government and Leader for fifty years; the first woman Prime Minister. I cannot absorb it all."[96] In his memoirs, Healey wrote of Thatcher:

> Once leader, she proved more like Mao Tse-tung than Jack Cade; she articulated and organised the instincts of the average Tory voter as successfully as Mao those of the Chinese peasantry. Her sayings will no doubt be collected some time in a Little Blue Book, perhaps by those Young Conservatives who share a faith in her Cultural Revolution as fervent as that which inspired Mao's Red Guards.[97]

These were tough words.

If Thatcher's victory has a connection to a revolution, it is the demise of a Keynesian Revolution that dominated British postwar politics. It mattered little that the finer points of economic theory remained mostly in the domain of think tanks. Ordinary British people knew little about Milton Friedman's monetarism or of the economists who pointed to the failure of Keynesianism to cure inflation. However, every day many of them experienced difficult economic times. Whether the source was Keynesianism or socialism, the progressive vision of government intervention resulted in a poor economy. A Labour Gaitstellite while a student at Oxford, political scientist Anthony King of the University of Essex clarified soon after the election why Labour lost:

> The British people deeply resent trade union power, increasingly dislike having to pay for even higher levels of government spending (except for a few of the basic social services) and not least are profoundly suspicious of nationalisation and government intervention in the economy generally.

Unfortunately, these causes were what Labour had stood for over the years.[98] Bernard Donoughue admitted that Keynesian state intervention could not solve economic problems and sometimes made things worse.[99] Former Labour MP Brian Walden, who became an admirer of Thatcher, put more focus on Thatcher and journalism. She was someone who took a different stand while also being careful not to be too different. For journalists to uncover the truth, they needed to ask, "Mrs. Thatcher, do you believe in a more unequal society?"[100] She wanted a higher standard of living for everyone, but she did not think this would happen if the government passed economic policies that attempted to force equality. A socialist message sounded compassionate, but many British voters were ready to send the Labour Party and trade union movement a message.

James Callaghan knew the tide had changed and Margaret Thatcher was ready. With her traditional conservatism stretching back to her childhood years and her receptiveness to new economic ideas that revealed the shortcomings of Keynesianism and socialism, she was confident enough, despite moments of caution, to pull the Tory Party from, in Anthony Benn's words, the "wishy-washy centre of British politics."[101] With genuine commitment she developed a case against socialism, and her rise to prime minister was because many British people were willing to take a chance and strike out in a new direction. As she explained, for voters, including skilled workers normally siding with the Labour Party, "it was a severely practical matter of choosing whether to rely on the comforting security of state provision or to make the sacrifices required to win a better life for themselves and their families."[102] Given the economic conditions of the previous five years, more voters went with the Conservative Party and a woman who had great faith in a market economy.

NOTES

1. Quoted in Tara Martin Lopez, *The Winter of Discontent: Myth, Memory, and History* (Liverpool: Liverpool University Press, 2014), 9.
2. Nelson, "Milton Friedman and U.K. Economic Policy," 493.
3. Quoted in Lopez, *The Winter of Discontent*, 20, 105.
4. Tara Martin, "The Beginning of Labor's End? Britain's 'Winter of Discontent' and Working-Class Women's Activism," *International Labor and Working-Class History*, no. 75 (2009), 50.
5. Cannadine, *Margaret Thatcher*, 25.

6. Quoted in Martin, "The Beginning of Labor's End?," 53.

7. Quoted in Martin, "The Beginning of Labor's End?," 56.

8. "Professor Milton Friedman Prescribes a Medicine for Britain," *The Listener*, 18 November 1976, 632–33, https://miltonfriedman.hoover.org/internal/media/dispatcher/215117/full.

9. "Professor Milton Friedman Prescribes a Medicine for Britain," 632–33.

10. See, Martin, "The Beginning of Labor's End?," 56. Shepherd, *Crisis. What Crisis?*, 59n2.

11. Shepherd, *Crisis. What Crisis?*, 31. Also, See Benn, *Conflicts of Interest*, 352–59.

12. Moore, *Margaret Thatcher*, 394.

13. Donoughue, *Downing Street Diary*, 391.

14. Lopez, *The Winter of Discontent*, 65–66.

15. Lopez, *The Winter of Discontent*, 72. Shepherd, *Crisis. What Crisis?*, 50.

16. Shepherd, *Crisis. What Crisis?*, 38, 40–41. Lopez, *The Winter of Discontent*, 76.

17. Lopez, *The Winter of Discontent*, 77–78.

18. Lopez, *The Winter of Discontent*, 80–81.

19. Callaghan, *Time and Chance*, 534.

20. MTF, Hansard HC [959/209-16], 28 November 1978, https://www.margaretthatcher.org/document/103788.

21. MTF, Hansard HC [960/932-42], 14 December 1978, https://www.margaretthatcher.org/document/103801.

22. Hansard HC [960/932-42], 14 December 1978.

23. Donoughue, *Down Street Diary*, 402.

24. Shepherd, *Crisis? What Crisis?*, 142.

25. Lopez, *The Winter of Discontent*, 116.

26. Shepherd, *Crisis. What Crisis?*, 75. The newspaper report was from January 8, 1979, and the author of the statement was Moss Evans, a General Secretary of the TGWU.

27. Shepherd, *Crisis. What Crisis?*, 83.

28. Wapshott and Brock, *Thatcher*, 167.

29. Campbell, *Margaret Thatcher*, 414.

30. Campbell, *Margaret Thatcher*, 420. Lopez, *The Winter of Discontent*, 86–87.

31. Quoted in Lopez, *The Winter of Discontent*, 94.

32. Quoted in Lopez, *The Winter of Discontent*, 95, 104.

33. Shepherd, *Crisis? What Crisis?*, 120.

34. Lopez, *The Winter of Discontent*, 106.

35. Shepherd, *Crisis? What Crisis?*, 119.

36. Lopez, *The Winter of Discontent*, 7. Martin, "The Beginning of Labor's End?," 57.

37. Martin, "The Beginning of Labor's End?," 58.

38. Shepherd, *Crisis? What Crisis?*, 126–28.

39. Donoughue, *Downing Street Diary*, 418, 427. On Callaghan's reaction to the photographs, see Shepherd, *Crisis? What Crisis?*, 128.

40. Lopez, *The Winter of Discontent*, 102.
41. Lopez, *The Winter of Discontent*, 89.
42. Shepherd, *Crisis? What Crisis?*, 82.
43. Quoted in Lopez, *The Winter of Discontent*, 170.
44. Shepherd, *Crisis? What Crisis?*, 108, 111, 114.
45. Shepherd, *Crisis? What Crisis?*, 118.
46. Lopez, *The Winter of Discontent*, 124.
47. Shepherd, *Crisis? What Crisis?*, 122.
48. Benn, *Conflict of Interests*, 433.
49. Christopher Hitchens, "The *Daily Mail* does it again," *New Statesman,* 2 February 1979, 136.
50. MTF, Hansard HC [960/1524-61], 16 January 1979, https://www.margaretthatcher.org/document/103924.
51. Donoughue, *Downing Street Diary*, 424.
52. MTF, Conservative Party Political Broadcast, Thatcher Archive: CCOPR 71/79, 17 January 1979, https://www.margaretthatcher.org/document/10392.
53. Moore, *Margaret Thatcher*, 399.
54. Shepherd, *Crisis? What Crisis?*, 81, 131–32.
55. Moore, *Margaret Thatcher*, 400–1.
56. MTF, HC S [Her Majesty's Government (Opposition Motion) (motion of confidence)], 28 March 1979, https://www.margaretthatcher.org/document/103983.
57. Moore, *Margaret Thatcher*, 400–1.
58. Moore, *Margaret Thatcher*, 402. Donoughue, *Downing Street Diary*, 480, 485, 490.
59. Young, *One of Us*, 137–38.
60. Butler and Kavanagh, *The British General Election of 1979*, 164.
61. Wapshott and Brock, *Thatcher*, 169.
62. Campbell, *Margaret Thatcher*, 408.
63. Moore, *Margaret Thatcher*, 402–3.
64. MTF, MT letter to David Cox, 3 April 1979, https://www.margaretthatcher.org/document/112289.
65. Campbell, *Margaret Thatcher*, 428.
66. Moore, *Margaret Thatcher*, 403–4.
67. Prior, *A Balance of Power*, 112.
68. MTF, Conservative General Election Manifesto 1979, 11 April 1979, https://www.margaretthatcher.org/document/110858.
69. MTF, General Election Press Conference (manifesto launch), 11 April 1979, https://www.margaretthatcher.org/document/104000.
70. Labour Party Manifesto, http://www.labour-party.org.uk/manifestos/1979/1979-labour-manifesto.shtml.
71. Butler and Kavanagh, *The British General Election of 1979*, 240.
72. Butler and Kavanagh, *The British General Election of 1979*, 245.
73. Quoted in Butler and Kavanagh, *The British General Election of 1979*, 239.
74. Thatcher, *Margaret Thatcher*, 243.
75. Moore, *Margaret Thatcher*, 406–7.

76. MTF, Speech to Conservative Rally in Cardiff, 16 April 1979, https://www.margaretthatcher.org/document/104011.

77. MTF, General Election Press Conference, 18 April 1979, https://www.margaretthatcher.org/document/104017.

78. Thatcher, *Margaret Thatcher*, 248–49.

79. MTF, Interview for Thames TV *TV Eye*, 24 April 1979, https://www.margaretthatcher.org/document/104040.

80. Thatcher, *Margaret Thatcher*, 250. Also, Moore, *Margaret Thatcher*, 412.

81. MTF, TV Interview for BBC *Campaign '79*, 27 April 1979, https://www.margaretthatcher.org/document/103864.

82. MTF, Speech to Conservative Trade Unionists, 29 April 1979, https://www.margaretthatcher.org/document/104053.

83. On Friedman, see Nelson, "Milton Friedman and U.K. Economic Policy," 492.

84. MTF, General Election Press Conference, 2 May 1979, https://www.margaretthatcher.org/document/104069.

85. General Election Press Conference, 2 May 1979.

86. Denham and Garnett, *Keith Joseph*, 324.

87. MTF, Keith Joseph talk given to the Bow Group, 5 February 1979, https://www.margaretthatcher.org/document/118814.

88. Socialists' lack of interest in discussing wealth creation was no surprise. For Joseph, the entrepreneur was the key to wealth creation. See Denham and Garnett, *Keith Joseph*, 78.

89. Quoted in Campbell, *Margaret Thatcher*, 366.

90. MTF, Milton Friedman letter to Ralph Harris, 4 December 1978, https://www.margaretthatcher.org/document/117139.

91. Campbell, *Margaret Thatcher*, 364, 369.

92. Moore, *Margaret Thatcher*, 413.

93. Butler and Kavanagh, *The British General Election of 1979*, 172.

94. "Gordon Burns recalls the innovative Granada 500 programme at the time of the 1979 General Election," 30 March 2015, https://www.granadaland.org/gordon-burns-recalls-the-innovative-granada-500-programme-at-the-time-of-the-1979-general-election-2/. MTF, TV Interview for Granada *Bolton 500*, 30 April 1979, https://www.margaretthatcher.org/document/103812.

95. Martin, "The Beginning of Labor's End?," 51.

96. Tony Benn, *Conflict of Interests*, 492, 494.

97. Healey, *The Time of My Life*, 488.

98. Shepherd, *Crisis? What Crisis?,* 162.

99. Donoughue, *Downing Street Diary*, 7.

100. Moore, *Margaret Thatcher*, 415.

101. Tony Benn, *Conflict of Interests*, 505.

102. Thatcher, *Margaret Thatcher*, 254.

Bibliography

Aiken, Jonathan. *Margaret Thatcher: Power and Personality*. London: Bloomsbury, 2013.

Bebbington, David W. *Evangelicalism in Modern Britain: A History from the 1730s to the 1980s*. London: Routledge, 1993.

Benn, Tony. *Against the Tide: Diaries 1973–76*. London: Hutchinson, 1989.

———. *Conflicts of Interest: Diaries 1977–80*. London: Hutchinson, 1990.

Blackaby, F.T., ed. *British Economic Policy, 1960–74*. London: Cambridge University Press, 1978.

Blake, Robert. *The Conservative Party from Peel to Thatcher*. London: Methuen, 1985.

Bose, Mihir. "Britain's Libel Laws: Malice Aforethought." *History Today* 63, no. 5 (May 2013).

Brittan, Samuel. *The Economic Consequences of Democracy*. London: Temple Smith, 1977.

Burk, Kathleen and Alec Cairncross. *Goodbye, Great Britain: The 1976 IMF Crisis*. New Haven, CT: Yale University Press, 1992.

Butler, David and Dennis Kavanagh. *The British General Election of 1979*. London: The Macmillan Press Ltd., 1980.

Caldwell, Bruce, ed. *The Collected Works of F.A. Hayek Volume II, The Road to Serfdom Text and Documents: The Definitive Edition*. Chicago: The University of Chicago Press, 2007.

Callaghan, James. *Time and Chance*. London: Collins, 1987.

Campbell, John. *Margaret Thatcher, vol. 1: The Grocer's Daughter*. London: Jonathan Cape, 2000.

Cannadine, David. *Margaret Thatcher: A Life and Legacy*. Oxford University Press, 2017.

Crines, Andrew Scott and Kevin Hickson, eds. *Harold Wilson: The Unprincipled Prime Minister?* London: Biteback Publishing, 2016.

Crosland, Anthony. *The Future of Socialism*. London: Constable, 2006.

Crotty, James. *Keynes Against Capitalism: His Economic Case for Liberal Socialism*. London: Routledge, 2019.

Davies, Liz. "Tony Benn: Liz Davies Pays Tribute to One of the Giants of the Labour Movement, Who Died in March 2014." *Socialist Lawyer*, no. 67 (2014).

Denham, Andrew and Mark Garnett. *Keith Joseph*. Chesham Bucks: Acumen, 2001.

Diamond, Patrick. *The Crosland Legacy: The Future of British Social Democracy*. Bristol: Bristol University Press, 2016.

Domitrovic, Brian. *Econoclasts: The Rebels Who Sparked the Supply-Side Revolution and Restored American Prosperity*. Wilmington, DE: ISI Books, 2009.

Donoughue, Bernard. *Downing Street Diary, Volume Two*. London: Jonathan Cape, 2008.

Economic Strategy – IMF, 29 November 1976, http://filestore.nationalarchives.gov.uk/pdfs/small/cab-129-193-cp-76-118-8.pdf.

Ellison, Nick. "The Conservative Party and Public Expenditure." In *The Conservative Party and Social Policy*, edited by Hugh Bochel. Bristol, UK: Bristol University Press, 2011: 41–60.

Evans, Richard J. *The Third Reich in Power*. New York: Penguin Books, 2005.

Friedman, Milton. "Has the Economic Tide Turned?," Glasgow: Strathclyde Business School, University of Strathclyde, 1978, https://miltonfriedman.hoover.org/objects/57654/has-the-economic-tide-turned.

———. "Is Inflation a Curable Disease?" Pittsburgh: Pittsburgh National Bank, Alex C. Walker Educational and Charitable Foundation, and the University of Pittsburgh Graduate School of Business, 1974. Alex C. Walker Memorial Lecture, 5 December 1974, https://miltonfriedman.hoover.org/internal/media/dispatcher/271086/full.

———. https://miltonfriedman.hoover.org/friedman_images/Collections/2016c21/IEA_1970.pdf.

Gamble, Andrew. *Britain in Decline: Economic Policy, Political Strategy and the British State*. London: The Macmillan Press Limited, 1981.

———. *The Free Economy and the Strong State: The Politics of Thatcherism*, Second Edition. London: The Macmillan Press Ltd., 1994.

Garnett, Mark. "Banality in Politics: Margaret Thatcher and the Biographers." *Political Studies Review* 5 (2007).

Goodlad, Graham. *Thatcher*. London: Routledge, 2016.

Goodman, Geoffrey. *From Bevan to Blair: Fifty Years Reporting from the Political Front Line*. London: Pluto Press, 2003.

"Gordon Burns Recalls the Innovative Granada 500 Programme at the Time of the 1979 General Election," 30 March 2015, https://www.granadaland.org/gordon-burns-recalls-the-innovative-granada-500-programme-at-the-time-of-the-1979-general-election-2/.

Grant, Wyn. "Economic Policy." In *James Callaghan: An Underrated Prime* Minister, edited by Kevin Hickson and Jasper Miles. London: Biteback Publishing, 2020.

Green, E. H. H. "Thatcherism: An Historical Perspective." *Transactions of the Royal Historical Society* 9 (1999): 17–42.

Greenspan, Alan. *The Age of Turbulence: Adventures in a New World.* New York: The Penguin Press, 2007.

Halcrow, Morrison. *Keith Joseph: A Single Mind.* London: Macmillan, 1989.

Hansard, Attack on Inflation, 11 July 1975, https://api.parliament.uk/historic-hansard/commons/1975/jul/11/attack-on-inflation#S5CV0895P0_19750711_HOC_20.

———. "Budget Resolutions and Economic Situation," Vol. 881, 14 November 1974, https://hansard.parliament.uk/Commons/1974-11-14/debates/7b2e7262-d47a-4e9b-bb97-6930de16b9f5/BudgetResolutionsAndEconomicSituation.

———. "Domestic Inflation," Vol 894 cc1189-200, 1 July 1975, https://api.parliament.uk/historic-hansard/commons/1975/jul/01/domestic-inflation#S5CV0894P0_19750701_HOC_172.

———. "Domestic Monetary Effects," 15 December 1976, https://api.parliament.uk/historic-hansard/commons/1976/dec/15/domestic-monetary-effects.

———. "Economic Prospects," 15 December 1976, https://api.parliament.uk/historic-hansard/commons/1976/dec/15/economic-prospects.

———. HC, 13 March 1962, Volume 655, columns 1161 and 1281, https://hansard.parliament.uk/Commons/1962-03-13/debates/0b7f180e-7ca5-48df-af80-b70ad6d7e82c/NationalInsuranceAndNationalAssistanceBenefits.

———. HC Deb 29 April 1974 vol 872 cc787-906, https://api.parliament.uk/historic-hansard/commons/1974/apr/29/london.

———. HC Deb 22 May 1975 vol 892 cc1637-768, https://api.parliament.uk/historic-hansard/commons/1975/may/22/the-economy.

———. Incomes Policy, 15 December 1976, https://api.parliament.uk/historic-hansard/commons/1976/dec/15/incomes-policy.

———. Inflation, 24 March 1977, https://api.parliament.uk/historic-hansard/written answers/1977/mar/24/inflation#S5CV0928P0_19770324_CWA_205.

———. 1803-2005 – People (B), Mr Nigel Birch, Economic Situation, HC Deb, 26 July 1961 vol 645 cc558-560, https://api.parliament.uk/historic-hansard/commons/1961/jul/26/economic-situation#S5CV0645P0_19610726_HOC_263.

———. Orders of the Day, Vol. 881, 14 November 1974, https://hansard.parliament.uk/Commons/1974-11-14/debates/4dde9703-2139-4911-8ed9-536c9fdff719/OrdersOfTheDay.

———. Ways and Means, column 282, 15 April 1975, https://hansard.parliament.uk/Commons/1975-04-15/debates/05a66797-c0a7-46f4-be2c-fe7885c2935c/WaysAndMeans.

Harris, Robin. *Not For Turning: The Life of Margaret Thatcher.* New York: St. Martin's Press, 2013.

Haseler, Stephen. *The Grand Delusion: Britain After Sixty Years of Elizabeth II.* London: I.B. Taurus, 2012.

Hayek, F.A. *A Tiger by the Tail: The Keynesian Legacy of Inflation.* San Francisco: Cato Institute, 1979.

Healey, Denis. *The Time of My Life.* London: Michael Joseph, 1989.

Healey's Finance Speech at Labour Party Conference, 30 September 1976, http://www.aparchive.com/metadata/youtube/6b4343969f4513ed15a0ac1c393ad851.

Heath, Edward. *The Course of My Life: My Autobiography*. London: Hodder & Stoughton, 1998.

Jenkins, Peter. *Mrs Thatcher's Revolution: The End of the Socialist Era*. London: Jonathan Cape Ltd, 1987.

Jobson, Richard. *Nostalgia and the Post-war Labour Party: Prisoners of the Past*. Manchester: Manchester University Press, 2018.

John Mendelsohn, M. P., http://discovery.nationalarchives.gov.uk/details/r/7a34baf9-b936-4e8f-bdc4-0a7304d494b5.

Johnson, Paul. *Modern Times: The World from the Twenties to the Nineties*. New York: Harper Perennial, 2001.

Jones, Daniel Stedman. *Masters of the Universe: Hayek, Friedman, and the Birth of Neoliberal Politics*. Princeton University Press, 2012.

Keegan, William. *Mrs Thatcher's Economic Experiment*. London: Allen Lane, 1984.

Keynes, John Maynard. *The General Theory of Employment, Interest, and Money*. New York: Harcourt, 1963.

Kynaston, David. *Austerity Britain, 1945-51*. New York: Walker and Company, 2008.

Leader's speech, Blackpool 1976 http://www.britishpoliticalspeech.org/speech-archive.htm?speech=174.

Letwin, Shirley. *The Anatomy of Thatcherism*. London: Fontana, 1992.

Lopez, Tara Martin. *The Winter of Discontent: Myth, Memory, and History*. Liverpool: Liverpool University Press, 2014.

Magee, Brian. "Tony Crosland as I Knew Him." *Political Quarterly* 81, no. 2 (April 2020).

Margaret Thatcher Foundation (MTF), Adam Ridley note for Keith Joseph, 26 June 1978, https://www.margaretthatcher.org/document/109763.

———. Adam Ridley paper, 30 June 1978, https://www.margaretthatcher.org/document/109764.

———. Adam Ridley paper for pay meeting, 16 March 1978, https://www.margaretthatcher.org/document/109759.

———. Article for *Young Kent Forum*, 1 October 1949. https://www.margaretthatcher.org/document/109511.

———. Budget Resolutions and Economic Situation, 11 April 1978, https://www.margaretthatcher.org/document/103653.

———. Centre for Policy Studies Management Committee Minutes, 20 June 1978, https://www.margaretthatcher.org/document/111956.

———. Conservative General Election Manifesto 1979, 11 April 1979, https://www.margaretthatcher.org/document/110858.

———. Conservative Political Centre Lecture ("What's wrong with politics?"), 11 October 1968, https://www.margaretthatcher.org/document/101632.

———. Conservative Party Political Broadcast, Thatcher Archive: CCOPR 71/79, 17 January 1979, https://www.margaretthatcher.org/document/10392.

———. Counter-Inflation Policy, 20 July 1977, https://www.margaretthatcher.org/document/103421.

———. Economic Reconstruction Group – Minutes of Meeting 16, 10 June 1976, https://www.margaretthatcher.org/document/110235.
———. Economic Reconstruction Group—Minutes of Meeting 18, 24 June 1976, https://www.margaretthatcher.org/document/110237.
———. The Economy, 25 July 1978, https://www.margaretthatcher.org/document/103736.
———. Economy: Adam Ridley note for MT, 5 March 1975, https://www.margaretthatcher.org/document/109954.
———. Economy: Fentiman Road Seminar, 18 May 1975, https://www.margaretthatcher.org/document/109968.
———. Economy: "Stepping Stones," 14 November 1977, https://www.margaretthatcher.org/document/111771.
———. General Election Press Conference, 18 April 1979, https://www.margaretthatcher.org/document/104017.
———. General Election Press Conference, 2 May 1979, https://www.margaretthatcher.org/document/104069.
———. General Election Press Conference (manifesto launch), 11 April 1979, https://www.margaretthatcher.org/document/104000.
———. Geoffrey Howe paper, 1 August 1976, https://www.margaretthatcher.org/document/110078.
———. Geoffrey Howe to MT, 30 July 1976, https://www.margaretthatcher.org/document/110076.
———. Geoffrey Howe to Sir Keith Joseph, 22 March 1976, https://www.margaretthatcher.org/document/110039.
———. Geoffrey Howe to Sir Keith Joseph, 2 July 1976, https://www.margaretthatcher.org/document/110067.
———. *Gravesend and Dartford Reporter*, 28 January 1950, https://www.margaretthatcher.org/document/100856.
———. Hailsham diary, 9 March 1977, https://www.margaretthatcher.org/document/111176.
———. Hailsham diary (Shadow Cabinet squabbles over Keith Joseph paper), 11 April 1975, https://www.margaretthatcher.org/document/111134.
———. Hansard, House of Commons PQs, 14 March 1978, https://www.margaretthatcher.org/document/103642.
———. Hansard HC [959/209-16], 28 November 1978, https://www.margaretthatcher.org/document/103788.
———. Hansard HC [960/932-42], 14 December 1978, https://www.margaretthatcher.org/document/103801.
———. Hansard HC [960/1524-61], 16 January 1979, https://www.margaretthatcher.org/document/103924.
———. Hayek to Sir Keith Joseph (talks for BBC), 23 March 1977, https://www.margaretthatcher.org/document/114625.
———. HC PQ, 6 November 1967, https://www.margaretthatcher.org/document/101590.

———. HC I, 29 January 1976, https://www.margaretthatcher.org/document/102946.

———. HC S [Budget Resolutions and Economic Situation], 17 April 1967, https://www.margaretthatcher.org/document/101551.

———. HC S [Her Majesty's Government (Opposition Motion) (motion of confidence)], 28 March 1979, https://www.margaretthatcher.org/document/103983.

———. HC S 2R [Coal Industry Bill], 28 November 1967, https://www.margaretthatcher.org/document/101594.

———. House of Commons PQs, 27 April 1978, https://www.margaretthatcher.org/document/103665.

———. Interview for *Hornsey Journal*, 21 April 1978, https://www.margaretthatcher.org/document/103662.

———. Interview for Thames TV *TV Eye*, 24 April 1979, https://www.margaretthatcher.org/document/104040.

———. John Hoskyns Letter to Sherman, 24 February 1976, https://www.margaretthatcher.org/document/111926.

———. Keith Joseph Memorandum to Chris Patten, 7 January 1976, https://www.margaretthatcher.org/document/111971.

———. Keith Joseph, Speech at Preston ("Inflation is Caused by Government"), 5 September 1974, https://www.margaretthatcher.org/document/110607.

———. Keith Joseph, Speech at Upminster ("This is Not the Time to be Mealy-Mouthed: Intervention is Destroying Us"), 22 June 1974, https://www.margaretthatcher.org/document/110604.

———. Keith Joseph Talk Given to the Bow Group, 5 February 1979, https://www.margaretthatcher.org/document/118814.

———. Keith Joseph to Geoffrey Howe, 19 July 1976, https://www.margaretthatcher.org/document/111232.

———. Keith Joseph to Various Colleagues, 4 May 1976, https://www.margaretthatcher.org/document/111230.

———. Keith Joseph to Willie Whitelaw, 17 March 1976, https://www.margaretthatcher.org/document/111226.

———. Labour Party Manifesto, http://www.labour-party.org.uk/manifestos/1979/1979-labour-manifesto.shtml.

———. Milton Friedman letter to Ralph Harris, 4 December 1978, https://www.margaretthatcher.org/document/117139.

———. MT Letter to David Cox, 3 April 1979, https://www.margaretthatcher.org/document/112289.

———. Norman Strauss Notes, 3 August 1976, https://www.margaretthatcher.org/document/220210.

———. Press Conference after Meeting President Ford, 18 September 1975, https://www.margaretthatcher.org/document/102464.

———. Press Conference after Winning Conservative Leadership (Conservative Central Office), 11 February 1974, https://www.margaretthatcher.org/document/102487.

———. Report of Conservative Backbench Finance Committee Meeting, 11 April 1978, https://www.margaretthatcher.org/document/109762.

———. *The Right Approach,* 4 October 1976, https://www.margaretthatcher.org/document/109439.

———. *The Right Approach to the Economy*, 8 October 1977, https://www.margaretthatcher.org/document/112551.

———. Scarman Report, 26 August 1977, https://www.margaretthatcher.org/document/111943.

———. Sherman Memorandum to CPS Management Board, 20 July 1978, https://www.margaretthatcher.org/document/111999.

———. Sherman Memorandum to Keith Joseph, 17 February 1976, https://www.margaretthatcher.org/document/111925.

———. Sir Geoffrey Howe speech in Kirtlington, 2 June 1978, https://www.margaretthatcher.org/document/109798.

———. Sir Geoffrey Howe Statement, 8 June 1978, https://www.margaretthatcher.org/document/109799.

———. Sir Keith Joseph to Hayek (talks for BBC), 1 February 1977, https://www.margaretthatcher.org/document/114623.

———. Sir Keith Joseph to MT, 25 February 1975, https://www.margaretthatcher.org/document/111215.

———. Sir Keith Joseph to Thorneycroft, 29 August 1978, https://www.margaretthatcher.org/document/111865.

———. Speech to British American Chamber of Commerce, 8 September 1977, https://www.margaretthatcher.org/document/103436.

———. Speech to Conservative Rally in Cardiff, 16 April 1979, https://www.margaretthatcher.org/document/104011.

———. Speech at Hove Town Hall, 1 September 1977, https://www.margaretthatcher.org/document/111945.

———. Speech at Kensington Town Hall, 19 January 1976, https://www.margaretthatcher.org/document/102939.

———. Speech at Roosevelt University, 22 September 1975, https://www.margaretthatcher.org/document/102465.

———. Speech in Chelmsford, 20 June 1977, https://www.margaretthatcher.org/document/111257.

———. Speech in Finchley (Conservative Leadership Election), 31 January 1975, https://www.margaretthatcher.org/document/102605.

———. Speech to Chelsea Conservative Association, 26 July 1975, https://www.margaretthatcher.org/document/102750.

———. Speech to Conservative Party Conference (1966), 12 October 1966, https://www.margaretthatcher.org/document/101520.

———. Speech to Conservative Party Conference (1967), 20 October 1967, https://www.margaretthatcher.org/document/101586.

———. Speech to Conservative Party Conference, 10 October 1975, https://www.margaretthatcher.org/document/102777.

———. Speech to Conservative Party Conference, 14 October 1977, https://www.margaretthatcher.org/document/103443.

———. Speech to Conservative Party Conference, 13 October 1978, https://www.margaretthatcher.org/document/103764.

———. Speech to Conservative Trade Unionists, 29 April 1979, https://www.margaretthatcher.org/document/104053.

———. Speech to Conservative Women's Conference, https://www.margaretthatcher.org/document/102694.

———. Speech to Finchley Conservatives, 19 March 1962, https://www.margaretthatcher.org/document/100958.

———. Speech to Finchley Conservatives, 1 October 1975, https://www.margaretthatcher.org/document/102774.

———. Speech to Institute of Bankers, 19 January 1977, https://www.margaretthatcher.org/document/103303.

———. Speech to Overseas Bankers, 7 February 1978, https://www.margaretthatcher.org/document/103609.

———. Speech to the Institute of Socio Economic Studies ("Let Our Children Grow Tall"), 15 September 1975, https://www.margaretthatcher.org/document/102769.

———. Speech to the National Press Club, 19 September 1975, https://www.margaretthatcher.org/document/102770.

———. Speech to Southampton Conservatives, 11 February 1977, https://www.margaretthatcher.org/document/103315.

———. Speech to Westminster Conservatives, 22 June 1977, https://www.margaretthatcher.org/document/103400.

———. Speech to Zurich Economic Society, 14 March 1977, https://www.margaretthatcher.org/document/103336.

———. "Stand by to Repel Coalition—Press-gangs," 1 June 1978, https://www.margaretthatcher.org/document/111993.

———. Stockton Lecture, 5 April 1976, https://www.margaretthatcher.org/document/110796.

———. TV Interview for BBC *Campaign '79*, 27 April 1979, https://www.margaretthatcher.org/document/103864.

———. TV Interview for Granada *Bolton 500*, 30 April 1979, https://www.margaretthatcher.org/document/103812.

———. TV Interview for NBC *Today,* 16 September 1975, https://www.margaretthatcher.org/document/102565.

Martin, Tara. "The Beginning of Labor's End? Britain's 'Winter of Discontent' and Working-Class Women's Activism." *International Labor and Working-Class History*, no. 75 (2009).

Middleton, Roger. "Brittan on Britain: 'The Economic Contradictions of Democracy' Redux." *The Historical Journal* 54, no. 4 (2011).

Middleton, Stuart. "'Affluence' and the Left in Britain, C. 1958–1974." *The English Historical Review* 129, no. 536 (2014).

Moon, David S. "The Oratory of Barbara Castle." In *Labour Orators from Bevan to Miliband*, edited by Andrew S. Crines and Richard Hayton. Manchester; New York: Manchester University Press, 2014.

Moore, Charles. *Margaret Thatcher: The Authorized Biography: Volume One*. London: Penguin Books, 2014.

Morgan, Kenneth O. *Callaghan: A Life*. Oxford: Oxford University Press, 1997.

Nasar, Sylvia. *Grand Pursuit: The Story of Economic Genius*. New York: Simon & Schuster, 2011.

Nelson, Edward. "Milton Friedman and U.K. Economic Policy: 1938-1979." *Federal Reserve Bank of St. Louis Review* 91 (5, Part 2) (September/October 2009): 465–506.

1951 Conservative Party General Election Manifesto, http://www.conservativemanifesto.com/1951/1951-conservative-manifesto.shtml.

Norton, Philip. "The Oratory of Enoch Powell." In *Conservative Orators: From Baldwin to Cameron*, edited by Hayton Richard and Crines, Andrew S. Manchester: Manchester University Press, 2015.

O'Hara, Glen. "'This Is What Growth Does': British Views of the European Economies in the Prosperous 'Golden Age' of 1951-73." *Journal of Contemporary History* 44, no. 4 (2009): 697–718.

Oliver, Michael J. "The Two Sterling Crises of 1964: A Comment on Newton." *The Economic History Review* 65, no. 1 (2012): 314–321.

Page, Robert M. "The Conservative Party and the Welfare State since 1945." In *The Conservative Party and Social Policy*, edited by Hugh Bochel. Bristol, UK: Bristol University Press, 2011: 23–40.

Pemberton, Hugh. "Relative Decline and British Economic Policy in the 1960s." *The Historical Journal* 47, no. 4 (2004): 989–1013.

Pressman, Steven. *Fifty Major Economists*, Third Edition. London: Routledge, 2014.

Prior, Jim. *A Balance of Power*. London: Hamish Hamilton, 1986.

"Professor Milton Friedman Prescribes a Medicine for Britain," *The Listener*, 18 November 1976, 632–633, https://miltonfriedman.hoover.org/internal/media/dispatcher/215117/full.

Ramsden, John. "'A Party for Owners or a Party for Earners?' How Far Did the British Conservative Party Really Change after 1945?" *Transactions of the Royal Historical Society* 37 (1987).

Reagan, Ronald. *An American Life: The Autobiography*. New York: Simon & Schuster, 1990.

Regan, David. "The Local Left and Its National Pretensions." In the *Policies of Thatcherism: Thoughts from a London Thinktank*, edited by Richard Haas and Oliver Knox. Lanham: MD: University Press of America, 1991.

Robbins, Lionel. *An Essay on the Nature & Significance of Economic Science* (1932), https://milescorak.files.wordpress.com/2020/02/robbins-essay-nature-significance-economic-science.pdf.

Sandbrooke, Dominic. "'Enoch Powell Speaks for Britain': The Press, the Public and the Speech." *The Political Quarterly* 89, no. 3 (July–September 2018).

Saville, John. "Hugh Gaitskell (1906-1963): An Assessment." *Socialist Register* 17 (1980): 148–169.

Schivelbusch, Wolfgang. *Three New Deals: Reflections on Roosevelt's America, Mussolini's Italy and Hitler's Germany, 1933-1939.* New York: Picador, 2006.

Scott, Peter M. and James T. Walker. "'Stop-go' Policy and the Restriction of Postwar British House-building." *Economic History Review* 72, no. 2 (2019): 716–737.

Shepherd, John. *Crisis? What Crisis?: The Callaghan Government and the British 'Winter of Discontent.'* Manchester: Manchester University Press, 2013.

Shirer, William. *The Rise and Fall of the Third Reich.* New York: Simon & Schuster, 2011.

Skousen, Mark. *Vienna & Chicago: Friends or Foes?—A Tale of Two Schools of Free-Market Economics.* Washington, DC: Regnery Publishing, Inc., 2005.

Sowell, Thomas. *Basic Economics: A Common Sense Guide to the Economy, Fifth Edition.* New York: Basic Books, 2016.

Swartz, Bill. "The Thatcher Years." *Socialist Register 1987: Conservatism in Britain and America. Rhetoric and Reality*, Vol. 23 (March 1987).

Tebbit, Norman. *Upwardly Mobile.* London: Futura, 1989.

Thatcher, Margaret. *Margaret Thatcher: The Autobiography.* New York: HarperPerennial, 2010.

Tomlinson, Jim. "British Government and Popular Understanding of Inflation in the Mid-1970s." *The Economic History Review* 67, no. 3 (2014): 750–768.

———. "The Iron Quadrilateral: Political Obstacles to Economic Reform under the Attlee Government." *Journal of British Studies* 34, no. 1 (1995): 90–111.

Toye, Richard. "From 'Consensus' to 'Common Ground': The Rhetoric of the Postwar Settlement And Its Collapse." *Journal of Contemporary History* 48, no. 1 (2013): 3–23.

———. *The Labour Party and the Planned Economy, 1931-1951.* Woodbridge, UK: Boydell & Brewer, 2003.

Vanaik, Achin. "Tony Benn (1925-2014): Committed Democratic Socialist." *Economic and Political Weekly* 49, no. 16 (2014): 25–29.

Walters, A. "A Life Philosophy." *The American Economist* 33, no. 2 (1989): 18–24.

Wapshott, Nicholas and George Brock. *Thatcher.* London: Macdonald & Co, 1983.

Wilson, Harold. *Final Turn: The Labour Government 1974-1976.* London: Weidenfeld and Nicolson, 1979.

Yergin, Daniel and Joseph Stanislaw. *The Commanding Heights: The Battle Between Government and the Marketplace That Is Remaking the Modern World.* New York: Simon & Schuster, 1998.

Young, Hugo. *One of Us: A Biography of Margaret Thatcher.* London: Macmillan, 1989.

Index

About the Author

Eric R. Crouse is professor of history and global studies at Tyndale University, Toronto, Canada. He is the author of six other academic history books.

Lightning Source UK Ltd.
Milton Keynes UK
UKHW022144240322
400579UK00003B/46